Claude Chabrol: Interviews

Conversations with Filmmakers Series
Gerald Peary, General Editor

Claude Chabrol
INTERVIEWS

Edited by Christopher Beach

University Press of Mississippi / Jackson

The University Press of Mississippi is the scholarly publishing agency of
the Mississippi Institutions of Higher Learning: Alcorn State University,
Delta State University, Jackson State University, Mississippi State University,
Mississippi University for Women, Mississippi Valley State University,
University of Mississippi, and University of Southern Mississippi.

www.upress.state.ms.us

The University Press of Mississippi is a member
of the Association of University Presses.

First printing 2020
∞

Library of Congress Cataloging-in-Publication Data available

LCCN 2019049802
ISBN 978-1-4968-2468-4 (hardcover)
ISBN 978-1-4968-2675-6 (trade paperback)
ISBN 978-1-4968-2676-3 (epub single)
ISBN 978-1-4968-2677-0 (epub institutional)
ISBN 978-1-4968-2678-7 (pdf single)
ISBN 978-1-4968-2679-4 (pdf institutional)

British Library Cataloging-in-Publication Data available

Contents

Introduction

> For someone who wants to make a film on a subject of his choice, two solutions
> present themselves. Depending on his aspirations, the filmmaker can tell the
> story of the French Revolution or that of a quarrel between neighbors . . . that of
> the last hours of a hero of the Resistance or the murder of a prostitute. . . . In my
> opinion, there are no large or small subjects, because the smaller a subject is, the
> more you can treat it with grandeur. In truth, there is only truth.
> —**Claude Chabrol**[1]

Claude Chabrol (1930–2010) was a founding member of the French New Wave,
or Nouvelle Vague, the group of filmmakers that also included Jean-Luc Godard,
François Truffaut, Eric Rohmer, and Jacques Rivette and that revolutionized French
filmmaking in the late 1950s and early 1960s. One of the most prolific directors of
his generation, Chabrol averaged more than a film a year from 1958 until his death
in 2010, directing over twice as many feature films as either Truffaut or Rohmer.

Perhaps the most striking difference between Chabrol and his New Wave
contemporaries can be seen in the way in which his films attempt to break
down the barrier between art cinema and popular cinema. Chabrol exhibited
simultaneously a desire to create films as works of art and an impulse to direct
films that would be commercially successful and accessible to the average viewer.
In fact, he expressed disdain for filmmakers whom he considered overly elitist in
their intellectual and artistic aspirations, and he often characterized himself as
a pragmatic craftsman who made films that had popular as well as intellectual
appeal. He was not particularly concerned about making films that were viewed
as failures by the critics, as long as he was allowed to continue working. He also
displayed a preference for what he called "small subjects." When he did attempt to
make a film based on a "large subject"—for example, his World War II film *La Ligne
de démarcation* (*Line of Demarcation*)—the results were generally disappointing.

The genre with which Chabrol is most often associated is the crime thriller.
Chabrol's interest in the thriller and its particular French variant the *film policier*
or *polar* has led to comparisons between his films and those of Alfred Hitchcock
and Fritz Lang. However, any attempt to define Chabrol's work too narrowly runs

the risk of oversimplifying what was a very complex set of stylistic and thematic tendencies. Although Chabrol directed a fairly large number of films in which criminal behavior and murder play a central role, a far smaller number of those films can be classified as traditional *policiers*. As he put it in a 1970 interview not included in this volume: "The working out of the plot of the *policier*, the suspense-based thriller, is for me purely intellectual, appearing only as a commodity."[2] Even before becoming a director, Chabrol had signaled his feelings about the thriller genre in an essay, entitled "Evolution of the Thriller," that he wrote in 1955 while on the editorial staff of *Cahiers du cinéma*.[3] In what would be a prescient comment on his own future career, Chabrol wrote that the best crime films were those that used the thriller plot "only as a pretext or a means, but never as an end in itself." The best films in the genre were those that were made not simply as variations on a particular plot or dramatic situation, but as explorations of ontological or metaphysical questions. As he would continue to make clear in a number of interviews, Chabrol was far less interested in the intricacies of plot than he was in the development of his characters, in the subtleties and perversities of human behavior, and in the ways that behavior exhibits itself within a wide range of social spheres—from the provincial village (*Le Beau Serge* and *Le Boucher*) to the bourgeois family (*La Femme infidèle* and *La Cérémonie*) to the more specialized domains of law, business, entertainment, and politics.

Chabrol's films are less widely known outside of France than those of Truffaut, Godard, and Rohmer, and his career is only now beginning to receive the critical attention it deserves.[4] It is my hope that this volume of his interviews (most of which are translated into English here for the first time) will be an important step toward a wider understanding of his films and of his unique place within French cinema of the past sixty years. As Chabrol himself freely admitted, not all of his films were equally successful, and his oeuvre is unusually uneven for a filmmaker of his stature. For the more devoted cinephiles who wish to venture beyond Chabrol's best-known films, the path is not always easy. A number of his films are difficult to find, and some have never been made available in DVD format.

The films for which Chabrol is most celebrated tend to fall into discrete phases of his career. The early New Wave period of 1958 to 1962 include *Le Beau Serge*—generally considered the first feature film of the Nouvelle Vague—as well as *Les Cousins*, *A double tour*, and *Les Bonnes Femmes*. In the "Pompidoulian" era of 1967 to 1971, Chabrol directed several of his most enduringly successful films: *Les Biches*, *La Femme infidèle*, *Que la bête meure*, *Le Boucher*, and *Juste avant la nuit*. Finally, Chabrol enjoyed an extended period of more consistent success in the last two decades of his career, when he made a series of memorable films including *L'Enfer*, *La Cérémonie*, *The Swindle*, *The Flower of Evil*, *The Bridesmaid*, and *Inspector Bellamy*. Separating these bursts of inspired filmmaking are long stretches in which Chabrol appears to have been searching for a subject compelling enough to produce a successful film. The 1970s was a particularly challenging decade for the filmmaker, one in which he seems to have taken an almost contrarian delight in making films that feel like flawed experiments rather than fully realized projects. It was not until the end of that decade, when he discovered both the explosive talent of a twenty-four-year-old Isabelle Huppert and the fascinating subject of the patricidal teenager Violette Nozière, that Chabrol began what would be a gradual resuscitation of his career. By then, he had been practically forgotten by the French critical establishment: he went twenty years—from 1962 to 1982—without an interview in *Cahiers du cinéma*, and even longer—from 1970 to 1995—without an interview in the rival review *Positif*.

Chabrol was strongly drawn to British and American literature, and books by Anglophone writers serve as underlying material for a number of his films, but this tendency in Chabrol's work can be overstated. I would take issue with François Truffaut's assertion that Chabrol's literary tastes made him "the least French of us all": in fact, Chabrol adapted more books by French authors than by Anglophone authors, and his adaptations of novels by such writers as Ruth Rendell, Charlotte Armstrong, and Ellery Queen are balanced by films based on the work of French writers, including one of the great classics of French fiction, Flaubert's *Madame Bovary*, two books by Chabrol's favorite writer Georges Simenon (the creator of the world-famous detective Maigret), and a novel by Simone de Beauvoir. Chabrol's most successful films are set in France and deal with contemporary French life; the interest of his films often lies in his minute observation of social, cultural, and political life in postwar France, and more particularly in his unrelenting examination of the French urban and provincial bourgeoisie. Though several of his films are set in distinct historical periods—from the mid-nineteenth century of *Madame Bovary* to the late 1910s of *Landru* to the mid-1930s of *Violette Nozière* to the early 1940s of *Une affaire de femmes*—Chabrol preferred to set his films in the contemporary era, where the opportunity to engage in relevant social critique was greatest, and where a cumbersome and expensive recreation of another era was not required.

The most compelling example of Chabrol's particular brand of cultural translation may be his 1995 film *La Cérémonie*, based on the novel *A Judgement in Stone* by the British writer Ruth Rendell. A study of British social classes in the 1970s, Rendell's novel is reimagined by Chabrol in an isolated village in Brittany, becoming another in his series of trenchant examinations of the French bourgeoisie. *La Cérémonie* is also a chilling depiction of a form of class warfare carried out on the level of the interactions between a domestic servant and the upper bourgeois family that employs her. One of Chabrol's most enduringly powerful films—and the film that effectively solidified Chabrol's reputation and introduced him to a new generation of viewers in the mid-1990s—*La Cérémonie* is clearly the work of an auteur who has orchestrated every detail of the dialogue, filming, and mise en scène to achieve the maximum dramatic impact.

The films Chabrol set in other countries, or made as international projects involving largely non-French actors, are less convincing. Chabrol worked with a number of well-known international stars—including Orson Welles and Anthony Perkins (*Ten Days' Wonder*), Mia Farrow (*Docteur Popaul*), Rod Steiger and Romy Schneider (*Les Innocents aux mains sales*), Franco Nero (*Les Magiciens*), Bruce Dern, Ann-Margret, and Maria Schell (*The Twist/Folies bourgeoises*), Donald Sutherland (*Blood Relatives*), Jodie Foster and Sam Neill (*Le Sang des autres*), and Alan Bates and Jennifer Beals (*Docteur M*)—but their performances in his films are almost never as effective as those of the French actors with whom he developed close and long-term working relationships. The films suffer as a result.

Chabrol was famous for not liking to give precise directions to his actors, preferring to cast actors whose performance styles best suited his projects and giving them relatively free rein to discover their own voices and ways of inhabiting the screen. In his interviews, Chabrol devotes a significant amount of space to his work with actors: one feels both the importance they had for him and the respect he had for their craft. (One notable exception was Romy Schneider, whose absence of a sense of humor and lack of affinity for her costar Rod Steiger apparently derailed Chabrol's intentions for *Les Innocents aux mains sales*.) Chabrol tended to keep his actors in his orbit, reusing their talents in a succession of different roles: by my count, he cast at least nineteen different actors in a minimum of three films, giving a remarkable consistency to the quality of acting in his films which serves as a complement to the consistency of their visual style.

Three actors were particularly important to Chabrol's career. The first was Stéphane Audran, to whom Chabrol was married from 1964 to 1980 and who appeared in twenty-two of his films. Audran gave a number of memorable performances, playing a range of different characters (often with the first name Hélène) with nuanced sensitivity. Michel Bouquet, a relatively understated actor whose subtle performances were ideally suited to the Chabrolian style of psychological realism, appeared in six of the director's films: his most iconic performance may have been in *La Femme infidèle*, where he played opposite Audran as a jealous husband who murders his wife's lover. And then, of course, there is Isabelle Huppert, the actress most strongly associated with Chabrol in the popular imagination and the most important muse in the second half of his career. Huppert provided memorable performances in seven of the director's films over a period of nearly thirty years, from *Violette Nozière* (1978) to *Comedy of Power* (2005). Other actors whose performances function as landmarks in Chabrol's career include

Bernadette Lafont, Jean-Claude Brialy, Juliette Mayniel, Michel Duchaussoy, Jean Yanne, François Cluzet, and Jean-Pierre Cassel.

Chabrol was a true cinephile, and his interviews display his love for the cinema and his fascination with films and their directors. The interviews are also filled with anecdotes about those with whom he collaborated, including the somewhat notorious figure Paul Gégauff, whose work as a screenwriter was a crucial contribution to fourteen of Chabrol's films. The interviews contain relatively less discussion of the technical side of filmmaking. Unlike a director such as Godard, whose interest was as much in the technical (and even technological) aspect of filmmaking as in his narratives and characters, Chabrol was not particularly known as a stylistic innovator, and he felt uncomfortable calling attention to his own filmmaking technique. Nevertheless, when viewed closely Chabrol's films do have a recognizable visual style: he scrupulously avoided the shot-reverse-shot technique, and his signature camera movement was the panning shot. (Godard remarked, in a review of *Les Cousins*, that Chabrol "*invented* the panning shot, the same way Alain Resnais invented the dolly shot, Griffith the close-up, or Ophuls the use of framing.") On the occasions when Chabrol does speak about technical matters, his passion for the art of cinema is obvious, as when he discusses a particularly challenging shot in *La Cérémonie* or an impressive Steadicam sequence shot at the beginning of *Comedy of Power*.

The interviews collected here cover nearly the entirety of Chabrol's filmmaking career—from 1962 to 2009—and they vary considerably in both length and content. I have included one interview devoted to a formal device—the flashback—which gives us a feeling for Chabrol's ability to speak articulately about a particular aspect of his filmmaking craft. Other interviews focus on a single film directed by Chabrol—including two interviews focusing on *La Cérémonie*: these interviews provide a more localized sense of how he approached a particular project. The longest interview in the volume, and the one that attempts a complete overview of the first half of Chabrol's career, was conducted by the editors of the now defunct journal *Cinématographe* in 1982. For readers less familiar with Chabrol's filmography, it provides a unique vantage point for understanding how the director viewed his own trajectory as a filmmaker.

Chabrol's characteristic "voice" is difficult to capture on the page, and it is even more difficult to capture in translation. His fondness for wordplay, jokes, and irony—not to mention his penchant for highly idiomatic speech—makes his language highly colorful and idiosyncratic. Chabrol's mistrust of conventional wisdom often leads him to make pronouncements that seem intended as much to shock his interlocutors as to elucidate, and he frequently questions established ideas and normative attitudes toward moral, ethical, and social behavior. His intelligence is wide-ranging, moving freely between philosophy, politics, psychology, literature, and history. His iconoclastic spirit, combined with his blend of sarcasm and self-deprecating humor, give his interviews a tone that hovers between a high moral seriousness and a cynical sense of hilarity in the face of the world's complexities.

As in other volumes in the Conversations with Filmmakers series, typographical and spelling errors have been silently corrected, but all of the interviews are included in their entirety and they have not been substantially edited for republication. In the essays that were originally published in French film journals and that have been newly translated for this volume, I have added a few explanatory footnotes in cases where I felt Chabrol's cultural references would be obscure to non-French readers.

CB

Notes

1. Chabrol, "Les petits sujets," *Cahiers du cinéma* 100 (1959).
2. Interview in *Nouvelles Littéraires*, August 1970.
3. Chabrol, "Evolution du film policier," *Cahiers du cinéma* 54 (1955).
4. See, for example, the books by Catherine Dousteyssier-Khoze and Jacob Leigh listed in the Selected Resources section of this volume.

Chronology

Unless otherwise indicated, the year of each film corresponds to the date of its first cinematic release in France.

1930   Born in Paris on June 24 to Madeleine Chabrol and Yves Chabrol, a successful pharmacist.

c. 1935   Begins viewing films at different Paris cinemas with his parents.

1939–44   Sent to live with his grandmother in the village of Sardent, in the Creuse region of central France.

1945–52   Pursues studies in literature, law, and pharmacy in Paris.

1952   Marries Agnès Goute—they will have two sons before divorcing in 1964. In 1957, the couple will inherit a fairly large sum of money from Agnes's parents, allowing them to start the production company Ajym Productions and to finance Chabrol's first film, *Le Beau Serge*.

1953–59   Writes film criticism and conducts interviews for *Cahiers du cinéma*. Among his fellow writers at the magazine are Eric Rohmer, Jean-Luc Godard, Jacques Rivette, and François Truffaut.

1955   Works as press agent for 20th Century-Fox in Paris.

1956   Serves as coscreenwriter and producer on Rivette's short film *Le Coup du berger*.

1957   With Rohmer, writes the first French study of Alfred Hitchcock [*Hitchcock* (Paris: Editions Universitaires)]. Begins work on *Le Beau Serge*, shot on location in Sardent between December 1957 and February 1958.

1958   *Le Beau Serge* released; Chabrol wins best director prize at the Locarno Film Festival, and the film wins the Prix Jean Vigo.

1959   *Les Cousins*; wins the Golden Bear at the Berlin International Film Festival. *A double tour* (*Leda*), Chabrol's first color film. Madeleine Robinson wins the Volpi Cup for best performance by an actress at the Venice Film Festival.

1960   *Les Bonnes Femmes*.

1961   *Les Godelureaux* (*Wise Guys*). Jean Rabier replaces Henri Decaë as Chabrol's cinematographer.

1962   *L'Oeil du Malin (The Third Lover)*.

1963   *Landru (Bluebeard)* and *Ophelia*.

1964   *Le Tigre aime la chair fraiche (Code Name: Tiger)*. Directs theatrical production of Shakespeare's *Macbeth* at the Theatre Montansier in Versailles. Marries his second wife Stéphane Audran—they will have one son before divorcing in 1980.

1965   *Marie-Chantal contre Dr. Kha (Blue Panther)* and *Le Tigre se parfume à la dynamite (Our Agent Tiger)*.

1966   *La Ligne de démarcation (Line of Demarcation)*.

1967   *Le Scandale (The Champagne Murders)* and *La Route de Corinthe (Who's Got the Black Box?)*

1968   *Les Biches (The Does)*. Stéphane Audran wins Best Actress award at Berlin International Film Festival.

1969   *La Femme infidèle (The Unfaithful Wife)* and *Que la bête meure (This Man Must Die)*.

1970   *Le Boucher* and *La Rupture (The Breach)*. Stéphane Audran wins Best Actress award at the San Sebastien Film Festival for her performance in *Le Boucher*.

1971   *Juste avant la nuit (Just Before Nightfall)* and *La Décade prodigieuse (Ten Days' Wonder)*.

1972   *Docteur Popaul (Scoundrel in White)*.

1973   *Les Noces rouges (Red Wedding)*; wins FIPRESCI Prize and is nominated for Golden Bear at the Berlin International Film Festival.

1974   *Nada (The Nada Gang)*. Directs two adaptations of stories by Henry James for television, as well as several episodes in the television series *Histoires insolites*.

1975   *Une partie de plaisir (Pleasure Party)* and *Les Innocents aux mains sales (Dirty Hands)*.

1976   Publishes a critical autobiography, *Et pourtant je tourne* (Paris: Robert Laffont). *Les Magiciens (Death Rite)* and *Folies bourgeoises (The Twist)*.

1977   *Alice, ou la dernière fugue (Alice or the Last Escapade)*.

1978   *Les Liens du sang (Blood Relatives)* and *Violette Nozière (Violette)*. Isabelle Huppert wins best actress award at the Cannes Film Festival and is nominated for a César (the French equivalent of the Oscar) for her performance in *Violette*. Stéphane Audran wins the César for best supporting actress.

1979   Directs two episodes of the television series *Fantomas*.

1980   Directs three episodes of the television series *Les Musiciens*. Publishes a novel, *L'Adieu aux dieux* (Paris: Encre). *Le Cheval d'orgueil (The Proud Ones)*.

1981	Directs television adaptation of Goethe's *Elective Affinities*.
1982	*Les Fantômes du chapelier* (*The Hatter's Ghost*).
1983	Marries his third wife, his longtime script supervisor Aurore Pajot.
1984	*Le Sang des autres* (*The Blood of Others*). Directs theatrical production of August Strindberg's *Dance of Death* at the Théatre de L'Atelier in Paris.
1985	*Poulet au vinaigre* (*Cop au Vin*).
1986	*Inspecteur Lavardin*.
1987	*Masques* and *Le Cri du hibou* (*The Cry of the Owl*).
1988	*Une affaire de femmes* (*Story of Women*). Nominated for Golden Globe Award for Best Foreign Language Film; also nominated for César for best director, best actress (Isabelle Huppert), and best supporting actress (Marie Trintignant).
1990	*Jours tranquilles à Clichy* (*Quiet Days in Clichy*) and *Dr. M.*
1991	*Madame Bovary*. Nominated for Golden Globe Award for Best Foreign Language Film.
1992	*Betty*.
1993	*L'Oeil de Vichy* (*The Eye of Vichy*), Chabrol's only documentary film.
1994	*L'Enfer*.
1995	*La Cérémonie*. Nominated for the César for best film, director, screenplay, actress (Isabelle Huppert and Sandrine Bonnaire), supporting actress (Jacqueline Bisset), and supporting actor (Jean-Pierre Cassel); Isabelle Huppert wins the award for best actress. At the Venice Film Festival, Huppert and Bonnaire share the Volpi Cup for best actress.
1997	*Rien ne va plus* (*The Swindle*); Michel Serrault wins Lumière Award for best actor. Special issue of *Cahiers du cinéma* dedicated to Chabrol to honor the release of his fiftieth feature film.
1999	*Au coeur du mensonge* (*The Color of Lies*).
2000	*Merci pour le chocolat*; wins Prix Louis-Delluc for best French film of the year, and Isabelle Huppert wins Lumiere Award for best actress.
2003	*La Fleur du Mal* (*The Flower of Evil*).
2004	*La Demoiselle d'honneur* (*The Bridesmaid*).
2005	Chabrol receives the Prix René-Clair from the Académie Française for his lifetime achievement in cinema.
2006	*L'Ivresse du pouvoir* (*Comedy of Power*), Chabrol's seventh and final film with Isabelle Huppert.
2007	*La Fille coupée en deux* (*The Girl Cut in Two*).
2009	*Bellamy* (*Inspector Bellamy*). Chabrol receives the Berlinale Camera award for lifetime achievement.
2010	Chabrol dies in Paris on September 12 and is buried in Père-Lachaise cemetery.

Filmography

This filmography includes all the films directed by Chabrol for cinematic release, but it does not include films and series episodes made for television. It also does not include films in which Chabrol appeared as an actor but was not the director, though it should be noted that Chabrol had an active side-career as an actor, appearing in over thirty films by other directors as well as several of his own films.

The information provided here is not meant to be exhaustive: those interested in more complete information about Chabrol's films (for example, a full listing of cast and crew) can consult the website imdb.com.

In cases where the films were released in English-speaking countries under a different title, I have provided both the French and English titles.

LE BEAU SERGE (1958)
Production: **Claude Chabrol** (Ajym Films)
Director: **Claude Chabrol**
Screenplay: **Claude Chabrol**
Cinematography: Henri Decaë
Editing: Jacques Gaillard
Music: Emile Delpierre
Cast: Gérard Blain (Serge), Jean-Claude Brialy (François), Bernadette Lafont (Marie), Michèle Méritz (Yvonne), Claude Cerval (priest), Jeanne Perez (innkeeper), Edmond Beauchamp (Glomaud), André Dino (doctor), Philippe de Broca (Jacques Rivette de Chasuble)
Length: 93 minutes

LES COUSINS (1958)
Production: **Claude Chabrol** (Ajym Films)
Director: **Claude Chabrol**
Screenplay: **Claude Chabrol**, with dialogue by Paul Gégauff
Cinematography: Henri Decaë
Production Design: Jacques Saulnier and Bernard Evein
Editing: Jacques Gaillard
Music: Paul Misraki

Cast: Gérard Blain (Charles), Jean-Claude Brialy (Paul), Juliette Mayniel
(Florence), Claude Cerval (Clovis), Guy Decomble (bookseller), Corrado
Guarducci (Italian count), Geneviève Cluny (Geneviève), Michele Meritz
(Vonvon), Stéphane Audran (Françoise), Jean-Pierre Moulin (Philippe)
Length: 110 minutes

A DOUBLE TOUR/ LEDA (US)/ WEB OF PASSION (UK) (1959)
Production: Robert and Raymond Hakim (Paris Films), Titanus Films
Director: **Claude Chabrol**
Screenplay: Paul Gégauff, based on the novel *The Key to Nicholas Street* by
Stanley Ellin
Cinematography: Henri Decaë
Production Design: Jacques Saulnier and Bernard Evein
Editing: Jacques Gaillard
Music: Paul Misraki
Cast: Madeleine Robinson (Thérèse Marcoux), Jacques Dacqmine (Henri
Marcoux), Jean-Paul Belmondo (Laszlo Kovacs), Antonella Lualdi (Léda), Jeanne
Valerie (Elizabeth Marcoux), André Jocelyn (Richard Marcoux), Bernadette
Lafont (Julie), Laszlo Szabo (Waldo), Mario David (the milkman)
Length: 100 minutes

LES BONNES FEMMES (1960)
Production: Robert and Raymond Hakim (Paris Films), Panitalia
Director: **Claude Chabrol**
Screenplay: Paul Gégauff, based on an original idea by **Claude Chabrol**
Cinematography: Henri Decaë
Production Design: Jacques Mély
Editing: Jacques Gaillard
Music: Paul Misraki and Pierre Jansen
Cast: Bernadette Lafont (Jane), Stéphane Audran (Ginette), Clotilde Joano
(Jacqueline), Lucile Saint-Simon (Rita), Ave Ninchi (Madame Louise), Pierre
Bartin (Monsieur Belin), Sacha Briquet (Henri), Mario David (André), Claude
Berri (Jane's boyfriend), Albert Dinan (Albert), Jean-Louis Maury (Marcel),
Serge Bento (deliveryman)
Length: 95 minutes

LES GODELUREAUX/ WISE GUYS (1960)
Production: International Production, Cocinor, SPA Cinematografia
Director: **Claude Chabrol**

Screenplay: Eric Ollivier, Paul Gégauff, and **Claude Chabrol**, based on the novel *Godelureaux* by Eric Ollivier
Cinematography: Jean Rabier
Production Design: Charles Mérangel
Editing: James Cuenet
Music: Pierre Jansen
Cast: Jean-Claude Brialy (Ronald), Charles Belmont (Arthur), Bernadette Lafont (Ambroisine), Jean Galland (Arthur's uncle), Jean Tissier (the president), Sacha Briquet (Henri), Sophie Grimaldi (the fiancée), Stéphane Audran (the dancer), André Jocelyn (young man)
Length: 99 minutes

L'AVARICE (in the sketch anthology *Les Sept péchés capitaux/ The Seven Deadly Sins*) (1961)
Production: Gibé-Franco-London-Titanus
Director: **Claude Chabrol**
Screenplay: Félicien Marceau
Cinematography: Jean Rabier
Production Design: Bernard Evein
Editing: Jacques Gaillard
Music: Pierre Jansen
Cast: Danièle Barraud (prostitute), Jacques Charrier (Antoine), Jean-Claude Brialy (Arthur), Jean-Pierre Cassel (Raymond), Claude Rich (Armand)
Length: 18 minutes

L'OEIL DU MALIN/ THE THIRD LOVER (1961)
Production: Georges de Beauregard (Rome-Paris Films)
Director: **Claude Chabrol**
Screenplay: **Claude Chabrol**, with the collaboration of Paul Gégauff
Cinematography: Jean Rabier
Editing: Jacques Gaillard
Music: Pierre Jansen
Cast: Jacques Charrier (Albin Mercier), Stéphane Audran (Hélène Hartmann), Walter Reyer (Andreas Hartmann), Daniel Boulanger (policeman)
Length: 80 minutes

OPHELIA (1962)
Production: Boreal Films
Director: **Claude Chabrol**
Screenplay: Paul Gégauff, with dialogue by **Claude Chabrol**

Cinematography: Jean Rabier
Editing: Jacques Gaillard
Music: Pierre Jansen
Cast: Alida Valli (Claudia Lesurf), Claude Serval (Adrien Lesurf), Juliette
Mayniel (Lucie), André Jocelyn (Yvan Lesurf), Jean-Louis Maury (Sparkos),
Sacha Briquet (gravedigger), Liliane David (barmaid), Pierre Vernier (hotel
manager), Serge Bento (François)
Length: 105 minutes

LANDRU/ BLUEBEARD (1962)
Production: Georges de Beauregard (Rome-Paris Films), Compagnia
Cinematographia Champion
Director: **Claude Chabrol**
Screenplay: Françoise Sagan and **Claude Chabrol**
Cinematography: Jean Rabier
Editing: Jacques Gaillard
Production Design: Jacques Saulnier
Music: Pierre Jansen
Cast: Charles Denner (Landru), Danielle Darrieux (Berthe), Michèle Morgan
(Célestine), Juliette Mayniel (Anna), Catherine Rouvel (Andrée), Mary Marquet
(Madame Guillin), Stéphane Audran (Fernande), Hildegarde Neff (German
woman), Denise Provence (Célestine's sister), Serge Bento (Landru's son), Jean-
Louis Maury (Officer Belin), Françoise Lagagne (Madame Landru), Mario David
(prosecutor)
Length: 115 minutes

L'HOMME QUI VENDIT LA TOUR EIFFEL/ THE MAN WHO SOLD THE
EIFFEL TOWER (in the sketch anthology *Les Plus belles escroqueries du monde/
The World's Most Beautiful Swindlers*) (1963)
Production: Pierre Roustang (Ulysse Productions), Primex, Vides
Cinematographica, Toho, Caesar Film
Director: **Claude Chabrol**
Screenplay: Paul Gégauff
Cinematography: Jean Rabier
Editing: Jacques Gaillard
Music: Pierre Jansen
Cast: Jean-Pierre Cassel (the swindler), Francis Blanche (the buyer), Catherine
Deneuve, Jean-Louis Maury, Sacha Briquet, Philomene Toulouse
Length: 18 minutes

LE TIGRE AIME LA CHAIR FRAICHE/ CODE NAME: TIGER (1964)
Production: Christine Gouze-Rénal (Progefi)
Director: **Claude Chabrol**
Screenplay: Roger Hanin
Cinematography: Jean Rabier
Editing: Jacques Gaillard
Music: Pierre Jansen
Cast: Roger Hanin (Louis Rapière, a.k.a. The Tiger), Sauveur Sasportes
(Baskine), Daniela Bianchi (Mehlica Baskine), Maria Mauban (Madame Baskin),
Stéphane Audran (singer), Roger Dumas (Duvet) Pierre Moro (Ghislain), Mario
David (Dobrovsky)
Length: 85 minutes

MARIE-CHANTAL CONTRE DOCTEUR KHA/ BLUE PANTHER (1965)
Production: Georges de Beauregard (Rome-Paris Films), Producciones DIA,
Mega Films, Maghreb Unifilms
Director: **Claude Chabrol**
Screenplay: **Claude Chabrol** and Christian Yve, based on a character created by
Jacques Chazot, with dialogue by Daniel Boulanger
Cinematography: Jean Rabier
Editing: Jacques Gaillard
Production Design: Guy Littaye
Music: Pierre Jansen
Cast: Marie Laforet (Marie-Chantal), Francisco Rabal (Paco Castillo), Serge
Reggiano (Ivanov), Charles Denner (Johnson), Roger Hanin (Bruno Kerrien),
Akim Tamiroff (Doctor Kha), Stéphane Audran (Olga), Pierre Moro (Hubert),
Claude Chabrol (barman), Antonio Passalia (Sparafucile), Robert Burnier (Swiss
gentleman)
Length: 110 minutes

LA MUETTE (in the sketch anthology *Paris vu par . . . / Six in Paris*) (1965)
Production: Bardet Schroeder (Films de Losange)
Director: **Claude Chabrol**
Screenplay: **Claude Chabrol**
Cinematography: Jean Rabier
Editing: Jacqueline Raynal
Production Design: Eliane Bonneau
Cast: Stéphane Audran (the wife), **Claude Chabrol** (the husband), Gilles
Chasseau (the son), Dany Saryl (the maid)
Length: 14 minutes

LE TIGRE SE PARFUME A LA DYNAMITE/ OUR AGENT TIGER (1965)
Production: Christine Gouze-Rénal (Progefi), Dino de Laurentiis, Producciones
Balcazar
Director: **Claude Chabrol**
Screenplay: Roger Hanin, with dialogue by Jean Curtelin
Cinematography: Jean Rabier
Editing: Jacques Gaillard
Music: Jean Wiener
Cast: Roger Hanin (The Tiger), Michel Bouquet (Vermorel), Margaret Lee
(Pamela), Roger Dumas (Duvet), Jean-Marc Caffarel (Colonel Pontalier), Georges
Rigaud (Commander Damerec), Michaela Cenali (Sarita Sanchez), **Claude
Chabrol** (doctor), Assad Bahador (Hans von Wunchendorf), Carlos Casaravilla
(Ricardo Sanchez)
Length: 85 minutes

LA LIGNE DE DEMARCATION/ LINE OF DEMARCATION (1966)
Production: Georges de Beauregard (Rome-Paris Films), SNC Productions
Director: **Claude Chabrol**
Screenplay: Colonel Rémy and **Claude Chabrol**
Cinematography: Jean Rabier
Editing: Jacques Gaillard and Monique Fardoulis
Production Design: Guy Littaye
Music: Pierre Jansen
Cast: Maurice Ronet (Pierre, Comte de Grandville), Jean Seberg (Mary,
Comtesse de Grandville), Stéphane Audran (Madame Lafaye), Jacques Perrin
(Michel), Mario David (Urbain), Roger Dumas (passer), Noel Roquevert
(innkeeper), Jean-Louis Maury and Paul Gégauff (Gestapo agents), Reinhard
Koldeheff (Major von Pritsch)
Length: 120 minutes

LE SCANDALE/ THE CHAMPAGNE MURDERS (1967)
Production: Raymond Eger (Universal-France)
Director: **Claude Chabrol**
Screenplay: Claude Brulé and Derek Prouse, based on an idea by William
Benjamin, and with dialogue by Paul Gégauff
Cinematography: Jean Rabier
Editing: Jacques Gaillard
Production Design: Rino Mondellini
Music: Pierre Jansen
Cast: Anthony Perkins (Christopher Belling), Maurice Ronet (Paul Wagner),

Stéphane Audran (Jacqueline), Yvonne Furneaux (Christine Belling), Christa Lang (Paula), Catherine Sola (Denise), Suzanne Lloyd (Evelyn Wharton), Henry Jones (Mr. Clarke), George Skaff (Mr. Pfeiffer)
Length: Two versions of the film were shot simultaneously, and edited to different lengths: the French-language version is 110 minutes, and the English-language version is 98 minutes

LA ROUTE DE CORINTHE/ WHO'S GOT THE BLACK BOX? (1967)
Production: André Génovès (La Boétie), Orion Films, Compagnia Generale Finanzaria Cinematographica
Director: **Claude Chabrol**
Screenplay: Daniel Boulanger and Claude Brulé, based on the novel by Claude Rank
Cinematography: Jean Rabier
Editing: Jacques Gaillard and Monique Fardoulis
Production Design: Marilena Aravantinou
Music: Pierre Jansen
Cast: Jean Seberg (Shanny), Maurice Ronet (Dex), Christian Marquand (Robert Ford), Michel Bouquet (Sharps), **Claude Chabrol** (Alcibiade), Antonio Passalia (the killer), Saro Urzi (Khalhides), Paolo Justi (Josio)
Length: 90 minutes

LES BICHES (1968)
Production: André Génovès (La Boétie), Alexandra Produzione Cinematographiche
Director: **Claude Chabrol**
Screenplay: **Claude Chabrol** and Paul Gégauff
Cinematography: Jean Rabier
Editing: Jacques Gaillard
Production Design: Marc Berthier
Music: Pierre Jansen
Cast: Stéphane Audran (Frédérique), Jacqueline Sassard (Why), Jean-Louis Trintignant (Paul), Henri Attal (Robègue), Dominique Zardi (Riais), Serge Bento (bookseller), Nane Germon (Violetta)
Length: 88 minutes

LA FEMME INFIDELE/ THE UNFAITHFUL WOMAN (1969)
Production: André Génovès (La Boétie), Cinegai S.P.A.
Director: **Claude Chabrol**

Screenplay: **Claude Chabrol**
Cinematography: Jean Rabier
Editing: Jacques Gaillard
Production Design: Guy Littaye
Music: Pierre Jansen
Cast: Stéphane Audran (Hélène Desvallées), Michel Bouquet (Charles Desvallées), Maurice Ronet (Victor Pégala), Michel Duchaussoy (Officer Duval), Guy Marly (Officer Gobet), Stéphane di Napoli (Michel, the son of Charles and Hélène), Serge Bento (detective), Henri Marteau (Paul), Louise Chavalier (maid), Louise Rioton (Charles's mother), Donatella (Charles's secretary)
Length: 95 minutes

QUE LA BETE MEURE/ THIS MAN MUST DIE (1969)
Production: André Génovès (La Boétie), Rizzoli Films
Director: **Claude Chabrol**
Screenplay: Paul Gégauff and **Claude Chabrol**, based on the novel *The Beast Must Die* by Nicholas Blake
Cinematography: Jean Rabier
Editing: Jacques Gaillard
Production Design: Guy Littaye
Music: Pierre Jansen
Cast: Michel Duchaussoy (Charles Thénier), Jean Yanne (Paul Decourt), Caroline Cellier (Hélène Lanson), Anouk Ferjac (Jeanne Decourt), Maurice Pialat (police inspector), Marc di Napoli (Philippe Decourt), Guy Marly (Jacques), Stéphane di Napoli (Charles's son)
Length: 113 minutes

LE BOUCHER (1970)
Production: André Génovès (La Boétie), Euro International Film
Director: **Claude Chabrol**
Screenplay: **Claude Chabrol**
Cinematography: Jean Rabier
Editing: Jacques Gaillard
Production Design: Guy Littaye
Music: Pierre Jansen
Cast: Stéphane Audran (Helene), Jean Yanne (Popaul), William Guérault (Charles, the schoolboy), Roger Rudel (police inspector), Mario Beccaria (Léon Hamel), Antonio Passalia (Angelo, the singer)
Length: 95 minutes

LA RUPTURE/ THE BREACH (1970)
Production: André Génovès (La Boétie), Euro International Film, Ciné Vog
Director: **Claude Chabrol**
Screenplay: **Claude Chabrol**, based on the novel *The Balloon Man* by Charlotte
Armstrong
Cinematography: Jean Rabier
Editing: Jacques Gaillard
Production Design: Guy Littaye
Music: Pierre Jansen
Cast: Stéphane Audran (Hélène Régnier), Jean-Pierre Cassel (Paul Thomas),
Jean-Claude Drouot (Charles Régnier), Michel Bouquet (Ludovic Régnier),
Marguerite Cassan (Emilie Régnier), Annie Cordy (Madame Pinelli), Jean
Carmet (Monsieur Pinelli), Katia Romanoff (Elise Pinelli), Michel Duchaussoy
(Hélène's lawyer), Catherine Rouvel (Sonia), Mario David (Gérard Mostelle),
Margo Lion, Louise Chevalier, and Maria Pichi (the three Fates)
Length: 124 minutes

JUSTE AVANT LA NUIT/ JUST BEFORE NIGHTFALL (1971)
Production: André Génovès (La Boétie), Cinegai S.P.A.
Director: **Claude Chabrol**
Screenplay: **Claude Chabrol**, based on the novel *The Thin Line* by Edward Atiyah
Cinematography: Jean Rabier
Editing: Jacques Gaillard
Production Design: Guy Littaye
Music: Pierre Jansen
Cast: Michel Bouquet (Charles Masson), Stéphane Audran (Hélène Masson),
François Périer (François Tellier), Dominique Zardi (Prince), Henri Attal
(police officer Cavanna), Paul Temps (Bardin), Jean Carmet (Jeannot), Daniel
Lecourtois (Dorfmann), Patrick Gillot (Auguste Masson), Brigitte Perrin
(Joséphine Masson)
Length: 106 minutes

LA DECADE PRODIGIEUSE/ TEN DAYS' WONDER (1971)
Production: André Génovès (La Boétie)
Director: **Claude Chabrol**
Screenplay: Eugene Archer and Paul Gardner, based on the novel *Ten Days'
Wonder* by Ellery Queen, with dialogue by Paul Gégauff
Cinematography: Jean Rabier
Editing: Jacques Gaillard
Production Design: Guy Littaye

Music: Pierre Jansen
Cast: Orson Welles (Théo Van Horn), Marlène Jobert (Hélène Van Horn), Anthony Perkins (Charles Van Horn), Michel Piccoli (Paul Régis), Guido Alberti (Ludovic Van Horn)
Length: 110 minutes

DOCTEUR POPAUL/ SCOUNDREL IN WHITE (1972)
Production: André Génovès (La Boétie), Cerrito Films, Rizzoli Films
Screenplay: **Claude Chabrol** and Paul Gégauff, based on the novel *Meurtre à loisir* by Hubert Monteilhet
Cinematography: Jean Rabier
Editing: Jacques Gaillard
Production Design: Guy Littaye
Music: Pierre Jansen
Cast: Jean-Paul Belmondo (Paul Simay), Mia Farrow (Christine), Laura Antonelli (Martine), Daniel Ivernel (Berthier), Daniel Lecourtois (Christine's father), Marlène Appelt (Carole), Michel Peyrelon (Joseph)
Length: 105 minutes

LES NOCES ROUGES/ RED WEDDING (1973)
Production: André Génovès (La Boétie), Canaria Films
Director: **Claude Chabrol**
Screenplay: **Claude Chabrol**
Cinematography: Jean Rabier
Editing: Jacques Gaillard
Production Design: Guy Littaye
Music: Pierre Jansen
Cast: Stéphane Audran (Lucienne Delamare), Michel Piccoli (Pierre Maury), Claude Piéplu (Paul Delamare), Clotilde Joano (Clotilde Maury), Eliana de Santis (Hélène Delamare), François Robert (Auriol), Ermanno Casanova (political advisor), Pippo Merisi (Berthier)
Length: 90 minutes

NADA/ THE NADA GANG (1973)
Production: André Génovès (La Boétie), Italian International Films
Director: **Claude Chabrol**
Screenplay: Jean-Patrick Manchette and **Claude Chabrol**, based on the novel by Jean-Patrick Manchette
Cinematography: Jean Rabier
Editing: Jacques Gaillard

Production Design: Guy Littaye
Music: Pierre Jansen
Cast: Fabio Testi (Buonaventura Diaz), Maurice Garrel (André Epaulard), Michel Duchaussoy (Marcel Treuffais), Mariangela Melato (Veronique), Michel Aumont (Goemond), Didier Kaminka (Meyer), Lou Castel (D'Arey), André Falcon (The Minister), Lyle Joyce (Ambassador Richard Poindexter)
Length: 110 minutes

UNE PARTIE DE PLAISIR/ PLEASURE PARTY (1974)
Production: André Génovès (La Boétie), Sunchild, Gerico Sound
Director: **Claude Chabrol**
Screenplay: Paul Gégauff
Cinematography: Jean Rabier
Editing: Jacques Gaillard
Production Design: Guy Littaye
Music: Matthieu Chabrol
Cast: Paul Gégauff (Philippe), Daniele Gégauff (Esther), Clémence Gégauff (Elise), Paula Moore (Sylvia), Michel Valette (Katkof), Giancarlo Sisti (Habib), Cécile Vassort (Annie), Mario Santini (Rosco), Pierre Santini (Michel)
Length: 100 minutes

LES INNOCENTS AUX MAINS SALES/ DIRTY HANDS (1975)
Production: André Génovès (La Boétie), Terra Filmkunst, Jupiter Generalia Cinematografica
Director: **Claude Chabrol**
Screenplay: **Claude Chabrol**, based on the novel *The Damned Innocents* by Richard Neely
Cinematography: Jean Rabier
Editing: Jacques Gaillard
Production Design: Guy Littaye
Music: Pierre Jansen
Cast: Romy Schneider (Julie Wormser), Rod Steiger (Louis Wormser), Jean Rochefort (Albert Légal, attorney), Paolo Giusti (Jeff Marle), François Maistre (police officer Lamy), Pierre Santini (police officer Villon), François Perrot (Georges Tohrent)
Length: 120 minutes

LES MAGICIENS/ DEATH RITE (1976)
Production: Tarak Ben Amar (Carthago Films), Mondial Te-Fi, Maran Films
Director: **Claude Chabrol**

Screenplay: Paul Gégauff, **Claude Chabrol,** and Pierre Lesou, based on the
novel *Invitation au meurtre* by Frédéric Dard
Cinematography: Jean Rabier
Editing: Monique Fardoulis and Luce Grunenwald
Production Design: André Labussière
Music: Pierre Jansen
Cast: Stefania Sandrelli (Sylvie), Franco Nero (Sadry), Jean Rochefort (Edouard),
Gert Frobe (Vestar), Gila von Weitershausen (Martine)
Length: 90 minutes

FOLIES BOURGEOISES/ THE TWIST (1976)
Production: Barnabé Productions, Gloria Films, CCC Filmkunst
Director: **Claude Chabrol**
Screenplay: Ennio De Concini, **Claude Chabrol**, Norman Enfield, and Maria Pia
Fusco, based on the novel *Le Malheur fou* by Lucie Faure
Cinematography: Jean Rabier
Editing: Monique Fardoulis
Production Design: Maurice Sergent
Music: Manuel de Sica
Cast: Stéphane Audran (Claire Brandels), Bruce Dern (William Brandels),
Jean-Pierre Cassel (the editor), Maria Schell (Gretel), Charles Aznavour (Dr.
Lartigue), Curd Jurgens (the jeweler), Ann-Margret (Charlie Minerva), Sydne
Rome (Nathalie), Francis Perrin (Robert Sartre)
Length: 105 minutes

ALICE OU LA DERNIERE FUGUE/ ALICE OR THE LAST ESCAPADE (1977)
Production: Filmel, P. II. P. G.
Director: **Claude Chabrol**
Screenplay: **Claude Chabrol**
Cinematography: Jean Rabier
Editing: Monique Fardoulis
Production Design: Maurice Sergent
Music: Pierre Jansen
Cast: Sylvia Kristel (Alice Caroll), Charles Vanel (Henri Vergennes), André
Dussollier (young man in the park), Fernand Ledoux (old man, doctor), Jean
Carmet (Colas), Thomas Chabrol (thirteen-year-old boy), Bernard Rousselet
(Alice's husband)
Length: 93 minutes

LES LIENS DU SANG/ BLOOD RELATIVES (1978)
Production: Filmel, Cinevideo, Classic Film Industries
Director: **Claude Chabrol**
Screenplay: **Claude Chabrol** and Sydney Banks, based on the novel *Blood Relatives* by Ed McBain
Cinematography: Jean Rabier
Editing: Yves Langlois
Production Design: Annie Pritchard
Music: Pierre Jansen and Howard Blake
Cast: Donald Sutherland (Inspector Steve Carella), Stéphane Audran (Mrs. Lowery), Donald Pleasence (James Doniac), Aude Landry (Patricia), Lisa Langlois (Muriel Stark), Laurent Malet (Andrew Lowery), David Hemmings (Armstrong), Micheline Lanctot (Mrs. Carella)
Length: 100 minutes

VIOLETTE NOZIERE/ VIOLETTE (1978)
Production: Eugène Lépicier (Filmel), Denis Héroux (FR3 Cinévidéo)
Director: **Claude Chabrol**
Screenplay: Odile Barski, Hervé Bromberger, and Frédéric Grendel, based on the book by Jean-Marie Fitère
Cinematography: Jean Rabier
Editing: Yves Langlois
Production Design: Jacques Brizzio
Music: Pierre Jansen
Cast: Isabelle Huppert (Violette Nozière), Stéphane Audran (Germaine Nozière), Jean Carmet (Baptiste Nozière), Lisa Langlois (Maddy), Jean-François Garreaud (Jean Dabin), Guy Hoffman (the Judge), Jean Dalmain (Emile), Bernadette Lafont (prison inmate)
Length: 124 minutes

LE CHEVAL D'ORGEUIL/ THE PROUD ONES (1980)
Production: Georges de Beauregard (Bela and TF1)
Director: **Claude Chabrol**
Screenplay: Daniel Boulanger and **Claude Chabrol**, based on the book by Pierre-Jakez Hélias
Cinematography: Jean Rabier
Editing: Monique Fardoulis
Production Design: Hilton McConnico
Music: Matthieu Chabrol
Cast: Jacques Dufilho (Alain, the grandfather), François Cluzet (Pierre, the

father), Bernadette Le Saché (Anne-Marie, the mother), Paul Le Person
(Gourgon, the mailman), Ronan Hubert (Pierre-Jacques at age seven), Arnel
Hubert (Pierre-Jacques at age eleven), Michel Blanc (Corentin Clavez), Georges
Wilson (narrator), Dominique Lavanant (Marie-Jeanne, the midwife)
Length: 120 minutes

LES FANTOMES DU CHAPELIER/ THE HATTER'S GHOST (1982)
Production: Horizon Productions, S. F. P. C., Antenne 2
Director: **Claude Chabrol**
Screenplay: **Claude Chabrol**, based on the novel by Georges Simenon
Cinematography: Jean Rabier
Editing: Monique Fardoulis
Production Design: Jean-Louis Poveda
Music: Matthieu Chabrol
Cast: Michel Serrault (Léon Labbé), Charles Aznavour (Kachoudas), François
Cluzet (Jeantet), Monique Chaumette (Madame Labbé), Aurore Clément
(Berthe), Isabelle Sadoyan (Madame Kachoudas), Christine Paolini (Louise),
Fabrice Ploquin (Valentin), Jean Champion (Senator Laude)
Length: 120 minutes

LE SANG DES AUTRES/ THE BLOOD OF OTHERS (1984)
Production: Denis Héroux, John Kemeny, ICC, Antenne 2, Films A2, Téléfilm
Canada
Director: **Claude Chabrol**
Screenplay: Brian Moore, based on the novel by Simone de Beauvoir
Cinematography: Richard Ciupka
Editing: Yves Langlois
Production Design: François Comtet
Music: François Dompierre and Matthieu Chabrol
Cast: Jodie Foster (Hélène Bertrand), Sam Neill (Bergman), Stéphane Audran
(Gigi Grandjovan), Michael Ontkean (Jean Blomart), Lambert Wilson (Paul
Perrier), Alexandra Stewart (Madeleine), Jean-François Balmer (Arnaud), John
Vernon (General von Loenig), Marie Bunel (Yvonne Klotz)
Length: 180 minutes

POULET AU VINAIGRE/ COP AU VIN (1985)
Production: Marin Karmitz (MK2 Productions)
Screenplay: Dominique Roulet and **Claude Chabrol**, based on the novel *Une
mort en trop* by Dominique Roulet
Cinematography: Jean Rabier

Editing: Monique Fardoulis
Production Design: Françoise Benoit-Fresco
Music: Matthieu Chabrol
Cast: Jean Poiret (Jean Lavardin), Michel Bouquet (Hubert Lavoisier),
Stéphane Audran (Madame Cuno), Lucas Belvaux (Louis Cuno), Pauline Lafont
(Henriette), Jean Topart (Dr. Morasseau), Caroline Cellier (Anna Foscarie),
Andrée Tainsy (Marthe), Jean-Claude Bouillaud (Gérard Filliol), Joséphine
Chaplin (Delphine Morasseau)
Length: 110 minutes

INSPECTEUR LAVARDIN (1986)
Production: Marin Karmitz (MK2 Productions), Films A2, Télévision Suisse
Romande, CAB Productions
Director: **Claude Chabrol**
Screenplay: **Claude Chabrol** and Dominique Roulet, based on the character
created by Dominique Roulet
Cinematography: Jean Rabier
Editing: Monique Fardoulis and Angela Braga-Mermet
Production Design: Françoise Benoit-Fresco
Music: Matthieu Chabrol
Cast: Jean Poiret (Jean Lavardin), Jean-Claude Brialy (Claude Alvarez),
Bernadette Lafont (Hélène Mons), Jacques Dacqmine (Raoul Mons), Jean-Luc
Bideau (Max Charnet), Hermine Clair (Véronique Manguin), Pierre-François
Dumeniaud (Marcel Vigouroux), Florent Gibassier (Francis)
Length: 100 minutes

MASQUES (1986)
Production: Marin Karmitz (MK2 Productions), Films A2
Director: **Claude Chabrol**
Screenplay: **Claude Chabrol** and Odile Barski
Cinematography: Jean Rabier
Editing: Monique Fardoulis
Production Design: Françoise Benoit-Fresco
Music: Matthieu Chabrol
Cast: Philippe Noiret (Christian Legagneur), Bernadette Lafont (Patricia
Marquet), Robin Renucci (Roland Wolf), Anne Brochet (Catherine), Monique
Chaumette (Colette), Roger Dumas (Manu), Pierre-François Dumeniaud (Max)
Length: 100 minutes

LE CRI DU HIBOU/ THE CRY OF THE OWL (1987)
Production: Civite Casa Films, Italfrance Films, TF1
Director: **Claude Chabrol**
Screenplay: **Claude Chabrol** and Odile Barski, based on the novel *The Cry of the Owl* by Patricia Highsmith
Cinematography: Jean Rabier
Editing: Monique Fardoulis
Production Design: Jacques Leguillon
Music: Matthieu Chabrol
Cast: Christophe Malavoy (Robert), Mathilda May (Juliette), Jacques Penot (Patrick), Jean-Pierre Kalfon (police officer), Virginie Thévenet (Véronique), Patrice Kerbrat (Marcello), Jean-Claude Lecas (Jacques), Agnès Denèfle (Suzie)
Length: 102 minutes

UNE AFFAIRE DE FEMMES/ STORY OF WOMEN (1988)
Production: Marin Karmitz (MK2 Productions), Films A2, Films du Camélia, La Sept, Sofinergie
Director: **Claude Chabrol**
Screenplay: Colo Tavernier O'Hagan and **Claude Chabrol**, based on the book by Francis Szpiner
Cinematography: Jean Rabier
Editing: Monique Fardoulis
Production Design: Françoise Benoit-Fresco
Music: Matthieu Chabrol
Cast: Isabelle Huppert (Marie), François Cluzet (Paul), Marie Trintignant (Lucie), Nils Tavernier (Lucien), Dominique Blanc (Jasmine), Marie Bunel (Ginette)
Length: 110 minutes

JOURS TRANQUILLES A CLICHY/ QUIET DAYS IN CLICHY (1990)
Production: Italfrance Films
Director: **Claude Chabrol**
Screenplay: Ugo Lenzio, with dialogue by **Claude Chabrol**
Cinematography: Jean Rabier
Editing: Monique Fardoulis
Production Design: Marco Dentici
Music: Matthieu Chabrol
Cast: Andrew McCarthy (Joey), Nigel Havers (Karl), Stéphane Audran

(Adrienne), Stéphanie Tchou-Cotta (Colette), Anna Galiena (Edith), Barbara De Rossi (Nys), Isolde Barth (Ania), Eva Grimaldi (Yvonne)
Length: 120 minutes

DOCTEUR M/ DR. M (1990)
Production: Adolphe Viezzi (Clea Productions), Soly-Fic, FR3, NEF Filmproduktion, Ellepi Films, Zweites Deutsches Fernsehen, La Sept, Téléfilm
Director: **Claude Chabrol**
Screenplay: Sollace Mitchell and **Claude Chabrol**, based on an original story by Thomas Bauermeister
Cinematography: Jean Rabier
Editing: Monique Fardoulis
Production Design: Wolfgang Hundhammer and Dante Ferretti
Cast: Alan Bates (Dr. Heinrich Marsfeld), Jennifer Beals (Sonja Vogler), Hanns Zischler (Moser), Jan Niklas (Lt. Klaus Hartman)
Length: 116 minutes

MADAME BOVARY (1991)
Production: Marin Karmitz (MK2 Productions), CED Productions, FR3 Films
Director: **Claude Chabrol**
Screenplay: **Claude Chabrol**, based on the novel by Gustave Flaubert
Cinematography: Jean Rabier
Editing: Monique Fardoulis
Production Design: Michèle Abbé-Vanier
Music: Matthieu Chabrol
Cast: Isabelle Huppert (Emma Bovary), Jean-François Balmer (Charles Bovary), Christophe Malavoy (Rodolphe Boulanger), Jean Yanne (Monsieur Homais), Lucas Belvaux (Léon Dupuis), Jean-Louis Maury (Lheureux)
Length: 140 minutes

BETTY (1992)
Production: Marin Karmitz (MK2 Productions), CED Productions, FR3 Films, Canal+
Director: **Claude Chabrol**
Screenplay: **Claude Chabrol**, based on the novel by Georges Simenon
Cinematography: Bernard Zitzermann
Editing: Monique Fardoulis
Production Design: Françoise Benoit-Fresco
Music: Matthieu Chabrol
Cast: Marie Trintignant (Betty Etamble), Stéphane Audran (Laure),

Jean-François Garreaud (Mario), Yves Lambrecht (Guy Etamble), Christiane
Minazzoli (Madame Etamble)
Length: 103 minutes

L'OEIL DE VICHY/ THE EYE OF VICHY (1993)
Production: Jean-Pierre Ramsey Levi, Fit Productions, Institut National de
L'Audiovisuel, TF1 Films, Canal+, Sylicone, Sofica Bymages, Centre National de
Cinématographie
Director: **Claude Chabrol**
Screenplay: Jean-Pierre Azema and Robert Paxton
The film was made entirely from archival footage, with voiceover narration by
Michel Bouquet.
Length: 110 minutes

L'ENFER (1994)
Production: Marin Karmitz (MK2 Productions), SA/CED Productions, France 3
Cinéma, Cinemanuel, Canal+
Director: **Claude Chabrol**
Screenplay: Henri-Georges Clouzot, with the collaboration of José-André
Lacour; adaptation and additional dialogue by **Claude Chabrol**
Cinematography: Bernard Zitzermann
Editing: Monique Fardoulis
Production Design: Emile Ghigo
Music: Matthieu Chabrol
Cast: Emmanuelle Béart (Nelly), François Cluzet (Paul), Marc Lavoine
(Martineau), Nathalie Cardone (Marylin), André Wilms (Dr. Arnoux), Christiane
Minazzoli (Madame Vernon), Dora Doll (Madame Chabert), Mario David
(Duhamel), Jean-Pierre Cassel (Vernon)
Length: 100 minutes

LA CEREMONIE (1995)
Production: Marin Karmitz (MK2 Productions), Prokino Filmproduktions,
Zweites Deutsches Fernsehen, France 3 Cinéma, Olga Films
Director: **Claude Chabrol**
Screenplay: **Claude Chabrol** and Caroline Eliacheff, based on the novel *A
Judgement in Stone* by Ruth Rendell
Cinematography: Bernard Zitzermann
Editing: Monique Fardoulis
Production Design: Daniel Mercier
Music: Matthieu Chabrol

Cast: Isabelle Huppert (Jeanne), Sandrine Bonnaire (Sophie), Jacqueline Bisset (Catherine Lelièvre), Jean-Pierre Cassel (Georges Lelièvre), Virginie Ledoyen (Melinda Lelièvre), Valentin Merlet (Gilles Lelièvre), Julien Rochefort (Jérémie), Dominique Frot (Madame Lantier)
Length: 111 minutes

RIEN NE VA PLUS/ THE SWINDLE (1997)
Production: Marin Karmitz (MK2 Productions)
Director: **Claude Chabrol**
Screenplay: **Claude Chabrol**
Cinematography: Eduardo Serra
Editing: Monique Fardoulis
Production Design: Françoise Benoit-Fresco
Music: Matthieu Chabrol
Cast: Isabelle Huppert (Betty), Michel Serrault (Victor), François Cluzet (Maurice Biagini), Jean-François Balmer (Monsieur K), Jackie Berroyer (Robert Chatillon), Jean Benguigui (Guadeloupe gangster), Mony Dalmes (Signora Trotti), Thomas Chabrol (hotel desk clerk)
Length: 105 minutes

AU COEUR DU MENSONGE/ THE COLOR OF LIES (1998)
Production: Marin Karmitz (MK2 Productions)
Director: **Claude Chabrol**
Screenplay: **Claude Chabrol** and Odile Barski
Cinematography: Eduardo Serra
Editing: Monique Fardoulis
Production Design: Françoise Benoit-Fresco
Music: Matthieu Chabrol
Cast: Sandrine Bonnaire (Viviane Sterne), Jacques Gamblin (René Sterne), Valeria Bruni-Tedeschi (Frédérique Lesage), Bulle Ogier (Evelyne Bordier), Antoine de Caunes (Germain-Roland Desmot), Bernard Verley (Inspector Loudun)
Length: 113 minutes

MERCI POUR LE CHOCOLAT (2000)
Production: Marin Karmitz (MK2 Productions), France 2 Cinéma, Canal+
Director: **Claude Chabrol**
Screenplay: Caroline Eliacheff and **Claude Chabrol**, based on the novel *The Chocolate Cobweb* by Charlotte Armstrong
Cinematography: Renato Berta

Editing: Monique Fardoulis
Production Design: Ivan Niclass
Music: Matthieu Chabrol
Cast: Isabelle Huppert (Marie-Claire Muller), Jacques Dutronc (André Polonski), Anna Mouglalis (Jeanne Pollet), Rodolphe Pauly (Guillaume Polonski), Brigitte Catillon (Louise Pollet)
Length: 101 minutes

LA FLEUR DU MAL/ THE FLOWER OF EVIL (2003)
Production: Marin Karmitz (MK2 Productions), France 3 Cinéma, Canal+
Director: **Claude Chabrol**
Screenplay: Caroline Eliacheff, Louise Lambrichs, and **Claude Chabrol**
Cinematography: Eduardo Serra
Editing: Monique Fardoulis
Production Design: Françoise Benoit-Fresco
Music: Matthieu Chabrol
Cast: Nathalie Baye (Anne Charpin-Vasseur), Benoît Magimel (François Vasseur), Suzanne Flon (Aunt Line), Bernard Le Coq (Gérard Vasseur), Mélanie Doutey (Michèle Charpin-Vasseur), Thomas Chabrol (Matthieu Lartigue)
Length: 104 minutes

LA DEMOISELLE D'HONNEUR/ THE BRIDESMAID (2004)
Production: Alicelio, France 2 Cinéma, Canal Diffusion
Director: **Claude Chabrol**
Screenplay: Pierre Leccia and **Claude Chabrol**, based on the novel *The Bridesmaid* by Ruth Rendell
Cinematography: Eduardo Serra
Editing: Monique Fardoulis
Production Design: Françoise Benoit-Fresco
Music: Matthieu Chabrol
Cast: Benoît Magimel (Philippe Tardieu), Laura Smet (Stéphanie "Senta" Bellange), Aurore Clément (Christine Tardieu), Bernard Le Coq (Gérard Courtois), Solène Bouton (Sophie Tardieu), Anna Mihalcea (Patricia Tardieu)
Length: 111 minutes

L'IVRESSE DU POUVOIR/ COMEDY OF POWER (2006)
Production: Alicelio, France 2 Cinéma, A.J.O.Z. Films
Director: **Claude Chabrol**
Screenplay: Odile Barski and **Claude Chabrol**
Cinematography: Eduardo Serra

Editing: Monique Fardoulis
Production Design: Françoise Benoit-Fresco
Music: Matthieu Chabrol
Cast: Isabelle Huppert (Jeanne Charmant-Killman), François Berléand (Michel Humeau), Patrick Bruel (Jacques Sibaud), Robin Renucci (Philippe Charmant-Killman), Thomas Chabrol (Félix), Jean-François Balmer (Boldi)
Length: 110 minutes

LA FILLE COUPEE EN DEUX/ THE GIRL CUT IN TWO (2007)
Production: Alicelio, France 2 Cinéma
Director: **Claude Chabrol**
Screenplay: Cécile Maistre and **Claude Chabrol**
Cinematography: Eduardo Serra
Editing: Monique Fardoulis
Production Design: Françoise Benoit-Fresco
Music: Matthieu Chabrol
Cast: Ludivine Sagnier (Gabrielle Deneige), Benoît Magimel (Paul Gaudens), François Berléand (Charles Saint-Denis), Mathilda May (Capucine Jamet), Caroline Silhol (Geneviève Gaudens), Valeria Cavalli (Dona Saint-Denis), Marie Bunel (Marie Deneige), Etienne Chicot (Denis Deneige)
Length: 115 minutes

BELLAMY/ INSPECTOR BELLAMY (2009)
Production: Alicelio, France 2 Cinéma
Director: **Claude Chabrol**
Screenplay: Odile Barski and **Claude Chabrol**
Cinematography: Eduardo Serra
Editing: Monique Fardoulis
Production Design: Françoise Benoit-Fresco
Music: Matthieu Chabrol
Cast: Gérard Depardieu (Paul Bellamy), Marie Bunel (Françoise Bellamy), Clovis Cornillac (Jacques Lebas), Jacques Gamblin (Noel Gentil/ Emile Leullet/ Denis Leprince), Vahina Giocante (Nadia Sancho), Marie Matheron (Madame Leullet)
Length: 110 minutes

Claude Chabrol: Interviews

Interview with Claude Chabrol

Michel Mardore / 1962

From *Cinéma* 64 (March 1962): 6–18. Translated from the French by CB.

Michel Mardore: Claude Chabrol, you have the floor.

Claude Chabrol: The beers they serve in France are pathetic. Do you see this little stoneware pot? Well, in Germany it would be big enough to hold a liter or more of beer. I had the chance to experience that in Munich during the shooting of *The Third Lover* (*L'Oeil du Malin*). We announced that there were 300,000 people in the film, and that was not a joke. I simply filmed the Beer Festival, where there really were 300,000 people. That's better than any of the super-productions, right?

MM: Did you shoot that just to bring a picturesque note into the film?

CC: No. It is a picturesque element, but above all it is part of the substance of the film. This event is quite repugnant—you know, the Germans are very fond of it because of folklore and tradition, but on another level they are not very proud of it—and its character jibes perfectly with the meaning of the film. *The Third Lover* is definitely quite anti-German. I show how a German man, placed in a certain situation, can only act in a certain way. In my film, the husband takes the big kitchen knife, well sharpened, and goes quite calmly to cut his wife's throat. That is a way of saying that the Germans are fearsome people, rather disturbing, and it is better to give them a wide berth. They have a terrifying logic inside them.

MM: Aren't you afraid of publicly displaying the things you have contempt for? People really criticized you for a certain interview you gave after the release of *Les Bonnes Femmes*.

CC: Because I said that the public was stupid? What does that mean? I had to tell the people that they were stupid, because it's true. Why should they get upset if you explain to them, for example, that they are stupid because they read idiotic things all day long? They should know that that isn't contempt. I had some reasons for being in a bad mood after the reception my film *Les Bonnes Femmes* had gotten.

Because I love to joke around, people think that, in my films, I am making fun of people.

MM: To be precise, as people discovered a "message" in your film, some of them thought you were showing contempt for the characters who seemed to be complicit in their own social alienation.

CC: I had to present some very cruel situations. In order to avoid falling into sentimentality, in order to preserve an objective vision, I had to force myself to take a certain distance. People believed that it was out of meanness, or "fascism." Nothing could be more false.

Also, the puerility of some of the things they criticized in the film bowls me over. They were astonished, for example, by the absence of customers in the household appliance store. But customers were pointless, all the more so because the salesgirls don't give a damn about the customers since they aren't paid on a percentage basis. You can imagine fifty guys arriving in a line: "Miss, I would like a refrigerator." "Yes, sir. Should I wrap it?" etc. I find those spectators who want to verify the accuracy of people's movements in a film to be ridiculous. Parisians are very fastidious when it comes to Paris, but who verified the movements around San Francisco that Hitchcock chose in *Vertigo*? I am for unrealism, trickery. You have to cheat in order to get at what is essential.

MM: There is always something strange or fantastic in your films!

CC: Let's be clear: realism already contains everything. Have you noticed that ringing sound that has been going off insistently, for a few minutes, at regular intervals? Well, in this café, isn't that a bit bizarre? That is the fantastic.

The feeling of strangeness can be obtained by putting useless details together. Since the customers of the store play no role in the lives of the salesgirls, I left them out. That absence doesn't seem natural, and it contributes to the feeling of unease. The whole film is built on rejections of this kind. The film gives the impression of being loose, while it is in fact tightly constructed, without any useless details. I sincerely consider it my greatest success. The mise en scène is much more pared down, more understated than in my previous films, without sacrificing any of its meaning. Because, I ask you, if the framing of a shot, a shooting angle, or a camera movement is gratuitous or interchangeable, what is the point of cinema?

MM: What do you think of your first films?

CC: It's very simple: *Le Beau Serge* is unbearable. But it at least served a purpose: it completely de-Christianized me. I had filled the film with an imbecilic symbolism. I had to do it so that I could get rid of it. Now, it's over. And then, at the time, I wanted to put in too many things which collided with each other. I had made a three-hour film, which I had to reduce to a normal length. That is unfortunate, because it was a hundred times more boring in the full-length version, but also a hundred times more authentic. I had, among other things, a ten-minute documentary on baking bread. It was very boring, but also more accurate, more true. In this context, my "religious" intentions worked better. Now, finally, I am cured of the pastors of cinema: I locked the church that Gérard Blain wanted to enter in *Les Cousins* in order to get revenge on *Le Beau Serge*.

MM: I think *Les Cousins* will hold up better.

CC: Not in my opinion; it has too many mistakes. First of all, it was an antifascist film which was obviously understood as a fascist film.

MM: Because of Paul Gégauff?

CC: Not at all: Gégauff is not a fascist, but rather a legend! But he is very anarchistic, and he loves to speak German, to dress up as a German officer, etc. At a reception, you might very well surprise him in a hallway disguised as Adolf Hitler. In 1945, at the "Bal du Scandale," he dressed up as an officer of the Third Reich. That cast a shadow on him, but it was a "scandalous ball," wasn't it? Some of the things in the film that are attributed to him because of his reputation were not written by him: for example, the scene where Jean-Claude Brialy recites a poem in German.

MM: Isn't the Brialy character a fascist and yet also sympathetic?

CC: Yes, but that is entirely my fault. In the screenplay, he is a character along the lines of Jean-Marie Le Pen, though distinguished by the fact that Brialy has a remarkable elegance and "class," while Le Pen looks more like a butcher. But Brialy is so sympathetic that, in the shooting, it was impossible for me to make him into a bastard.

MM: The scene where he wakes up the young Jewish man while imitating an SS officer is hard to interpret.

CC: Yes, that is a typical moment. Brialy is not acting that way out of cruelty. In a more or less voluntary way, I pushed his role toward a lack of conscience in order to make him more antipathetic.

MM: Is that why the film doesn't seem to you to be a success?

CC: No, it's above all because of its unevenness. The best scenes are the ones with two or three characters. I don't know how to make groups or crowds act.

MM: So, one would think, the subject of *A double tour* appealed to you?

CC: Of course, I was delighted to be able to show this family in the process of destroying itself. Since I didn't really like the couple played by Jacques Dacqmine and Madeleine Robinson at all, I took particular pains with them. For the scene of their argument, I made Madeleine Robinson cry for a quarter of an hour. As these were not very interesting characters, I inflicted horrible colors on them: greenish tones, etc.

You know, Madeleine Robinson is quite a character in real life. I remember a crew member who, bare-chested, was sweating a lot while carrying a piece of the set. She went up to him and started licking his back with big strokes of her tongue, saying, "That's good. It's salty . . ." I love whatever is monstrous. I would love to be able to put that kind of detail in a film. I can very well see a "grande dame of the cinema," like Edwige Feuillère, doing that. But Edwige Feuillère would certainly refuse. It's too bad.

The funniest thing was that we were basing it on a crime novel, and that the story soon revealed itself to be that of a true-life event that had happened in the region where we were shooting! Even better, in the villa where we were shooting, using the real décor, there was the portrait of one of the ancestors who looked like Dacqmine to an astonishing degree!

Henri Decaë and I allowed ourselves a lot of technical experiments, and even some daring moves. In order to show the theatrical aspect of the situation, in the shot of the big storm scene, there is a flash of lightning that reveals everything: the set, the hangers, the projectors, etc.

I prefer that kind of mistakes to mistakes in the casting: for example, the role played by Jean-Paul Belmondo had been written for Brialy. Belmondo looked too much the part of the enfant terrible, which took away the effect of surprise and contrast, and the character of the Hungarian that he played was badly integrated into the story.

MM: Why did you agree to direct *Wise Guys* (*Les Godelureaux*)?

CC: That's a long story. A new producer who had seen *Les Cousins* asked me to choose a subject for a film. That morning, I had received Eric Ollivier's book [*Les Godelureaux*, 1959], of which I had read only the cover copy, that didn't seem bad to me: the youth of Saint Germain, etc. I gave it to the producer to read, and he told me that Brialy would be perfect in the role of Ronald. Ronald was a name that I liked, I have to admit. And so I read the book, where Ronald takes up two or three pages at most: it was very bad, rigorously unusable. The project sat around for nearly two years. Then the producer came back on the attack. Since I needed money, I decided to make the film. Gégauff and I tried to propose other subjects, but there was nothing we could do since the film had already been sold abroad (this was before the failure of *Les Bonnes Femmes*).

We shot it as a joke, retaining nothing from the novel. Even time was against us: at the ocean, it was raining, and in the mountains it was snowing. In conclusion, I only like one scene, which is the one where Brialy and Bernadette Lafont go to look for a bottle of cognac. The rest has no interest in my eyes.

MM: Was your sketch in *The Seven Deadly Sins* also just done for the sake of making money?

CC: Yes and no. The sets were so horrible that I took a series of closeup shots of faces to try to hide the ugliness. But I like the outlandishness of the premise: a group of polytechnic students who join forces to pay for a prostitute. Twenty-five polytechnic students: that's not bad!

MM: Now we've come to *The Third Lover*. Was it just an "anti-German" film?

CC: In reality, it is a film about envy. I would have liked to have chosen Envy as my deadly sin for my sketch if they hadn't given me Avarice.

The character played by Jacques Charrier is a loser who goes to take a job in Germany. He attaches himself to a couple, with whom he is soon sharing a certain intimacy. The husband is a well-known writer, and Charrier starts envying everything about him: the celebrity, the money, the success, the comfort, and the wife, who is a French woman with whom he falls in love. Since he is a born voyeur, he follows her and discovers that she is cheating on her husband with a fop. He takes photos. Blackmail: if she won't sleep with him, he will show the photos to the husband. She holds fast. He shows the photos. The husband kills his wife. It is a murder by proxy.

MM: What is the relation of this to the Germanic mindset?

CC: It's that a German, in the way he is conditioned, and with his heredity, etc., could only act in this way. It is a logical progression of events. I am in favor of logic (and I mean logic and not fatalism), as opposed to randomness or chance. But don't think that it's tied to psychological analysis. In fact, I don't like psychology either. It's a waste of time, and it reduces everything to a case study. If we wanted to put it that way, Charrier's character in the film is a neuropath. You could explain him psychoanalytically, but that doesn't interest me. I avoid branching out in this way. It's not like it was at the time of *Le Beau Serge*. I make an hour and a half film that lasts an hour and a half, and I go toward what is essential.

It was the same problem for the style of the film. It was the experience of *Les Bonnes Femmes*, but pushed further, with an added rigor: either static shots or shots with unusual camera movements. (In *Les Bonnes Femmes*, at the Jardin des Plantes, I did a tracking shot interrupted by a closeup, which is heresy). In *The Third Lover*, there is less flashy virtuosity, and more of a serious approach. My only luxury is a certain turn toward expressionism in the cinematography. I admit that I like that.

MM: What is it that primarily interests you in the film?

CC: Several things. For example, the ambiguity of appearances. Charrier is always smiling—you know his famous dimple—and he is impenetrable. The woman, who is an upstanding woman, becomes a bitch in heat the moment she finds herself at the Beer Festival that I was telling you about earlier. We hardly changed anything— only her hairstyle—and she becomes another character altogether. These are closed characters. In one scene, Charrier doesn't go swimming because he doesn't want to admit that he doesn't know how to swim.

It's funny, but I have been asking myself for a long time why I wrote this scene, and I now know that the same thing happened to me during the war with a friend who didn't know how to swim. I had him climb into a boat which took on water and sank. We only saved him when it was absolutely necessary. This event really struck me, and then I completely forgot about it.

MM: And what about *Ophelia*? Why use the Shakespearian title?

CC: Because it was the story of a Hamlet character. Juliette Mayniel is Ophelia, and André Jocelyn, who also played the neurotic young man in *A double tour*, is Hamlet. His mother is played by Alida Valli, and the role of the stepfather is played by Claude Cerval, who already appeared in *Le Beau Serge* and *Les Cousins*. But be careful! It's not a question of a modern transposition of Shakespeare's tragedy, because I believe, in principle, that the genre of adaptation is stupid and artificial, and that it can only have dismaying results. Thus it is a question of giving the appearance of an adaptation, but there is always a discrepancy. I'll give you one absurd example: the action takes place in a village that is called "Erneles"—this name is the anagram of Elseneur [the French spelling of Elsinore], but it is missing the "u," and therefore it is a false anagram. The spectator could be duped, but that is precisely the subject of the film: it is somewhere between reality and myth, and there is no real connection to the play. From this inadaptation the dramatic conflict is born, at the border between the real and the imaginary.

The protagonist, Ivan, is a sick man who rejects the real world. After the death of his father, he persuades himself that he is living the story of Hamlet, that he *is* Hamlet, and he tries to make the exterior world conform to the image of his madness; he tries to bring others into his game. And because they are unsatisfied with their real existences, these others accept it, except for the girl he has baptized with the name of Ophelia, and who in the end incarnates the triumph of reason. I pushed really far into finding parallels: for example, Ivan/Hamlet is shooting a 16mm film which becomes the "film within the film," just as Shakespeare has the "play within the play" at the moment when Hamlet accuses his stepfather. But these troubling parallels are deceiving: in fact, if there are coincidences that surprise the spectator, it's always Ivan who has brought them about. Some of the equivalences are pure buffoonery. So, the character who has agreed to be Polonius is obsessed with getting rid of jay's nests. He climbs up into trees and destroys the nests. But he has a heart problem, and one day, while he is in a tree trying to reach a jay's nest, he dies. He dies and remains caught in the tree!

MM: What is the tone of the film? Is it tragic farce?
CC: If there is comedy in it, it would be a fairly atrocious, monstrous form of comedy. I will tell you how the film begins. Before the credits, we see people going into church for the funeral of Ivan's father. At the end of the credits, they are coming out of the church, wearing the same clothes, but with a marigold pinned to their boutonnieres: they are coming out from the wedding of Ivan's mother with his uncle, of whom she had become enamored. That has the feeling of a farce, but it is true on a deep level: the only difference between a funeral and a wedding is the flower in the boutonniere.

For lovers of serious literature, I highlighted this quote: "And Bellerophon became melancholic—alone he wandered on the banks of the Allion—devouring his soul and fleeing the paths frequented by men."

MM: What will your next film be?
CC: I always have a lot of projects, but the most serious one is the one I am preparing with Françoise Sagan. It will be the story of Landru. In the beginning, we were going to write a kind of romanticized life of George Sand. But we very quickly realized that it wasn't much fun to write about the emotional high points of a suffragette. So, we preferred to work on Landru, who at least had a sense of humor. Do you know the answer that he gave to his lawyer before his execution? The lawyer said that he had defended him as if he were a brother, and he begged him to tell him whether he had—yes or no—killed all those women. So, Landru answered: "That, my dear, I will never tell you: that is my little piece of baggage!"

Sagan has marvelous ideas. When Landru went to the country with a prospective victim, he always bought one one-way ticket and one round-trip ticket. Sagan came up with the idea that he ended up being recognized by the cashier who gives out the tickets. So, the third time that he comes up to the ticket counter, before he has asked for anything, the guy gives him his round-trip ticket and his one-way ticket with a knowing wink.

MM: You are known as a joker, and your adversaries claim that you are even making fun of the cinema.

CC: That's one opinion, but for me the cinema is very important in the midst of the chaos in which we are living. For me, every film is a proof of the nonexistence of chaos, since it brings chaotic elements into organization.

You see, people criticize me, no doubt, for not being "engaged" with the problems of the contemporary world, but I have my own little philosophy about History: I haven't forgotten that if I don't deal with politics, politics will deal with me. Therefore, my honor is safe. Also, to make pronouncements about "engaged cinema" is to deny the existence of censorship, because such a cinema could not express itself under the reign of censorship. Yet those who want an engaged cinema also affirm that censorship exists. There is a contradiction there.

And then, seriously, in taking on subjects about which opinions are very sensitive, it would be too easy to engage in blackmail by intimidation: "I am taking on an important subject, and therefore my film is important, and therefore I am an important man . . ." You see, without making value judgements, I believe that it is obscene for someone to say, for example, about a film on the concentration camps: "This actor plays the role of the deportee very well." I think it is useless to demean the people who really lived it in their own bodies for a second time. For my part, I would prefer to try to understand, to discern, those who have demeaned them. In my opinion, pounding defenseless spectators with such general ideas is a cowardly way of behaving.

Interview with Claude Chabrol

Jean-André Fieschi and Mark Shivas / 1963

From *Movie* 10 (July 1963): 16–20. Translated from the French by Garry Broughton and Mark Shivas.

Question: What do you think of your first film, *Le Beau Serge*, these days?
Claude Chabrol: I still quite like the opening, and I quite like the village in the Creuse region where I stayed during the war. I hate the ending.

Q: It was quite symbolic, though, wasn't it?
CC: But it didn't come out very honest. In my mind it corresponded to something quite precise, something one often comes across in the world, but . . .

Q: What were the things that mainly interested you in the making of the film?
CC: First of all, there was the village which I knew well, and I liked the people there very much. That part of it I enjoyed doing a lot. But at the same time, I was learning the technical side, and that lost us lots of time!

Q: Haven't a lot of documentary things about the village been cut out during the montage?
CC: At the outset, the film was at least two and a half hours long. Luckily, I showed it to some people and they said, "Aie, aie!" So I cut three quarters of an hour. And in comparison with the original scenario I'd already cut half an hour. So it would have lasted three hours. It was cut mainly in the transitions, and then there were two things which took up a hell of a lot of time. The cutting was done so that the film could be more successful commercially, but I took care to make sure that the topography of the village was respected. So in order to get to one place to another, even if it meant going right across the village, one went right across, following the guy or whoever it might be. That took plenty of time! There were things like the baking of bread and scenes in the bistro with people talking among themselves that had nothing to do with the subject of the film but seemed to me to be indispensable

at the time. I'm sure that even the tables of the bistro were of very old wood, and so much wine had been spilt on them that they had an antique color. Henri Decae had rendered this color so well that I would have liked to have it in the film. But then everything would have been interminable.

Q: Had you ever worked with actors before? Rivette began, for instance, with actors in a short film.
CC: No, I hadn't done anything interesting. Short films aren't really the same. But for *Le Beau Serge* I mainly chose friends and old hams. In using those people, I realized that I liked barnstormers and actors who exaggerated a little. I always encourage them to grimace. If you are afraid you go (he makes an expression of horror by shrinking back and eyes popping); if you are happy you go (he throws up his hands in glee). It's because of this taste of mine that from time to time the actors grimace. The ones I used in *Le Beau Serge* were good, but not good at that.

Q: Do you prefer to use their natural mannerisms?
CC: Yes, there was a way in which Jean-Claude Brialy runs. That was very useful to me. It was when I saw him run like that that I made him wear the scarf, because it suited him. That was nowhere in the script. Gérard Blain rolls his shoulders like this (Chabrol shows roll of shoulders) when he walks, so I told him to walk faster to accentuate the fact. Little guys with complexes about their size often do things like this to make themselves look bigger. Hawks must have noticed this too in *Hatari*. On top of all this rolling motion, he was always supposed to be drunk as well, seeming to lean on one leg first and then on the other.

Q: Did you have more technical than acting problems?
CC: I had my main problem with that infernal device they call the camera-blimp! That was dreadful. All the same, there are one or two things I like. In the camera movements, there are some that don't serve any purpose: when a man walks across the main square, I put down all the tracking rails I had, maybe four hundred, five hundred meters of rail! I had already intended to do lots of camera movement—travelling shots which started here and ended there, crossing the main square, ending by going through a door into a house! Fantastic! As the camera followed the actor through the door, he was obliged to walk on the rails—clack, clack—and you could see them too! Then we had to go through little doors inside which there was no room for anything much more than the camera. Poor Rabier, he had a hell of a time working on the framing.

Q: What was it about the subject of *Les Cousins* that interested you particularly?
CC: I had both *Les Cousins* and *Le Beau Serge* prepared at the same time; in fact,

I had the idea for *Les Cousins* but I couldn't do it because it would have been too expensive. Construction-wise, *Le Beau Serge* was at once too long and without enough incident for its length. The pieces about the stepfather were added later. *Les Cousins* was just three pages long when written down. The situations were more compact. It has more construction. *Le Beau Serge* was economical and it was good on the village, but the story was rather tricked up. The people in *Les Cousins* were real.

Q: What do you especially like in *Les Cousins*?
CC: I'm very fond of the *tomates à la Provencale*, and I quite like the second surprise-party. The man who breaks the chains—things like that. The background in the party—nothing quite like it on the screen for twenty years—I think I broke all records there! There's everything there—Wagner, girls with bare feet, the lot!

Q: Weren't there repercussions from that film?
CC: Not particularly. There was a little. People didn't think there were any fascists in France then: they were that stupid. Now they can see that it was true.

Q: The characters?
CC: I like the character played by Brialy, and I like Carolus (Blain) quite well. It's sad that a chap as frank as he ends up a victim of his own foolishness.

Q: Is Paul Gégauff's part in it mainly concerned with the characters or with the construction of the script?
CC: It's not the construction which is Paul's part, but the dialogue, which is real Gégauff dialogue. It succeeds in saying in two pages what would have taken me four to say. That's very useful because it allows you to do a lot more in the same amount of time. And also by Gégauff are one or two little things such as the scene where they talk about the erotic quality of their skin. The whole story depends on this, he would say: it's a story about skin texture. He wrote that scene in about half an hour.

Q: Didn't he have any ideas as a scenarist?
CC: No, no, no ideas of construction.

Q: So the symmetrical construction of the film is your work?
CC: Yes, I like symmetry. I like it when everything comes together at the end, but one shouldn't strive for symmetry. It annoys me to strive for "rhymes." It's good working with Gégauff because he takes a delight in destroying casuistry. I like what Paul does.

Q: What was it that appealed in the subject of *A double tour*?
CC: I read Stanley Ellin's book when I was doing my military service, and there was one thing which I found very remarkable then: a chap who's very conformist and then suddenly takes off rejoicing into nature. The subject was impossible. There was one thing in it about a key which locks a granary. I have never understood whether the important thing was that it was locked or that it was unlocked! So I cut that out. And I amused myself with the mythological aspects of the story: Leda, and there were swan references in the house. Then there was the scene of the row between the man, Dacqmine, and his wife, the first version of which was refused by the Hakims who were producing the film: it was much more horrible than the scene we eventually shot. It was entirely physical with the bloke saying to his wife, "You are a mess, your armpits smell bad," and other nasty things. Finally, there was the character of the Hungarian, Lazslo (Jean-Paul Belmondo). He interested me. But at the same time, this was a mistake because the film would have done better at the box office without him. It didn't do badly, but without this bizarre guy, spectators would have been less upset by the film. He was a worrying element, spending his time saying and doing outrageous things to offend people.

Q: In *A double tour* André Jocelyn plays the role of a person who excludes or destroys beauty, a person who seems to crop up quite a lot in your films—in *The Third Lover* (*L'Oeil du Malin*) and *Ophelia* as well.
CC: Jocelyn represents a certain type in French society—the son of a good family, rather degenerate, a bit queer. Jocelyn is good at portraying that kind of character. But let's imagine a young chap who's intelligent, sensitive, kind, handsome, who lives in a milieu which is unintelligent, insensitive, ugly, hard, and yet he cannot abandon the milieu because his roots, his family are in it. When he comes face to face with something that contradicts what he has been brought up to, it's inevitable and normal that he will try to destroy it. In *The Third Lover*, it's a bit different: the wish for destruction comes more from the man's mediocrity than from anything else. The reaction is to turn their destruction outwards, preferring to fire on others. One finds the same sort of thing in present-day politics—the young people who have become "plastiquers." I'm sure their origins aren't so different from those of the Jocelyn character in *A double tour*: they're people who have problems inside themselves, inside their families. That sort of character interests me a great deal.

Q: It's the opposite in *Ophelia*, isn't it; it's a bit like *Vertigo*, where the character wants to make his dream concrete and thus destroys the real thing?
CC: It's very much like *Vertigo*, and that's a film which I admire very much. I saw it again when I was making *Ophelia*, and I found it totally unbearable. I found

ridiculous arguments so that I could say to myself, "What is all this driveling nonsense?" But the arguments I used to myself when I was making *Ophelia* were also ridiculous.

Q: *Vertigo* certainly had its influence, because there were many things in *The Third Lover* . . . there were very similar shots.
CC: Oh yes.

Q: And the color in *A double tour*: the field of poppies. You said the main problems were Decae's.
CC: There's one thing which I hate about color films: people who use up a lot of their despairing producer's money by working on the color in the laboratory to bring out the dominant hues, or to make color films where there isn't any color. The hell with them! I like to have the screen full of color, twenty colors on the screen at once, fifty colors. There are no dominants, despite what people have said.

Q: It must have been hard for Decaë.
CC: Yes, but the result was very faithful . . . and it was horribly complicated. I mean the golds and the interiors, with the windows with the colored glass giving the faces three colors at once. The relationship between the interiors and the Provence exteriors was very important, and coordinating the ideas of the decorator and costumier, the cameraman and director, is especially important in color movies, and much more difficult than for a black and white film. I like making black and white films in natural surroundings, but I much prefer shooting a color film inside a studio where the colors are easier to control. Some colors are very difficult to render, and you must compensate to get the color you want on the screen. It's pretty complicated, but not so much for me as for the cameraman. I say to him, "You see this, you see that. I want that exactly rendered as it is. Is that possible?" In the studio there are no troubles about the sun going in!

Q: *A double tour* is very exact in the colorings of the South of France.
CC: It was also very important to get the decors right for the South. There were family photos in the house we used, and the paternal grandfather of the house looked exactly like Dacqmine.

Q: Were you happy with the actors there?
CC: That was rather complicated. Everything was prepared, the locations were chosen and all that. My first choice for Leda was Suzy Parker, but she didn't fit in with the décor at all. So Antonella Lualdi was chosen. The plot had to be modified a bit: she became an Italian who had known a Hungarian in Japan. Rather

remarkable! I also wanted Charles Boyer for the Dacqmine part. On the other hand, Madeleine Robinson was just what I wanted.

Q: Jean-Paul Belmondo's gastronomic orgy was quite something.
CC: Yes, I've often noticed that in films people don't really stuff themselves full when they're eating. So now I work on the principle of having at least one meal in all my films. After all, one must eat. And after all, again, it's very scenic. It's difficult to put across on film, to get everyone in the shot without cutting to and fro. I've often thought of having a table made with a hole in the middle for the camera to film meal scenes!

Q: *Les Bonnes Femmes* is perhaps your most "symmetrical" film.
CC: Symmetrical? From the symmetrical point of view it's symmetrical!

Q: In the montage, or what?
CC: In my last version there was a final quarter of an hour of flashes of people in the street leaving their work between six and seven. That was cut. At the outset it was more symmetrical. The whole thing came full circle.

Q: Most people either think that *Les Bonnes Femmes* is a masterpiece or they're violently against it.
CC: I wanted to make a film about stupid people that was very vulgar and deeply stupid. From that moment on I can hardly be reproached for making a film that is about stupid people. I don't think that it's a pessimistic film. I'm not pessimistic about people in general, but only about the way they live. When we wrote the film the people were, for Gégauff, fools. It was a film about fools. But at the same we could see little by little that if they were foolish, it was mainly because they were unable to express themselves, establish contact with each other. The result of naivety, or a too great vulgarity. People have said that I didn't like the people I was showing, because they believe that you have to ennoble them to like them. That's not true. Quite the opposite: only the types who don't like their fellows have to ennoble them.

Q: But the cinema is an art of identification, and that makes it annoying for the spectator. And that is perhaps the reason for the film's failure commercially.
CC: As the film shows vulgar people, who explain themselves instinctively without any kind of mask, so spectators and critics talk about "excess." But the girls aren't shown as idiots. They're just brutalized by the way they live. They're simple girls who are impressed by "savoir faire," by people who *do* things, tricks and conjurers

for example. Maids and shop girls love this sort of thing. The poetical side doesn't really interest them. You see much more grotesque things going on every day than you do in *Les Bonnes Femmes*. Actually, it wasn't a *group* of girls in the film. In effect, it was one girl. *Les Bonnes Femmes* is the one I like best of all my films. I like *Ophelia*, but I prefer *Les Bonnes Femmes*. *Ophelia* wasn't quite what we wanted. I think it was shot too late. It should have been made sooner and nearer the time when I had the idea. And then it wasn't shot just *where* I would have liked: the chateau I had wanted had been sold and that was annoying. And we had changed the scenario around too much by the time the film was made. But I like *Ophelia* very much.

Q: I have the impression that you aren't very fond of *Wise Guys* (*Les Godelureaux*). **CC:** It's a failure. From the start it was of an unfathomable idiocy. It was about uselessness, and its lack of success came from the fact that it was useless. It should never have been started. Gégauff wrote a scenario of extraordinary uselessness! There are things in it I like quite well: the charity party. The film would only have made any sort of sense if it had lasted five hours and people had walked out all the way through so that there was no one left at the end. If the film had been a complete success there would have been three hundred people in the cinema at the beginning and only three at the end. But you can't make films on that principle, so it should never have been made at all. The film is very close to absurdity, and what I really wanted can best be seen in a scene which was cut of Ambroisine (Bernadette Lafont) and the bottle of cognac. Ambroisine takes a bottle of cognac and hides it behind a curtain. Then she says, "I'd like a glass of cognac. I can't find it. Go and get it." Her idea is to mess Brialy about. They go off to the kitchen for it, but a third man, who's reading some kind of Latin at the same time, follows them and finds them kissing in the kitchen. So they pretend to be looking for the cognac. They are unable to find it, and continue their useless game all over the house, in all the rooms. In the end they give up and go back to the first room. Of course, nobody liked that scene, and there was no reason why they should have been happy with it. But then the whole film was about uselessness, about nothingness. *The Third Lover* was a bit the same. It was about a pitiful man and the story was seen from his point of view. And so the film was, in a way, also pitiful, mean.

Q: Did *The Third Lover* cost a lot to make? **CC:** No, very little, but it lost a lot!

Q: Did you enjoy showing the scenes of the beer festival? **CC:** I had to shoot it very quickly in one day only. And then I had 200,000 people on the screen at once. More than *Ben-Hur*!

Q: What did you think of the character played by Jacques Charrier? Are you against him?

CC: Charrier knew he was playing an unsympathetic character and did his best to make him sympathetic. Charrier is very usable as an actor.

Q: What about *Avarice*, the sketch from *The Seven Deadly Sins*?

CC: Ah yes, that meant a fortnight in St. Tropez for me. The producers liked the sketch and the public liked it too. Making it helped me a lot. But I made it too quickly, in six days and nights, and got very tired doing it. I'm very happy about the girl who played the young prostitute. She's very gifted, very true, very gentle. She was a virgin then. Still is, I hope.

Q: What is the difference between the projected version of *Ophelia* and the one that was finally made?

CC: I pushed it more towards having fun. The original version was more serious. I had the film *Hamlet* interposed into it. I put the guards back in and a bit where they chase Jocelyn, who puts on a cap to make them think he's breaking into the grounds of the chateau. I was obliged to change some of the scenes between Ivan (Jocelyn) and the girl (Juliette Mayniel). I like Juliette, but she wasn't quite what I had in mind at the outset for the part. I wanted a girl with a sort of angelic quality, more ethereal, so that one should understand the impossibility of any erotic quality there. I like the little film within the film and the reception that goes with it because it's more normal than the rest of the film. The hero is normal in comparison with the rest of them. He's not at all mad. In the context of the other monstrous people around, the relationship of Jocelyn and Mayniel is not all that strange.

Q: What about *Landru*? That's something else again!

CC: The women? There are two sorts of women in *Landru*: victims and nonvictims. I must be careful, but . . . there are sixteen victims, I think. One, two, three, four, five important ones. Some one sees only rapidly, their heads, and then the smoking chimney. The last one he brings back. He doesn't kill her because the circumstances are unfavorable.

I didn't realize that Landru's first words would be so surprising. You see him going about his business, looking for furniture, as is his job, trying to make some money to take home to his family; he goes home, takes the paper from his wife; everything is quiet and then he roars, "I would like a small cup of chocolate," and I tell you that is very frightening! He says it in a very savage voice.

He's very fastidious about his work. He's very sweet from time to time. Landru is a good father, though. He doesn't let his family go wanting.

The colors and the decors are pastel, but from time to time there are colors which are acid—worrying colors. Everything is pretty, pastel, and then suddenly there's a color which has nothing to do with the rest, expressing anguish. When he goes for the replies to his advertisement for lonely women, there's a little set which is an *entresol* so that you see only the women's hats and heads as they walk along the pavement outside. And those you see through a red window. On a screen of twenty or twenty-five square meters there are sixteen square meters of red. The red shocks because it is out of place there.

I don't like stories which attempt to demythify a myth. But Landru . . . is he a myth or is he a man? A man transformed into myth. So when one makes a film about Landru, does one transform the myth into a man, or must one transform the man into myth? That's the question! So there are both in this film. For the first time in World Cinema, we see Before Our Very Eyes the metamorphosis from man into myth!

After *Landru* I have a sketch in *The World's Most Beautiful Swindlers*, a farce about a guy who sells the Eiffel Tower in Germany to scrap merchants for the value of the iron. He has a small Eiffel Tower in his garden. Very beautiful. The first shot is the Eiffel Tower covered in snow. Then an enormous nose of a watering can appears and pours water over it! And you see that it's not snow but soap and the man is washing down his Eiffel Tower. After that he puts a cover over it! He sells it at a false price because the iron has a sort of myth attached to it, even though the myth is not saleable to a scrap-merchant. I had to make it in CinemaScope. The Eiffel Tower fits into the shape of the screen so beautifully.

Interview with Claude Chabrol

Michel Ciment, Gérard Legrand, and Jean-Paul Török / 1970

From *Positif* 115 (April 1970): 4–18. Reprinted by permission; translated from the French by CB.

Editor's note: The interview begins with Chabrol talking about his recently released film *Le Boucher*.

Claude Chabrol: The first idea I had was to shoot in the town of Les Eyzies. I had a memory of being enchanted by it. But it had become a touristic little city, which didn't work for the film. So we looked around, and we found Trémolat. I wanted a village with caves nearby. And since I wanted to use the people from the village, I didn't want them to live far from the prehistoric remains. And I wasn't wrong, because they have a comportment which is not that different from the healthy comportment of past eras. It seems that there are five hundred inhabitants (so the mayor said), but we always saw the same fifty. We took the village as it was, without changing anything. The butcher shop really exists. The only thing that we changed was that, as often happens in small towns, the town hall was in the same building as the school, and because that bothered me we changed the post office into the town hall and we also put the teacher's apartment in the building that was the marriage hall. Which didn't prevent us from having the wedding celebration there, and it is the first time that a married couple were ever brought together in the presence of a bed! There were even a few people who sat on the bed, which was quite a beautiful thing; but it was completely normal in this town, which was quite playful, quite joyful. These are not people who are put off by little details of that kind.

Question: You wanted to show the repercussions that such a bloody event as the killing of young women can have on the population of a village, with the idea that actually it doesn't have the effect we generally think.
CC: I knew that in the Périgord region I would find villages where it is like that. In the country, contrary to what one believes—except in certain less sympathetic

places—it is very rare that such events upset the lives of people. In general, they continue to live normally; it is not at all true that there are old women who get together in the evening and gossip. If the old women get together it is to play cards and eat cheese; it's not to talk about what the butcher's wife did with the priest and stuff like that. For example, in Trémolat the priest was sleeping with the wife of the mailman and the mailman threw him in the Dordogne River. Well, that was fine, and the priest dried out his clothes and life went on as before.

Q: What prompted you to choose the character of the schoolteacher, and to show the school environment?
CC: I have always been interested in secular schools, and I wanted one day to make a film about the teachers in the first secular schools. As soon as I thought of the butcher, I wanted there to be a schoolteacher, and I thought: "I see what it's going to be: the teacher and the butcher. We're going to remake *Marty*, with all the stupidities that were in *Marty*: the nice butcher smiled at the schoolteacher, who . . ." I have rarely seen ugly young women schoolteachers; contrary to what people think, young women teachers are pretty.

Q: We're laughing because all three of us are married to schoolteachers!
CC: Yes, it's no joke, it's true: they're not at all bad-looking. It's a venerable tradition that schoolteachers are like that. Of course, there are a few who aren't. Thirty years later, if they don't find happy scoundrels like you.

Q: And what about the character played by Jean Yanne? He is to some extent the opposite of the character played by Mario David in *Les Bonnes Femmes*, but at the same time did you want to use that character again?
CC: Yes, that's right. But with the character played by Mario David in *Les Bonnes Femmes*, we never try to understand him; he isn't the subject of the film. Whereas in *Le Boucher* . . . I don't want the spectators to have preconceived ideas. And if there is one thing that scares people in the movie theater, it is the sadistic murdering villain, the horrible monster. And I wanted to have it so that at the end of the film people would be shocked by his death, and they would think: "Oh, the poor man!" and they would completely understand what the teacher gives him. Though logically, if I had presented a sadistic killer, saying, "There, you see the woman there? She's going to knock him off," people would have said, "What a horrible piece of filth!"

Q: *Le Boucher* is the opposite of René Clément's film *Rider on the Rain*.
CC: It is the opposite, and, I would almost say, "fortunately."

Q: Is that why you showed only one side of the character? We only ever see him in his "nice" aspect.

CC: It's not Jekyll and Hyde; and anyway, when he kills it would happen very quickly and it would not be very pretty to see. Of course, we could have shown the bulging eyes (Chabrol makes a horrible grimace), the slime on the mouth, and the knife in the hand, but that is not what is interesting; it was the fact that he has his thing that he does. . . . And it was not a butcher knife that he uses, but an army knife.

Q: And also, that would have unbalanced the story, which is focused on the village, whereas the murders are committed outside of it.

CC: He doesn't kill in the village, and the only inhabitant of the village he kills is the bride, and he kills her for very precise reasons, because it is on the wedding day that he meets Miss Hélène; and we might also wonder if the fact that he kills her at the exact moment when the teacher arrives with the children is because the bride surprises him while he is watching Hélène like a wild beast, and he goes crazy. He is up on top when the teacher comes out of the caves with her students; we hardly see him, but he is there.

Q: Fritz Lang, in *M*, doesn't show the murders either, but he describes the character in terms of his pathological aspect, while Losey, in the remake, tries to make him much more pitiable.

CC: Yes, but I don't find my character pitiable. He's a guy who has not had good luck. There is the fact that he is a butcher, and his father must not have been much fun—just between us—and he spent fifteen years in the army. Just think about how the grunts chow down, and when they chow down they can forget a little. It's a break; even during wartime they relax while they eat. Well, he still had to be *chopping* at mealtime! That's not a great life, and it must create an obsession.

Q: Is there, in your opinion, a relationship, from the moment when he meets the teacher, between the fact that he falls in love with her and the murders? Are the two things connected?

CC: There is certainly a relationship. He had no doubt committed other crimes before, but further away. And then he has a tendency to reproach himself. Even the first crime that we hear about was, it seems—this is one of the rare dates in the film which is precisely identified—committed on Sunday: logically, the wedding happened on Saturday and it is on Monday that he brings her the leg of lamb. Thus, he could have killed on Sunday, which is to say on the day following the first meeting. So there is a relationship. But I didn't want to underline it, because underlining that kind of thing serves no purpose. Simenon, who is very good in that kind of case, always leaves it vague. I've read a certain number of books which deal with killers, village flayers and stranglers, and he leaves the direct relationships that might exist between certain characters and the crimes rather vague. The period that most interests us begins at the moment of the wedding, with the three crimes that he commits afterwards, which is to say from the moment when they really meet, because they certainly have seen each other before. Based on what we had established as the chronology, he must have come into the village about a week ago. And the village was very happy to see the son of the butcher take up his business.

Q: There is an object that plays a very precise role in the relationship between the teacher and the murders: the cigarette lighter. At the moment when she gives him the lighter, we say to ourselves: "Okay, it's a plot device that is pretty naïve: he's going to lose it and that's how she'll discover that . . ." In reality, it's much more complicated: it's a device with many triggers, because there is a first time when he loses it and a second time when he finds it. This is quite intentional, is it not?
CC: He wants her to know, and at the same time he wants to efface the fact that she knows. In his head, when he finds the lighter, there is nothing to worry about. After all, he is a simple man: he is not educated at one of the top schools. There is a double state of unconsciousness in him. He tells himself on the one hand, "Shit! She found the lighter; I will take back the proof because I don't want her to know." But that's idiotic. And then he also says to himself, "I will take it because I want her to know." Everything is mixed up for him. But I believe that he cannot hold himself back from taking it. It seems to me very logical that he would take it. Also, he has the certitude that it is his lighter, because her behavior has changed.

Q: There was a scene where she started crying. The second time is when he comes down the stairs and says: "There is no longer any reason why it should stop." And she completely understands, and he stops in the dark.
CC: Oh yes: I love that! When he says: "Why do you want it to stop?" It's so hopeless. There, I wanted to shoot in the dark. It's awful: this unhappy man who plunges into the darkness.

Q: In *La Femme infidèle*, there is also a lighter. Is that just a coincidence?
CC: No, no! It isn't a coincidence, but it is very strange. I didn't notice the connection until afterwards. In *La Femme infidèle*, I used the lighter for a very personal reason. I said to myself: "I am going to bring in a plot line that depends completely on one point: the fact of smoking, the smoke from a cigarette. I'm going to bring in a weird-looking lighter, and that will be the plot line." But I didn't analyze it at all. And then I noticed that in the stupid dictionaries of psychoanalysis the lighter represents the need to warm oneself, and that is valid for both of the films. In

the first film, I knew that it was very important: that's why I put in a huge lighter. When the husband notices that his wife gave it to the other man, he can't stand it. It represents warmth, the household. And it's exactly the same thing in *Le Boucher*, where she gives him the lighter in order to establish contact with him—because from her side it is not so simple either—and where he loses it almost at the same moment as she finds it.

Q: It is also, in smaller form, a version of the oven in *Landru*. It seems to us that in *La Femme infidèle* and in *Le Boucher*, which are two films that you wrote by yourself, there is no meanness toward the characters.
CC: It's very simple: when I want cruelty, I get Gégauff. Paul has a tremendous quality of putting "spice" into the screenplay. He knows very well how to spice it up; he knows how to make someone ridiculous. He says it's me, but in reality it's him: he can make a character completely ridiculous and hateful in two seconds. There are things that I would not dare to do on my own; for example, in *Que la bête meure* I came up with the suggestion that Yanne's character had the shits, and that is why he had to swing by. Well, I never would have dared to do that by myself. And by the way, that's the big contribution we made to the book: other than that, the rest . . .

Q: Jean Yanne said in an interview that during the shooting you had a tendency to push more on the "sympathetic" aspects of the character.
CC: Yes, of course, because if you make too much of a monster out of a guy, people will say: "Oh well, that kind of person doesn't really exist." I have already been criticized for making him too much of a caricature, but he's not a caricature at all. He was mostly beneath the level of caricature and almost less extreme than the reality. There are guys who are a lot scarier than that! The evil eyes of a guy who really struck me were those of a former mail and telegraph minister, who had been a government deputy from Périgord, named Yves Guena. Guena's evil eye was incredible, at least equal to that of Yanne in *Que la bête meure*.

Q: It seems like *Le Boucher* is much closer to *La Femme infidèle* than to *Que la bête meure*.
CC: My ideal would be to make a film like a drop of water, and everything would be in that drop of water. It's like the nut in the Charles Trenet song. When I write a screenplay by myself, that is really my obsession: I eliminate things nonstop. On the other hand, when I work with Paul, it's because I need the contribution of something more, so I prefer accumulation rather than elimination. But what I personally look for is the simplest possible plot.

Q: One could really feel that in *The Third Lover*.

CC: That was the same kind of thing. *The Third Lover* could have been really beautiful if we had had enough money to do it properly.

Q: Isn't the very clear form that is in your mise en scène a way of reinforcing your tendency to show characters who are wearing masks? Because the more your characters wear masks, the more the form of the film has to be clear.

CC: That's right. But the form of a film can also come as a reaction to something. There is a kind of rotten fussiness in films nowadays which makes me want to throw up. You can't watch the film and understand anything; it's atrocious. So I said to myself: "For god's sake, since you can't understand anything in other people's films, you'll at least understand them in mine." So I try to have a real clarity, a total clarity, in the narrative. But at the same time, psychological analysis is imbecility, because when someone analyzes someone else psychologically, it's always himself that he is analyzing. So we have to create a character out of his demeanor. But at that moment, to avoid having characters who lack depth and consistency, we have to—when we want to have a transparent form—pay close attention to having the elements of the film be very visible to the spectator, without insisting too much on them. So there's a thing which is quite easy to do, which is to use kinds of camera movement that do not have the function of reframing the shot. So, since they don't have that function, they have to have another. That helps with fluidity, and at the same time it allows us to be there at the right moment. It's practical. It's hard work, believe me, really hard work. It's more complicated than just moving the camera around into every corner, taking the camera into the fireplace. . . . That really annoys me!

Q: Do you know the saying of Billy Wilder: "I never put the camera in the chimney unless I'm telling the story of Santa Claus"?

CC: Often, you see films where you ask yourself: "Why did he make that shot? What is its purpose?" Actually, it doesn't have any purpose, so, all right, you can make it just for the pleasure of it, but for me, the pleasure is not in making shots just for the pleasure of it, but in bringing my pleasure inside the shot. Logic is something that fascinates me, because it can disappear, and the minute things start to disappear they interest me.

Q: We have already noted that in the case of *Que la bête meure*, in which, it seems to us, your admiration for Hitchcock took a back seat to your admiration for Lang.

CC: Yes, absolutely. It really made me laugh when they told me that *La Femme infidèle* was a bit Hitchcockian; it wasn't at all. And even when there is suspense, as in *Le Boucher*, for example, it is completely resolved with a shot that is totally simple. Even if before that there are little things—boom boom booms, little sorts of things, low-angle shots and things like that—the shot that is the most frightening is a static shot and a relatively closeup shot, and that's also why it is frightening.

Q: *Le Boucher* may not be Hitchcockian in terms of suspense, but could one ask if it isn't more profoundly Hitchcockian in terms of one of its themes: the admission of guilt; the necessity of admitting guilt?

CC: He has to explain himself when he feels that he is going to die. There is no "necessity of admitting," because he kills himself so that he won't see her anymore. It's almost a Christian reaction on the part of the butcher, but it's a normal reaction because in these little villages there is a deep structure of Christian education which subsists in people and gives them a sense of sin, of horror, of original shame. In the Dordogne, it is a bit less prevalent because of the proximity of the vestiges of prehistoric times, when the problem of shame did not present itself if one wanted to survive. And shame, in the case of the butcher, is the intervention of a notion of Christian civilization within the interior of an individual who is above all a barbarian, a prehistoric man. I prefer the prehistoric man to the Christian. I'm more in favor of the Cro-Magnon than of . . . what's his name . . . Pope Paul VI, who seems to come from well before the Cro-Magnon era.

Q: There is something that we find in your recent films, which is characters who go to the limits of themselves.

CC: I like to go to the far end of principles. Already, in stupid films like the *Tiger* series, I liked to go to the furthest end of stupidity. It was good stupidity. Let's bury ourselves in stupidity up to our necks and even above them if needed, but let's not do things halfway. For example, in the spy stories, the stupidity was more important than the spying. Within this genre, *Who's Got the Black Box?* (*La Route de Corinthe*), which was the most stupid of all, was also the most successful in doing this, but it's completely useless. A total uselessness. But that uselessness did not come about through a search for uselessness, which proves that stupidity always gets you: that's why you have to get out of it as soon as possible. You are only stupid so that stupid people will give you money so that you can make less stupid films; but to get stupid people to give you their money you have to do stupid things, and the more stupid the films are the more the stupid people will give you their money. But the stupidity wins out in the end, and it becomes *so* stupid that even the stupid people won't go along with it. One could even formulate it as a math problem: "Given that you need 47 percent stupidity so that a stupid film does not completely fall apart with its stupid premise, and that you need only 20 percent stupidity for a film with a nonstupid subject, but the overall stupidity is such—the ambient stupidity, that of the producers and so on—that people prefer the stupid subjects that are made with stupidity to the nonstupid subjects that are made without stupidity, what would you estimate to be the ideal amount of stupidity to make a film that is stupid enough to attract stupid people without chasing them away?"

Q: That isn't always true, because your "nonstupid" films still do quite well, don't they?

CC: Yes. But be careful! People are not intrinsically stupid; it's stupidity that makes them that way. You have intelligent producers who say: "Well, I'm doing badly at the moment. I need to do something stupid." They really reason like that. And they end up making such stupidities that they themselves become stupid.

Q: To come back to the films that you hold more dear: it seems undeniable that you have a passion for characters who go to the limit.

CC: First of all, because there is a logic to it. And then, I've always wondered why there are things that prevent people from going to their limits. Like the rules of war. They are really a burlesque. From the moment when we begin to be in a state of madness there is no reason not to go to the limit. And when we go to the limit, people are astonished. "You never should have done that!" And then those same people, in order to be able to be crazies, imbeciles, and bastards, put up bastard-protection around themselves. But when there is someone who won't play the game, then, oh boy, they're really bothered. I like people who say: "All right, since we're doing this, let's do it all the way!" For example, in *La Femme infidèle*, the husband learns that his wife is cheating on him. He could choose to close his eyes, kill his wife, cry, or go away, etc. There is one very simple solution, which is to go kill the guy, but he could also go shake his hand if he wants.

Q: That would have conformed better to the laws of society.

CC: Yes, and Michel Bouquet's character is more sympathetic to me from the moment when he hits the guy.

Q: You could say the same thing about Jean Yanne's character in *Que la bête meure*. He's a bastard, but he is not a hypocrite. The stew is disgusting, and he says: "The stew is disgusting."

CC: No, no: he only needs to get a new cook! He's a character who is completely invested in society. When I asked Jean Yanne why he liked the guy, he had an argument for defending him. His answer was: "Listen, this is a guy who supports his family; he has a wife who does nothing and who doesn't seem quite normal; he has his old mother to take care of, and a kid who isn't doing well in school; so he has the right to distract himself a little with his sister-in-law, who is a little floozy. And when a little boy throws himself against the car, he's not going to risk the life of his family by denouncing himself." That was a perfect defense of the character, but one that relies on a very contemporary conception of society.

Q: In your work, there is a hatred of the family, which you express above all through your child characters, as in *Que la bête meure* and *La Muette*; on the other hand, there is a defense of marriage, as in *La Femme infidèle*.
CC: They have nothing to do with each other. I'm not against the nuclear family, and I find that it has become a complete object of ridicule. The best proof of that is that there are people who spend their time sleeping around right and left with unhappy floozies, which is terrible. I am of a more monogamous temperament, but it is very difficult to be monogamous; you have to find a woman who suits you perfectly, with whom you feel perfectly at ease, who is not tired when you come home in the evening. And then you can live very well. It's something that has become completely disfigured, but I find that it is very simple: a man, a woman, kids—it's perfect!

Q: That's what the last shot of *La Femme infidèle* means: it is a backward tracking shot which is not a tracking shot that signifies a going away, but one that signals a coming together.
CC: The actual tracking shot is going backwards, but it is combined with a forward zoom.

Q: Do you think that there was a new departure, perhaps after *Les Biches*, or after *The Champagne Murders* (*Le Scandale*), following the period of the *Tiger* films?
CC: No, not with *The Champagne Murders*, which I was only able to get through by bullshitting the producer. You know, in the beginning *The Champagne Murders* was supposed to be about a crime committed in a nudist camp. They came to pitch me that, and since I was in great need of money I said: "That's a really good idea, and here's how we're going to hide the weapon. . . ."

Q: So it was *Les Biches* that was a new start?
CC: Yes, it was more of a safe bet, but yes, it was *Les Biches*.

Q: There's one thing that's a bit annoying in *Les Biches*: the character played by Trintignant, who is perhaps not fleshed out enough.
CC: He's not fleshed out at all, but I wanted him to be a very fluid character. He is a man-object. The screenplay of *Les Biches* is constructed exactly like that of *Les Cousins*. There is one scene that is exactly the same. It's when Stéphane Audran and Trintignant come home to the girl who was expecting to have to wait for a long time because they are going to stay out together. Gégauff and I shared the

task of writing the screenplay: I was in charge of Stéphane's character and he was in charge of the girl. And he absolutely wanted her to be crazy. He said: "These girls are all crazy." And he was right; it's true that they are completely unhinged.

Q: There had already been a preoccupation with insanity in your previous films. Is it because insanity is the counterbalance to idiocy?

CC: I am in favor of balance, but it is not balance as most people see it. For most people, balance is a form of imbalance. There is the type of person who says: "I have work to do for the next three weeks; I want to see my friends, but I won't see them because I have work to do." That is a total lack of balance. I find that balance is a complete liberty which doesn't impinge on the liberty of others. Of course, one has to be politically centrist to do that. But centrism is not at all what one thinks it is. People imagine that the center is where we are now, but that is in fact an unacceptable form of the extreme right. The true center could be a twentieth-century form of Marxism . . .

Q: Yes, but then that would not be the center. It would not be what people call the center.

CC: People are looking for balance, but their center of balance is completely unbalanced. The best proof of that is that they all say they are the center, and yet they don't hold the same opinions. The center is the least palpable of political positions.

Q: But what for you *is* the real center?

CC: I see that a regime would be very balanced once there is a reasonable division of wealth, and I believe that it is better for each person to have his own little house rather than a low-rent apartment. We don't think that is possible because we don't realize the extravagant wealth that is possessed by a minority of individuals. It is very mysterious, and it is total madness.

Q: You have a lot of nostalgia for small-town life.

CC: Well, yes, because in a small town there are hardly any rich people. Things are divided up well, everyone lives well, everyone has a car, and over time it becomes a better car: first it was a little *deux-chevaux*, and now they all have Peugeot 404s. In a while, with the Common Market, they will all have a Mercedes.

Q: That was what was best in *La Ligne de démarcation*: the town, and then the scene where Noel Roquevert sings "La Marseillaise."

CC: That was beautiful, and I was the one who added the "The Internationale." I said to Colonel Rémy: "We need to have both; we can't just have the Marseillaise;

there are also members of the FTP."[1] He said, "Yes, that's true!" The personality of Colonel Rémy was one of the most staggering I have ever known. My only task was to keep the film from becoming a German propaganda film. Because this good colonel, who is a man of the far right, had a grand theory: the bad guys are the Gestapo, and the Wehrmacht are very reasonable people. And the actor who plays the German army officer was always wanting to exonerate himself. He was always saying: "I was sick during the war, you know." And then he wanted to add little phrases, like "Madame Baroness, I will leave you now: Mr. Hitler is calling." I would tell him: "No, it's fine as it is." He and Rémy had written a scene where the Gestapo was criticizing a Wehrmacht guy for not being tough enough with the French population, and the Wehrmacht guy answered, "No, they have always acted properly, and I want to be proper with them." The scene was going to be like that. I had no desire to shoot the scene, but they bugged me about it so much that at the end of the filming I wanted to make them happy. Only I hadn't put film in the camera! To make things even funnier, I told the sound editor: "Look, we're going to start shooting, and at the end of the take you're going to say that it didn't work, that the sound was too faint." So the director of photography is walking around with his unit, we do the clapboard, and the scene begins.

The German soldier says: "I will not betray my honor!" And the guy from the SS says: "The National-Socialist Party has a different conception of honor!" "But the Count has always been very proper . . ."

Basically, it was monumental stupidity. We get to the end of the take, and Guy Chichignoud, the sound editor, says: "I would like to start again, because one of you is good for the sound, but the other is too soft." So we set it up again. And one of them is braying like a donkey, and the other one raises the level of his voice too. And then Chichignoud comes back and says: "Okay, now it's the opposite: this one is good, but the other one is slightly too soft." And by the end they were both yelling and screaming; they were making absolutely amazing noises, and everyone on the set was crying with laughter. And there was Colonel Rémy in his armchair in the corner, listening to what he had written. And he was beating out the measure of the speeches with his cane.

The premiere of the film was amazing. Rémy had arranged to have it shown under the auspices of the Rhine and Danube veterans association. They had an interview on Europe I television, and Rémy went on the air with two men who had smuggled Jews out, who told their stories. And then they told me I had a meeting at the Elysée Club at six o'clock with Monique Berger.[2] Rémy, who always has long ears and who is a big gourmand, said to himself: "Maybe there will be a cocktail party." And at six, at the Elysée Club, I had my back turned to the door, and I see Monique Berger's eyes turn into marbles: it was Rémy, who had marched in, flanked by his two smugglers, covered with medals like Soviet generals. "Where is the cocktail party?" Rémy asks. "There is no cocktail party." "Oh, well, then I guess we were wrong." And they left, with their medals clinking, which made an extraordinary noise. And that evening at the Moulin Rouge, when I arrived for the premiere, there were thirty of them on each side dressed like that, with their flags, their berets, and medals here and there: it was absolutely stupefying. And Colonel Rémy went to present the film in 150 different places. At the end of the screening, he would sell copies of his book *La Ligne de démarcation*, and inscribe it to people.

Q: To come back to your most recent films: in terms of the narration, there is always a character who is a witness; for example, in *La Femme infidèle* it's the husband, and in *Le Boucher* we see everything through the eyes of the teacher.
CC: It's better to see things through the eyes of someone, and I'm not sure that mine are so much more interesting. Seeing it through the eyes of a character whom we can see allows us to be more objective. I am enormously suspicious of anything that is autobiography. As in all my films, there are autobiographical elements, things that I have seen or heard, in other words received in a certain way that has given them a personal form, and if we don't want to cheat this form has to come from another person as intermediary, so we have to create an additional mirror. Because the same fact can have a different interpretation: a thing that seemed to me to be despicable may not be, and a thing that seemed pleasant is perhaps really despicable. The fact that the hero of an adventure is also the witness to the events is not new, you know: it is the case in a good number of novels.

Q: Henry James pushed that to its extreme, but it's implicit in the nineteenth-century novel in general.
CC: And it's also great for cinema. I find that the principles of cinematic writing are very close to those of the nineteenth-century novel, in any case much more so than to the *nouveau roman* or the modernist novel.

Q: That poses the whole problem of modern cinema. Certain art critics think, for example, that when there is a rupture in the style of painting, it is no longer possible to paint in the same way, and people try to apply this to the cinema, saying that now you cannot film in the same way. But you demonstrate that the opposite is true, and you are not alone.
CC: It isn't true because the cinema hasn't even arrived at a form. So when we try to destroy the form, it's kind of funny. There are guys who say, "I'm doing research on how to find new forms," but we haven't yet found the defining forms. Let them find those, and afterwards we'll see.

Q: There is a whole theory which claims that cinema found its form with Eisenstein, and then there was an immense parenthesis with American cinema, and now that this parenthesis has finally been closed we can move in a good direction, etc.

CC: That is a false theory, because, for example, the young Russian filmmakers hated Eisenstein. They said that he was a half-witted formalist—which they were a bit wrong about—and they supported their friend Dovzhenko. I am rather of their opinion. I think I read that in *Positif*. But what is a serious problem is that the young filmmakers who are fiddling with forms before they really exist care as little about Eisenstein as about Dovzhenko. That's what is wrong. For them, all that is shit, and they have to find new forms even though nothing exists, nothing is defined. The other arts have existed for hundreds of years. Of course, their forms have been defined, developed, overdeveloped, and possibly even ossified, although . . . But in terms of cinema, it's a joke. If you look at the films made in 1956, out of a hundred there are five that were well made. So the film critics write their filmological criticism. Because if I am reading *Positif*, I am also reading *Cinéthique*, *Cahiers du cinéma*, and *Cinéma 63* . . . or no . . . *Cinéma 70*. And I saw an issue of *Cinéthique* that was absolutely priceless: it consisted of studying the relationships that there could be between the conception of a cinema of the future proposed by *Cahiers du cinéma* and their own conception at *Cinéthique*. I'm not joking. One can only laugh out loud.

Q: They're making a kind of conglomeration of the form and the system.

CC: That's it. The form belongs to the system. But every form tries by definition to be comprehensible. In order to change that, you would have to change the form of writing. The critics themselves would have to—and by the way, they tend to do it—express themselves in such a gibberish that no one who had not already left the system could understand. But in any case, they are forced to express themselves in one way or another, so they too are in the system. I have even seen some who use mathematical formulas to express themselves, and that really astonished me.

Q: Among recent films, which ones have interested you the most?

CC: Maurice Pialat's *Naked Childhood*. There were some absolutely new things in it. And John Boorman's *Point Blank*, because he used the Hollywood system to try to explode it a bit.

Q: There is one thing that seems to particularly fascinate you, which is crime, and the way in which you approach this subject corresponds to a very precise literary genre, which goes from Charlotte Armstrong to Nicholas Blake, passing through Ellery Queen's first novels. Let's call it a "literature of criminal behavior."

CC: Those people are writers, real writers. They are interested in the behavior of people who kill others. That is not the case with the authors of noir, who are content to tell the stories of murders. For me, it is interesting to have someone kill someone, but I want to know what is *happening* when someone kills someone. What is good in the novels we're talking about is that the plot is always very simple. And I have also noticed that the authors of the criminal novels I prefer are almost all of the same physical type (and I don't mean they look like me). And when I see films adapted from books by those people, I am sure that they are less good than what I could have done. I am thinking about two films based on Charlotte Armstrong books which were really mediocre: *The Unsuspected* by Michael Curtiz and *Don't Bother to Knock* by Roy Baker. Those were two sublime subjects. She also wrote an extraordinary book, *The Case of the Weird Sisters*: one sister didn't have arms, one was blind, and the third was deaf. And the detective had to figure out which of the three was the killer, simply as a function of her infirmity. That was superb. I also love John Dickson Carr, even though his books are more about deduction. Did you know that I was supposed to make *La Chambre ardente*? It was Julien Duvivier who made it, and I was pretty furious about it.

Q: Since we're talking about police mysteries: we have been talking a lot among ourselves about the ending of *Que la bête meure*. What is your interpretation?
CC: Well, in the scene at the restaurant, when the anchorwoman announces on the television, "We have some very sad news," Michel Duchaussoy lifts up his hand to Caroline Cellier to listen. Also, Fritz Lang never would have doubted for a second that he was the one who did it.

Q: In that case, his diary has been rigged.
CC: Obviously, that is the key to the whole thing. He rigs his diary so that he won't get nabbed. We can imagine that he is sacrificing himself for the boy, just as the boy is sacrificing himself for him, but it's the fact that he gets arrested that causes the boy to denounce himself, just as he denounces himself because the boy is arrested, and thus the connection between them gets established.

Q: Staying with *Que la bête meure*: don't you think that the choice to cast Jean Yanne, with everything he represents to the public, creates a certain ambiguity for the spectator?[3] On the one hand, there is the role as you intended it, which is extremely unsympathetic, and on the other hand there can be a certain complicity on the part of the public, which sees Yanne's personality . . .
CC: That sense of complicity exists. It's normal for the public to feel fairly close to Yanne's character.

Q: Yes, but doesn't that come from the fact that the public has a certain sympathy for Yanne himself, which comes from his radio and television persona? To put it another way, is the public able to separate the character from Yanne's image?

CC: That is the problem. I said to myself: "If I cast Yanne, who plays the clown on the radio, are people going to start laughing?" So I tried to take that apart by showing him having the accident even before we meet him, which makes it so the spectators begin the film by experiencing the accident. And I tried to take it apart a second time by having them laugh just before Yanne's arrival in the film, so that their laughter would stop at the moment when he comes on and would start again at the moment when they hear what he says. I thought that in this way I could make them forget about their image of Yanne. We took a lot of trouble to do that. Maybe we didn't succeed; maybe the Yannesque mythology held on, but I actually don't believe so. It's hard to say, because there are a lot of people whose mental processes are so influenced by everything that goes into their heads from morning till evening that you can't trust what they say. They say they laughed, when in fact it wasn't true. There's the exemplary case of René Clément's *Rider on the Rain*, where the audience came out of the theater saying, "Oh, it was so beautiful," while in reality they had been bored for two hours. That is a case of extraordinary collective half-wittedness. And I actually intend to benefit from that because it's very practical: I'm also going to pound that message home, saying, "You will see how beautiful it is!" You can read the little piece in *Le Figaro*: "*Le Boucher* is the best French film since the liberation." That's a bit over the top! Well, that's the beginning of pounding the message home.

Q: And you don't neglect any opportunity to do that yourself, since you said that you put three stars next to *Que la bête meure* in the journal *V. O.* in order to launch the film, even though it's a little magazine that only prints only twelve hundred copies.

CC: Yes, but among the people who read those twelve hundred copies, there are critics and organizers of cinema clubs who will see the three stars and think: "Well, *he* likes the film, so we better be careful what we say." There are also people who liked *Le Boucher* because they had learned that *La Femme infidèle* was doing well in America and was appreciated by American filmmakers. That's a very strange and very fascinating reaction.

Q: So *Positif* would also not lack importance for you. . . .

CC: *Positif* called me a fascist for ten years! (Chabrol makes various loud noises and sounds of protest.) Yes! Yes! There is an article in *Positif* where a guy, Marcel Oms, I believe, wrote something like: "Chabrol speaks about ugliness, and seeing his face it is clear that he knows something about it." Okay, so I'm no Adonis! I didn't know this guy, and then one day I saw *his* face. He's no great shakes either! In a strange way, I have to say that politically I was closer to *Positif* than to . . . And I was good friends with Ado Kyrou.[4]

Q: Let's talk a bit about color. What does it mean for you?

CC: First of all, a great advantage with producers. They love seeing the rushes in color: "Oo la la! I've never seen such a blue sky: it's so beautiful! I've never seen such a red dress!" Basically, stupid things. It's very practical to use color in the filming, because then we have peace on the set. That said, I believe that if someone wanted to make a beautiful black and white film, it would be very interesting, but we no longer have the time or the means, and the film stocks have become so fast that it is difficult to develop them and get enough subtlety (it was great when they were slower!). Also, nowadays black and white is associated with economizing, and if I said: "I want to make a black and white film that will cost more than a color film," no one would understand. So let's make films in color. But if we make films in color, let's not make them black and white. There is one thing that annoys me, which is guys who say: "I made a color film, but I made it as if it was black and white." I don't want to be mean, but I went to see Melville's *Army of Shadows*, which our French Herman has explained he treated like a black and white film. Bull crap! It's not a black and white film; it's everything other than black and white. It's not bad . . . well, the film is very austere. It's not a film which makes you want to say "Congratulations."

Q: How do you work with actors?

CC: For me, actors are a miracle. I find that you don't have to tell them anything. As long as they have read and understood the screenplay, and as long as you don't give them impossible movements and gestures, they do fine on their own. You have to tell them where to stand, so they feel like you've got their back, but you rarely need to give them directions on how to say lines; that would be ridiculous.

Q: You said earlier that you had written a sort of biography for the character of the butcher in *Le Boucher*. Do you often do that?

CC: I like to know where they come from. For example, I've always thought that the wife of the character played by Michel Bouquet in *La Femme infidèle* had been his secretary. She had to have a social status that was slightly below his.

Q: In *Le Boucher*, there is a dictation to the students of a text by Balzac. . . .

CC: Yes, it's from his novel *A Woman of Thirty*. It's a story about a heroine named Hélène, which works very well, and then there's an allusion to a marquis, which I use later in the masked ball sequence.

Q: And what about the commentary the teacher makes to the students about Balzac's ambition to recreate society?
CC: That's not mine; it's a prop for critics.

Q: We can still find common ground, if not with Balzac, then with Billy Wilder. The way in which you depict France is close to the way only Wilder has of putting America on display.
CC: Everything that is realistic attracts me enormously. That's why I am a great admirer of Wilder.

Q: The characters of policemen in your films are stunning in their reality.
CC: I don't like them, but I never show them as mean. In *Le Boucher*, I asked the chief of police, whom we see for an instant in the film: "If we have a policeman who comes from Bordeaux, and if I dress him like this, with a rolled neckband and a hat, would that be realistic?" He told me, "Yes, that's exactly right." And it's the first time—and I'm very proud of this—that a film respects the actual title of a policeman. You don't say "Inspector," but "Police Officer." If someone says, "I am Inspector Tapautour," you can say, "Please leave, sir, that's not true!"

Q: And what about the people from the village? How did things go with them?
CC: Great! You know, this place is very special. It's very different from villages in the Beauce region or in Brittany, where people are not so happy, where they have problems. Here, they have absolutely no problems. They came to watch the shoot, and they were delighted! They stayed as silent as death, which was fantastic. There were very few professional actors: there was the old woman who laughs in the bakery, who is the wife of the blacksmith. Aside from the teacher, the father-in-law, the boy in the school and the policeman, I only used people from the village.

Q: Why does the song "Capri, petite île" start up again after the last shot of the film?
CC: That was for commercial reasons. The ending is a bit sad, a bit heavy, and if there wasn't that song there people would leave the theater saying: "It's a little too sad; it's good, but a little too sad." So they hear, "Tra palam pam pam," and they say, "It was good, right?"

Notes

1. The FTP, or "Francs tireurs et partisans," was a communist group within the French Resistance
2. Monique Berger was a French journalist and film critic.

3. Jean Yanne (1933–2003) was a well-known radio and television personality in France, having performed in a series of popular parodies of historical events. He was to give some of his most memorable screen performances in Chabrol's films.

4. Adonis (Ado) Kyrou (1923–1985) was a Greek filmmaker and frequent contributor to *Positif*.

Chabrol Talks

Rui Nogueira and Nicoletta Zalaffi / 1970

From *Sight and Sound* 40.1 (Winter 1970–71): 3–6. Reprinted by permission of the British Film Institute.

Question: What stage have you reached with your current project, *Ten Days' Wonder* (*La Décade prodigieuse*), from the Ellery Queen novel?

Claude Chabrol: I still have to hear from Orson Welles, which is not easy since he only communicates by cable. Things were going all right, but we have had no reply from him for a week. We don't even know where he is any more. The project is still on, but I think we will probably have to delay the shooting. I've already cast Orson Welles and Cathérine Deneuve. I wanted Tom Courtenay as well, but he is acting in the theater. The English are always acting in the theater. They're always busy playing Shakespeare, which leaves me busy trying to find actors who are free. I've left it all very late really; but I went to sleep on it a bit because I was thinking about it. I am rather at the mercy of time, but not of money. The film is going to be expensive, but André Génovès and I have managed to set it up ourselves. There are no big American companies to come along and recut it or anything like that. We're completely free.

Q: Throughout your career you've shown noticeable loyalty to your collaborators, whether producer, cameraman, editor . . . to say nothing of the actress.

CC: That isn't loyalty. It's selfishness. I can't conceive of changing editors from film to film. It's hard enough to make yourself understood without having to start again from scratch on every picture. If you take the same people each time, they know what you want, and they are able to make much more of a contribution to the film. With the producer, it's even more a matter of selfishness. He leaves me alone. It's marvelous.

Q: Do you think that *Les Biches* marks a turning point in your career?

CC: Yes, in that it was the first film which I made exactly as I wished. Although the first film I made with Génovès was a frightful experience—the thing I made in Greece, *Who's Got the Black Box?* (*La Route de Corinthe*)—he kept to my making *Les Biches*. I was able to have the actors I wanted. Since the film did well, Génovès said to me, "We may as well do a third . . ." and we've just kept on.

Q: Can you tell me something about your beginnings as a critic, and how you came to be interested in films?
CC: Oh, God! That's all far away in the mists of time. My earliest memory of the cinema is Mervyn LeRoy's *Anthony Adverse*. I don't know if you recall it, but there is a fantastic detail in it: in the duel it is the old man who kills the young one. That had a tremendous effect on me. Then I was bowled over by Errol Flynn in *Captain Blood*; and as kids often do, I started to direct my friends: I was a real little Michael Curtiz. After that there was *Snow White and the Seven Dwarfs*. And I was very struck by Mickey Rooney in *Boys' Town*, directed by Norman Taurog—the story of Father Flanagan. Oh, that really moved me. Ever since that film I've always loved hysterical actors.

Q: But you weren't intended to go into movies?
CC: At that time I wasn't really intended for anything; because I was only eight. But during the war, when I was in the Creuse, between the ages of ten and fourteen, I established the "Cinema de Sardantais" (Sardent is where I later shot *Le Beau Serge*), along with another boy who was also evacuated from Paris. With a capital of 75,000 old francs which we'd collected from here and there, we bought a 16mm projector. Our shows took place in a barn, using rented films. Program director, exhibitor, and projectionist: those were my first jobs.

We were obliged to show a certain quota of German films because of some agreement with Goering or Goebbels, but to annoy the Germans we cheated the publicity, just like real exhibitors. Since no one in that part of the country knew anything about the cinema, we made them think that we were showing American films, and would advertise, for instance, "Heinrich George in an American super-production." After the war I came back to Paris and no longer worked with movies. But I adored cinema; so I went to the Lycée Montaigne, where Langlois was giving his first shows, and then to the Cinémathèque in the Avenue de Messine. I also went to the Ciné-Club du Quartier Latin, which was where I got to know Rohmer, Jean-Luc, and then Truffaut.

Q: The legend is that your meeting with the *Cahiers du cinéma* group took place at the Studio Montparnasse (at that time run by Jean-Louis Chéray) after the screening of a Hitchcock film; and that your great knowledge of the work and world of Hitchcock earned you a place with the magazine.

CC: No: that's a total myth. I was doing my secondary and advanced studies when the others were still in the first grade. I had married well—at that time I had a very rich wife. I was a gigolo and had to find some kind of work. Coming back after my military service (I had managed to get myself posted as a projectionist in Germany) I met up with my friends again, and they told me I ought to write things for *Cahiers*. The first piece I wrote was about *Singin' in the Rain*. It was only after the special Hitchcock number that the whole "Hitchcock metaphysic" myth started.

Q: And then you did the book on Hitchcock with Eric Rohmer?
CC: Rohmer did most of it. I did the English period; also *Notorious*, *Stage Fright* . . . and *Rebecca*, I think.

Q: Hitchcock apart, your heroes at this time were Wilder and Lang?
CC: I had a passion for Lang before Hitchcock. *The Testament of Dr. Mabuse* made a stunning impression on me. Subsequently, as Hitchcock's films accumulated, and Lang was directing less, my affections transferred themselves to Hitchcock. But without Lang, Hitchcock would not have existed.

Q: Staircases play a great part in your films, as they do in Wyler's.
CC: Yes, that's true: there are a lot of staircases in my films. Why? First, because I think staircases are beautiful; and then, as it happens, I have always lived with staircases. Before the war my parents had a duplex, so we had a staircase inside the flat; during the war I was stuck in a house with a staircase. So many things can happen on staircases. They are like a spinal column.

Q: And your experience as a projectionist?
CC: Yes, I know: I put a lot of projections in my films, but it's not at all with an idea of having films within films. Perhaps I simply like projections.

Q: Were you a good projectionist?
CC: Better than the projectionists around here, I have to admit, because down there the audience yelled when it was out of focus. Perhaps nowadays audiences don't know when it's deliberate or not, because of the "New Look." If someone says, "Here, it's all out of focus," you reply, "Oh no; the idea is to isolate that leaf down there." Then people exclaim, "Ah! It's intentional!" There is even a film which stays very hazy quite intentionally from beginning to end: Elio Petri's *A Quiet Little Place in the Country*.

Q: Does the fact that you have acted yourself help when you direct actors?
CC: A little; but indirectly. I can assess the feeling which it is possible to experience,

first in rehearsal and afterwards in shooting. And I have learned to recognize the moment when you have to stop an actor rehearsing and to start shooting a scene.

Q: I'm told that you are a big ham and always try to steal scenes in *La Muette*.
CC: Yes. I know who told you that. Steph (Stéphane Audran). It's true. We played together, and I quite outshone her in my sketch in *Six in Paris*. In *La Muette* you only notice me, and I am very much better. I do more than she does as well. I do marvels in fifteen minutes.

Q: How did you feel about acting in front of the camera in a scene of having a meal together, as in real life?
CC: But we've *never* had that kind of row, ourselves! On the contrary, I remember that Bardet Schroeder came to call on us one morning and said he wanted some little background noises. Stéphane and I were in bed, having breakfast, and we were just like a couple of dead fish in front of the microphone. It was very odd. We had a lot of fun over that.

Q: To what extent were you involved in Project No. 4 of the Etats Generaux of the cinema?[1] In *La Femme infidèle* you refer to this period of May–June 1968 by showing an inscription, "Vive le projet IV," scrawled in red paint on the roof of a car parked outside the King Club.
CC: I frankly believed in the project at that time. No, I didn't really believe in it, but I told myself, "After all, you never know; perhaps we'll get rid of these bastards and it will become possible to organize things seriously. So why not look at things in a healthy way and in a completely new light. It doesn't matter if it is utopian." So we devised a scheme for cinema exhibition which was really irreproachable. It could be put into operation tomorrow. It is childishly simple. You replace the road tax by a cinema tax; and there you are. The project did not get a majority vote—only a hundred votes—but if the Etats Generaux had lasted a month longer it would have been carried, because people would have realized that it was the only one of the projects that made sense.

We reckoned that there was only one possible drawback: the *clochards*. They might have come to take up a cinema seat simply to have somewhere to sit and snooze.

Q: Have you followed the CNP (Cinéma National Populaire) experiment?
CC: A bit, at the start, but it was clobbered before it began. The moment there is a program, a thing has no more interest.

The cinema ought to be like a *pissotière* (public urinal) or a café, with free admission. And exhibition ought to be automatic, rather like television. That would do away with critical selection, which is always misleading, since critics inevitably go wrong all the time. So good films would get as much chance of recognition as bad ones.

Q: In the present crisis in the French cinema—it really seems to be a permanent crisis—you are directing more regularly than you've ever done before. How do you account for your rather privileged situation?

CC: If my films stopped doing well, I would find myself shooting fewer films. As it is, my films make money. I'm glad for me, and sorry for the others.

The SRF (Société de Réalisateurs des Films) is by definition a bad thing, because they are all too much involved with each other, and now they are all writing one another's scripts. Albicocco's next film is written by Pierre Kast, and the last Kast one was written by Pollet. It's a sort of musical chairs. And their solution to the salvation of the French cinema is to hold conferences, poor chaps! Two fundamental things are necessary to save the French cinema: immediate tax relief, and the abolition of censorship. But these people are going to talk before those prerequisites are achieved! The others will be ahead of them for twenty years. I don't know if you have read the report of the Centre National du Cinéma about the Sirizi or Surizi or some such conference, between the Centre and the professional people. It had to be read to be believed. They say things like, "It is urgent to make films for a total public, for every kind of public. . . ." What in the world does that really mean?

Q: There's no rule to determine if a film is going to succeed or not.

CC: There is: a film is successful if there is nothing about it to stop it from being successful.

Q: Of course: but probabilities are still uncertainties. And on the other hand, who would have foreseen the success of *Easy Rider*?

CC: *Easy Rider* couldn't lose money. What is frightful about the cinema is that these people always play single numbers. "Ah! Play that number and you'll get back thirty-five times the stake!" It doesn't work. You have to play the even chances. You put money on black reckoning that black will come up, but you can also play the black and the red at the same time, *à cheval*, because that way you can't lose. You can only lose on the zero.

Q: What is your current position in relationship to the Nouvelle Vague?

CC: The Nouvelle Vague has become a rather dirty word these days. First of all, what is the Nouvelle Vague? The New Wave of what?

Q: I'm talking about the group which has built up around Godard, Truffaut, Rohmer, you. . . .

CC: Each of us has evolved in his own particular direction. Jean-Luc, who is a hardened celibate and suicide, commits his suicide in different countries because he loves to make film after film and didacticism after didacticism. That is fine, that's what he wants. François wants to stop now for a couple of years because he has just killed off Antoine Doinel. That's fine too. I don't say he's right to stop, but . . . Rohmer, on the other hand, never wanted to have an important position in the French cinema. He just wanted to make his *contes moraux* (moral tales), which is what he did.

Q: People are always eating in your films. Do you know Marco Ferreri, who also likes gastronomy?

CC: He's a great chef, Marco.

Q: Do you agree with him that gastronomy is really a neurosis for neurotics, allowing an escape from reality?

CC: Gastronomy? What a funny idea! What a weird argument! I've just one question: what would Marco do if he didn't eat? Would he or would he not escape reality? He would starve to death. He would die. So he would escape reality promptly and without delay. Quite the contrary, gastronomy is one of those rare things which are not neurotic. Marco loves eating. I don't know if he likes it in a neurotic fashion, but faced with a good cassoulet, he's never given me the impression of a neurotic.

Q: Why, contrary to your usual habits, do you make everyone eat so stingily in *La Rupture*?

CC: You are quite right: they don't eat in *La Rupture*. It's awful. For me that contributes to the uneasiness of the atmosphere. But in my next film, *Ten Days' Wonder*, there are going to be some very fine and elegant meals. I ought to say that *La Rupture* is a straightforward film that does not aim at any reverse twist in the ending. The good people stay good. The villain stays bad. The only thing that has a twist is the conspiracy, which turns back on the one who plans it rather than on the victim. But these are things which happen, don't they? I wanted to make a melodrama, a real melodrama. I wanted to stop people from saying, "The film reveals melodramatic tendencies." If there are tendencies, you might as well make a melodrama, which is to say, a tear-jerking drama with music. And the music covers the words. Then the people who don't like melodrama are going to say, "It's grandiloquent." Well, it's not grandiloquent. It's melodramatic.

Q: You always like to follow things through to their conclusions.

CC: Always. I like nuances, but *underneath*, I would be awfully shocked to read, for instance, "The film ends happily with these images." I always go a bit beyond the point where it "ends happily."

Q: There is no filmmaker more fervently anti-Nazi than Fritz Lang. Yet he was fascinated by Nazism. Well, I find that in a certain way you are fascinated by creeps.

CC: Yes; because I am so strongly anti-creep. Something which always annoys me in films is when supposedly intelligent people are made to act in a thoroughly stupid way just for the convenience of the scenario. You must know whether the character is stupid or intelligent, and make him act accordingly. My next film—supposing that I can find Welles again—will be interesting from this point of view, although it is not based on stupidity but on intelligence. The trap is just the same.

Q: There is another of your films which I like very much, exactly because of the treatment of creeps: *La Ligne de démarcation*. I know you don't like it at all, but . . .

CC: Actually, I like it more and more. I'll explain. I hated it for a long time because it really made me suffer physically to see all those creeps—even though I ate very well, and it was a nice place. They really were an extraordinary bunch of characters, but it took place in a context in which I would rather not have shown their awfulness.

I have a great respect for the Resistance of those times, but I only had two solutions for the treatment of the scenario by Colonel Rémy: either to send it up completely—which was impossible—or to treat it absolutely seriously, saying: "Okay. Here's a bunch of characters. Let's enjoy it!"—and it was really deadpan stuff. There's not a second of humor in *La Ligne de démarcation*, and at the same time there's not a second which is *not* a second of humor, because it is a film which is entirely serious and totally stupid. You know that the old French Resistance fighters—the film was promoted by "Rhin-et-Danube," a veterans' association— came to all the showings with their berets, their medals, and their flags, and they stood up and joined in when "La Marseillaise" came on at the end of the film. They were thrilled. And Colonel Rémy cried, "Oh, how beautiful it is! How true it is! This is really France!" Much of the Resistance was lunatic romanticism. In those times they were absolutely heedless. Networks were dismantled as fast as they were built up. Colonel Rémy was . . . it was "Groucho Meets the Gestapo." He is very, very nice, but an old reactionary.

Q: Why did so many of the Resistance people gravitate towards the Right?

CC: It comes from the fact that they were really nationalists. They didn't resist for the sake of liberty, so much as against the occupation of French soil.

Q: Before *Les Biches*, if you had asked anyone which of your films he preferred, he would probably have singled out *Les Bonnes Femmes*. But the film did not do very well.

CC: Yes. Not many people have seen it. There's no mystery about it, it's the first film over which I was really roughly handled. Recently Janine Bazin very much wanted me to do a broadcast in the series *Cinéastes de notre temps*; and then, it's stupid, but I simply couldn't face it. She had sent me some contemporary reviews of *Les Bonnes Femmes*. To my astonishment most of them said that it was an odious film. Lots of left-wingers found it simply Fascist. It was a film which insulted the working class, and I don't know what else.

Some critics decided also that in this picture I was trying to be a Fellini. There they were as wrong as they could be. While I love Fellini, one of the films I detest above all others in the world is *Notti di Cabiria*. It seems to me a completely untruthful film. The basic idea of *Les Bonnes Femmes* is exactly the same as that of *Notti di Cabiria*, but it is treated in a completely contrary way. By definition, there is no film further from Fellini than *Les Bonnes Femmes*. Well, there are critics who have found it "Fellinian," which is to say that one has found oneself face to face with total astonishing incomprehension.

Q: At a certain point, *Cahiers du cinéma*, in which you had made your start as a critic, dropped you . . . to take you up again . . . and now again drop you.

CC: It doesn't worry me, because in any case you never know these days if *Cahiers* likes you or not—it seems to me to have become quite impossible to understand what they think or what they write. They've succeeded in abandoning a bourgeois way of writing, but I think they have not yet achieved a proletarian style in composition.

Q: There are often quotations in your films: T. S. Eliot in *La Femme infidèle*, Balzac in *Le Boucher*, Racine in *La Rupture*.

CC: I'll be truthful. It's to give them substance. I need a degree of critical support for my films to succeed: without that they can fall flat on their faces. So, what do you have to do? You have to help the critics with their notices, right? So, I give them a hand. "Try with Eliot and see if you find me there." Or "How do you fancy Racine?" I give them some little things to grasp at. In *Le Boucher* I stuck Balzac there in the middle, and they threw themselves on it like poverty upon the world. It's good not to leave them staring at a black sheet of paper, not knowing how to begin. "This film is definitely Balzacian," and there you are: they're off. After that they can go on to say whatever they want.

Q: What is a character for you? At what point does a character begin to interest you?

CC: It isn't the character which interests me at the start—a character you can always fabricate. It's a sort of . . . not the plot . . . What interests me is to tease the audience along, to set it chasing off in one direction, and then to turn things inside out.

Q: And how do you work with Jean Rabier? Do you have much discussion before shooting?
CC: Not anymore. Now, he reads the script, then he finds out what he wants to know. I give him points of reference to American cameramen: "James Wong Howe this bit." "Fine." "Ernest Laszlo." "Okay." It's exceedingly practical.

Q: It may seem paradoxical, but your films do seem to betray a respect for the family unit.
CC: Ah! I like the family very much. I think it is a much misunderstood thing; very beautiful, and very delicate, like all beautiful things. So, I am for it. FOR! The bourgeois family is a farce, you realize. It doesn't exist. But a *real* family, that is something wonderful.

Q: Starting from the sketch in *La Muette*, it would be possible to imagine the following. The mother does *not* die when she falls down the stairs. The little boy grows up, becomes the character played by Jean-Claude Drouot in *La Rupture*, and kills his mother, by making her fall downstairs. The circle is completed.
CC: Yes, absolutely. It's the same world. There's no shadow of doubt about it. There is a direct connection of milieu between *La Muette* and *La Rupture*.

Q: In *La Femme infidèle*, it is only through a lie that the husband and wife can find each other again.
CC: Yes. You talk about appearances. They break at a given moment, and then each one goes half of the way towards rediscovering the other. Whereas the characters in *La Rupture* are just caricatures of families. They are like prison wardens, vampires.

Q: Why do you never give a film a really conclusive ending?
CC: Simply because it's never completely finished. You begin at some point, and so you have to stop at some point.

Q: You begin *La Rupture* with a hospital sequence, which could make one think back to the last scenes of *Le Boucher*.
CC: But I only noticed that afterwards. What is terrifying is that my next film will begin with spirits, like a reminder of *La Rupture*, but it is really by pure chance.

Q: Why are all your heroines called Hélène?

CC: It's a name which goes quite well in most countries and is familiar to most people; then it's a name I like; and moreover it comes from mythology. And finally, I tend to keep to the same names to make things easier. There's not only a Hélène in my films. There's always a Paul and a Charles as well. And Charles will never kill Paul. That is a basic postulate, and it really started with *Les Cousins*. One of the cousins was called Charles and the other Paul, and they were two completely contrasting characters. Now when I return to this duality of characters, I tell myself that it is unthinkable, given that I started off with a Charles who would not possibly kill a Paul, not to continue in this same way. One of them may have to do away with the other but you'll never see a Charles kill a Paul. Never.

Q: What importance do you attach to editing?

CC: Editing, in general, is the assembly of the watch—as far as I'm concerned, at least. There's a chap who puts the watch together. If he doesn't put it together well, the watch won't go. And if it comes into his head to change the positioning of the parts, it's quite certain that the watch won't go at all. I don't think that it is possible to retrieve films in the editing. And I shoot very little footage, so there are not many alternative solutions. In fact, there is only one way.

Q: Hal Wallis told me that, for him, a film cut in the editing is a mutilated film. Do you agree?

CC: Yes, but I also agree with Samuel Goldwyn, who said that once a scene is shot it always figures in the film, even if it is later cut out in the editing. That's a very interesting theory. Anyway, though I don't much like the second solution, it is as true as the first one.

Q: Your films tell stories that are very easy to follow. Should we deduce a reaction against the rather "elusive" manner of a certain type of new filmmaker?

CC: I don't much care for the "New Look," the "focusers," the focusing in the course of a shot, the mistiness. It must come from a great failure in the sense of composition.

When you have two people in a room, and one of them has to leave on tiptoe, morally on tiptoe, you have to know how to shoot it. There's another solution: to get the camera behind a vase of flowers, and focus on the vase. In reaction against this I like sharp, clear films. And I like understandable stories. There are films of which you might say, "This shouldn't be shown to a dog." The very least you can do is to try to be simple when you want to say complicated things. And you should never complicate something simple.

Notes

1. Project 4 was a plan to establish films and TV as public services independent of state
   control. Its three main proposals were: free admission to all films; equal opportunities for
   professional status within the industry; and cultural decentralization through regional
   centers, mobile cinemas for rural areas, and the abolition of exclusive first runs. It was
   envisaged that all film production would be financed out of a general tax.

Chabrol: Game of Mirrors

David Overbey / 1977

From *Sight and Sound* 46.2 (Spring 1977): 78–81. Reprinted by permission of the British Film Institute.

One of several cultural shocks which the English-speaking cinephile in France must survive is the singularly Gallic judgment on films and directors. The predilection of the French for Jerry Lewis is of course notorious. Perhaps less well-known in Britain and America is that the French, in general, do not hold the work of Claude Chabrol in very high esteem. The last of his films to have had generally good critical notices and solid box-office receipts was *Les Noces rouges* in 1973, seven films ago (not counting the medium-length films and various episodes shot for French television). It is ironic that French critics usually find Chabrol too commercial, while French filmgoers evidently do not find him commercial enough. On the other hand, a short cigarette advertisement parodying the Bogart film noirs of the 1940s (a "commercial" project if ever there was one) was so overwhelmingly popular with everybody, including the critics, that it played in Paris cinemas for over three years and was often advertised in newspapers as well as outside the cinemas.

A further irony is that, aside from earlier Chabrol films which have never been released in English-speaking countries, most American and English critics are now several films behind. *Pleasure Party* (*Une partie de plaisir*) is only now turning up on the "Ten Best" lists of the New York critics and (except for a London Festival screening) has not yet been shown in Britain. Thus, most critical evaluations of Chabrol in English are, at the very least, dated. A few years ago—during Chabrol's "third period"—this would have been a minor matter. Then he seemed to be composing variations on a theme in which stylistic nuances and plot manipulations were alternative approaches within a given psycho-philosophical range. With his last three films, however, Chabrol has reached a turning-point in his career, and has set off on a trek into new and rather startling areas.

Les Magiciens, which opened last May just before the Cannes Festival during that always disastrous week when film critics seem too busy to attend to their work, was a commercial catastrophe, running exactly one week in its Paris release. Those critics who bothered to review the film at all followed the lead of *Image et Son*'s André Cornard: "It is disappointing to see the auteur of *Le Boucher* wasting his talent and taking pleasure in filming no matter what. . . . Everything is false, superficial, boring . . . tourist publicity." Only the subject and its treatment seemed to have bothered this critic, however. He found the films still proof that Chabrol is a "great technical master."

And so he is; the director takes obvious pleasure in long tracking shots along a beach, a series of zoom shots wickedly exploring décor, and a fake magic act in which heads separate from bodies to float about. Despite the verdict of the French critics, the film is fascinating, both per se and as a pivotal work in Chabrol's career. Set in Tunisia on the island of Djerba, the film's three plot strands/themes are woven into a unified seriocomic melodrama: the impact of tourism on the local culture, not to mention the mentality represented by a particularly awful hotel in which the "natives" are unwelcome as guests but are fully exploited as servants; Chabrol's customary treatment of bourgeois marriage, adultery, and jealousy; and a magician with pretensions to clairvoyance who recounts his obscure but "prophetic" vision of a murder to a Machiavellian tourist who, in a fit of ineffable ennui, manipulates the conditions in which the envisioned murder will occur. This last is particularly interesting in that it throws into relief the whole subject of the relationship of mise en scène to fantasy and reality.

When Chabrol's next project, *Folies bourgeoises* (*The Twist*), was announced, it seemed possible that the subject would lend itself to a comic development of those same themes set within his omnipresent bourgeoisie, for the plot involved marriage and infidelity with husband and wife creating and "directing" fantasies to fee their jealousies and take their revenge. However, while his creation of the coolly fashionable Paris literati and the fantasies set in an avant-garde theater and the Crazy Horse Saloon continued to demonstrate technical mastery, the film seemed misfired and flat, more Vadim than Buñuel in its overpowering décor. Released widely throughout France, it received universally hostile reviews. The fact that is also did little business was at least partially explained by its June release date, for the French seem to devote the summer entirely to *les vacances*, leaving art to fend for itself without them for three months.

After five successive critical and commercial failures, Chabrol might have been excused had he run for cover by finding a "sure-fire" subject. Instead, returning to *Les Magiciens*, he re-engaged himself in the exploration of the fantastic. *Alice, ou la dernière fugue* begins where many of his bourgeois melodramas end: with the disintegration of an unhappy upper-middle-class marriage. Within months after the film had begun, however, this link to his earlier work is stretched to a fineness which only close criticism by an overenthusiastic auteurist could render visible.

Fleeing Paris and her outrageously bourgeois husband, Alice has car trouble on the road at night and takes refuge from a storm in an old dark house. Instead of gothic horror, she finds civilized sympathy dinner and a warm, dry bed—none of it sinister. It is only upon awakening the following morning that a series of odd and fantastic events begin to happen to her. She accepts everything without fear, and soon everything is "explained" to her. Although the film is France's entry this year in the Avoriaz Fantastic Film Festival, it might be argued that *Alice* is not so much within the genre as it is an extended contemplation, stripped of all psychology and plot tension, in which Chabrol examines death, transformation, identity, and the philosophical implications of the relationship between "reality" and film, through a series of extraordinarily sensual image aligned to each other by hard logic, playful irony, and a sympathy for the human condition which most critics (French *and* Anglo-Saxon) usually deny their director.

If irony seems a particularly French trait, then Chabrol is very French indeed. Even as he laughs (which is often) there is a glint in his eyes which suggests that part of himself is removed from the joke and that he is amused at himself for laughing in the first place. He speaks quickly, often finishing a sentence with the wave of a hand or the lift of an eyebrow while his mind and tongue are already at work on the next one. I have never seen a printed interview with him (including this one, alas) which has caught exactly the flavor of his conversation, peppered as it is with argot and well-placed vulgarities. It is not that he lies; indeed, he is astonishingly honest both about his own work and his reaction to the work of others. Simply, he loves pranks, jokes, paradoxes, and games. The evening following our conversation, Chabrol gave a brief interview on television in which he was asked some of the same questions. His answers were not necessarily contradictory to those which follow here; they were merely different.

David Overbey: In America and England, you are something of a cultural hero, but . . .
Claude Chabrol: Yes, I know. In France, not at all.

DO: Why is that? Because you hold a mirror up to the French and they don't like what they see?
CC: Not particularly. I think it's more complicated than that. Many of my films are simply not understood here as they are in the Anglo-Saxon countries. *Une partie de plaisir*, for example, was a complete flop here, while it had some success in America. It was of course very French and some nations like that; but more than that, here in France other, more passionate connections were made which have nothing to do with a work of art. Here they know me. You know, no one is a hero to his valet. The film was destroyed by the critics; they all know Paul Gégauff, and they don't like him.

DO: There was also *Les Magiciens*. I liked that film and thought it a scandal that it lasted exactly one week in Paris.

CC: I like it too. With that one the distributor went quite mad during that period. Anyway, the film was never given a chance. The producers were Arabs, and the credits were full of Arab names. "Tarak Ben Ammar presents." That irritated them. You know what I am talking about. Then another thing was my fault. I tried to give it an Anglo-Saxon flavor at the beginning even though the story wasn't at all Anglo-Saxon. Anyhow, the novel by Frédéric Dard on which the film was based finally didn't inspire me all that much. What interested me was going to Tunisia to explore the situation there. The French seemed to think that because the producers were Tunisian I was making a publicity film on the beauties of Tunisia, which wasn't the case at all. I was there to show the horrible side of things: look at that monstrous hotel and those awful people.

DO: You then made *Folies bourgeoises* (*The Twist*) in English.

CC: I've made more than one film in English—remember *The Champagne Murders* (*Le Scandale*)?—and they have always been catastrophes. I made *Le Scandale* in two versions but I made this horrible stupidity—*Folies bourgeoises*—in English only. It was all very complicated. The film got away from me quickly. I started it just as my contract ended, but I felt somehow morally obliged to make it anyway. It wasn't that I wanted to do it, though it could have been a good film. It should have—and could have—been made on a small budget.

DO: Have you made other films you think are bad?

CC: I've done a lot of bad films, but I was always aware of it; I knew they were bad while I was making them. I must make awful crap from time to time. It is professionally inescapable, but it bothers me to do such things with material I care about. I would rather take a garbage can and throw everything awful into it at once. Sometimes such a film will be very popular. I have made frightful rubbish which went down very well with critics and public alike.

DO: *Les Innocents aux mains sales*?

CC: Yes. I know it wasn't all that good and I didn't like a lot of things about it, but there was an enormous ambiguity about it. In my mind it was a comic film, but the actors wouldn't follow me. Except for the two cops and Jean Rochefort. The rest, no. Certainly not Rod Steiger and not Romy Schneider! Romy took it all seriously as some sort of tragedy, but it was just a gag. I wonder what happened to me. What was so good about the book (although it was a *bad* little thriller) was that the further it went the madder it got, and if we had captured that idea, that tone, it could have been comic and wonderful. I finally got fed up. I didn't even direct that film, finally; I played chess.

DO: But you almost always make comic films.

CC: Yes, I know that, but my actors have to know it too. In *Alice* they all knew it was a very serious film, but they also realized the necessity of a light touch.

DO: And *Le Beau Serge*? Is it true that you said you thought it was insupportable?

CC: Yes, and I still think so. It is the most tricked-up film I have ever made. It is sneaky, fabricated, manipulated. There is just enough pretension to make me uncomfortable, but that is not its main fault. It was premeditated not so much to make the film work but to get good notices and a nice advance on receipts. I needed the money so badly at the time that I made the film with that in mind, in order to allow myself to make others. You can sense that in it. I like the description of the countryside, but the rest not very much.

DO: In a recent *Sight and Sound* there was an article about your work by Fassbinder. Among other things, he said that there were no people in most of your films, only shadows. He claims that the later films exhibit a latent fascism which has always been implicit in your work; in *Docteur Popaul*, for example. He also objects to your use of the zoom, calling it something like "the saddest device in the cinema" and saying that if it didn't exist you would have invented it. Would you care to comment?

CC: What do you want, ping-pong? I see! No, I have no comments really. Well, as for fascism; Popaul is a fascist, yes. But does making a film about fascism make one a fascist? I'm very happy that Fassbinder thought it was worthwhile to waste his time writing about me. I shouldn't think that anyone as busy as he is would take the time. I certainly wouldn't.

DO: Do you like Fassbinder's films?

CC: From time to time. Of course, he invented the *plan fixe*. He has a certain merit. It is very difficult, after all, to make any film in Germany at all. I don't agree with what he said about me, but what he said is of no importance.

DO: And the French cinema? I asked Alain Resnais why the French cinema was sick, and he denied it, arguing that there are never more than five or six good directors working in any national cinema, and that those few are enough to keep a cinema healthy. Do you agree?

CC: In a sense I do. But the health of a cinema doesn't really come from its good directors; it comes from the good movies of its bad directors. In the great epoch of American cinema, that is exactly what happened. A nothing director sometimes ended up every four or five years making a good film. That was remarkable. In France we have the reverse situation, in which good directors are almost forced to make bad films. Either they are given bad scenarios, or they do it for the money or for personal reasons. There simply is not an industrial organization which allows for good films. One must understand this about France, and that's what I criticize. There should be one. It's primarily the fault of distributors and exhibitors who always try to find a new success by way of prior hits. That's the worst way.

DO: There is nothing then that you care for in current French films? Bresson, for example?
CC: Ah, Bresson! Yes, I detest Bresson. I think he's completely in the wrong. But yes, I see what you mean. He is at least seeking something. Most directors aren't even looking. They just tell a story; some of them do it very well. That's all right, but it's not enough. It's boring. There is a film by Maurice Pialat which I like, *La Gueule ouverte* (*The Mouth Agape*): that was magnificent. He makes no compromises. He is a madman that way.

DO: And the young filmmakers? Claude Miller's *La Meilleure façon de marcher* (*The Best Way to Walk*), for example?
CC: It's a good movie, but it's a *film putain*.[1] A first film has to be a *film putain*. If not, there will be no second film.

DO: There is a good deal of talk in France at the moment about the wonders of "*le nouveau naturel*." What is that exactly?
CC: There's where they give actors only a vague idea of what is supposed to be said: "You just got back from a holiday in St. Tropez, and you from Brittany. Now you'll have coffee together and talk about your holidays. Give me two minutes, please." The poor actors then have to make two minutes out of a cup of coffee. Voila "*le nouveau naturel*."

DO: I assume that in your case everything is written beforehand?
CC: Yes, there's very little improvisation. In *Alice*, for example, there is none at all. And even when there is some, it isn't really improvisation. Something might come up while we are shooting, such as an idea from an actor, but we always write it down and try it out first, so that's not improvisation. Then, when Stéphane Audran has a very long speech I always give it to her ahead of time so that she can rearrange it until she feels comfortable with it. She does what she wants, but it is a written text, so that isn't improvisation either. Anyway, it is already hard enough to get an actor to give a good performance without asking him to make up dialogue as well.

DO: You haven't made a film in black and white in fifteen years, yet I've heard you say you like black and white.

CC: I don't have enough money to shoot in black and white. It is very expensive now, a luxury, especially since the laboratories are now set up entirely for color processing. For a black and white film to be sold and shown, it has to be a really superlative film. But I love it very much. There are things one can do in black and white which are impossible in color. There is a purity of line, for example, that can't happen in color.

DO: You used to play with color, as in *A double tour*, but not so much anymore.
CC: Ah, yes. So long ago! Now it bothers me. I find it stupid to play in that way; perhaps I just got bored with it. It is stupid to think about putting a blue carpet there, a red one here, because while I want people to keep a certain distance from the film, the use of color in that way distances an audience too much. An audience and a film can be absolutely crushed by color, which gets the attention instead of more important things. In *Le Scandale* there was no red at all; but then at the very end everything was red. But that's a children game; it doesn't interest me anymore.

DO: *Alice* is dedicated to Fritz Lang. There is a sequence at the beginning in which the husband's face keeps reappearing, getting larger each time. That's from *The Testament of Dr. Mabuse*, I assume. Is there anything else of Lang which I missed?
CC: Well, it was *Mabuse*, which I saw early on at a ciné-club, that made me want to direct in the first place. That's true, not just sentiment. As for influences and homages: you know, very often what is important is not what one borrows nor that one imitates what someone else has done. In *Alice*, for example, I refused to do all the things that Lang had refused to do. Lang rejected false effects; I won't have them either. I had already decided to do the film that way, but Lang died while we were shooting *Alice*, and that strengthened my decision. I decided that if I liked the film I would dedicate it to Lang, and when I finished I found many things in it that were reminiscent of him. I wanted Lang to make a film here with my producer, and we had long discussions about projects. One of them had to do with death. Of course, he had already made a film about death, *Destiny*, which also had a wall like *Alice*.

DO: You know that one of Lang's last projects contained a sequence at the end in which colored balls fall from the sky during an LSD trip. That reminds me of *Juste avant la nuit*. Is there a connection?
CC: Well, he told me that story and I suppose it was in the back of my mind somewhere. You will just have to believe me when I tell you that when I shot my film I wasn't conscious of it, though of course it must have been there. You know, for that film Lang had in mind having a villain with an artificial heart—one made of iron.

DO: *Alice* is the first time, really, that you have worked with the fantastic.

CC: Yes, but I've wanted to do so for a long time, and I even had this exact subject in mind. I had a scenario about six years ago, but it was overloaded. I ended up suppressing things; I pruned it down to essentials and I like it better that way.

DO: And will you continue in this vein?

CC: Yes, although it is not the fantastic in itself that I am drawn to. Rather, there are certain fantasy writers who impress me. Borges, and the short fiction of Dino Buzzati. Not the fantastic itself, because one easily falls into the genre tricks— creaking doors, grimacing faces, horrors. I suppressed all that; no doors creak in *Alice*. Of course, there is no real tradition of fantasy cinema in France, nor is there any literary tradition. That's why I leaned so heavily on surrealist painters like Magritte.

DO: You heroine is named Alice Carrol. Lewis Carroll is obviously the reference.

CC: Yes, although Carroll lost an "l." Beware, for in your relationship to my film Lewis Carroll is a false trail. That's one of Chabrol's pranks. Oh yes, there is the broken windshield which reminds one of the mirror, and there are a few other "fantastic" occurrences. But no, the Lewis Carroll business is neither a path nor a key to anything in the film. That is the joke. Don't forget that the book Alice reaches for to read in the house is by Borges. That's much more important.

DO: And the Mozart on the soundtrack?

CC: That is also important. For me, Mozart has always been a composer of simple effects engaged in a search for miniscule, scarcely palpable beauty. He is also a composer who sensed putrefaction and decadence in the simplest things. That is why I chose him. I wanted to give a bizarre continuity of sound to the film. One can't really know why, but it is the concerto which continues throughout the film. The action of the film—the "real" action—lasts nine minutes and the concerto lasts nine minutes. I tried to create a moment of pure beauty when at the end Alice comes out of the salon with Charles Vanel to go up to bed. There is the sound of a violin. It is all of a most extraordinary beauty. I get a thrill when I see that, and I don't care what other people feel about it.

DO: Why did you choose Sylvia Kristel for Alice?

CC: I have an old vice. I like to impose challenges on myself. Everyone in France says that Sylvia is a beautiful woman but that she can't act and so has to show her ass all the time. I thought it would be interesting to dress her and to make her play something very difficult. Remember, she is always alone on the screen. In such cases the problem is not to feel the presence of the camera; with her, one never does. Then, I found a photograph of Carroll's original Alice, whom Sylvia greatly resembles. And also, the film is not really very commercial, and it wasn't such a bad idea to use a well-known star in it. I knew she was a good actress anyway. For some reason, Sylvia is really the only one in France who can get people to come to see skin flicks. A sort of grace, perhaps?

DO: *Alice* seems to end twice, first as Alice goes downstairs and through the door, and again when we see the car accident.
CC: I thought about the car for a long time. I put it in; I took it out. Finally I put it back again because it is very Cartesian. It doesn't explain a thing, of course. Odd, because people seem to think that the final shot explains everything, when the contrary is true. Of course, it helps to bring people back to a kind of reality.

DO: And what is reality when one speaks of a film, since film is by definition unreal?
CC: It's all a game that one plays. There are degrees of reality and unreality. It was amusing to begin the film with a quarrel between husband and wife: that corresponds to a reality. Such realism ends abruptly with a shot that is entirely unrealistic: when the credits come up on the screen to divide the couple, each of them standing in a doorway on either side of the corridor with the light silhouetting them from behind. At that point the jump is easy, but remember that realism is never reality anyway. It's just a game. A game of mirrors. Which is why I wouldn't use laboratory tricks in the film. Instead, towards the end when the décor and the staircase become deformed, I did it all in the camera with mirrors. You know, Magritte did a painting of a pipe, and underneath he wrote: "This is not a pipe." A woman said to him, "But of course that is a pipe." He asked her what one did with a pipe. She replied that one smoked a pipe. "Smoke that one," he said.

DO: Vanel's character "explains" things to Alice by saying, "We are the representations of your destiny. Not only representations: we also have our own existence. The difference is that we are transformable." What does that mean?
CC: That is really the definition of an actor. When an actor plays a role, doesn't he transform himself? I suppose it depends on the actor. In *Alice* there is a doubling of the actors in that they play roles which in turn play roles. As for transformation, the film is about passage, flight, movement through time and space. Thus there must be transformation; otherwise there is no film. The décor changes, but the passage itself implies a transformation from life to death—or rather a transformation of the dead to the living, because one could regard what happens to Alice in the house as life and what happens to her both before and after as death. What happens in the house could then represent her period of gestation. Does the film begin with her death or with her birth? There are many elements in the film to suggest the latter. She is, after all, coming out of the car the way a child comes out of the womb. It is

a mystery. What is interesting is not to know that she is dead, but death itself. It is a film which makes death sweet; it is never frightening.

DO: Yet isn't it a rather pessimistic film? There is the cyclist at the end who glances indifferently at the accident and pedals away.

CC: But that might be very optimistic! He sees she is dead. Perhaps he is going to get help, to find a telephone. After all, he pedals away very fast. No, the film is neither pessimistic nor optimistic. It is a logical series of events which will be intellectually satisfying only if one accepts the double point of view of fantasy and reality.

DO: Since you have become interested in the fantastic, does that mean that the bourgeois tales are finished?

CC: Just about, though I still have a couple of ideas in mind along that line. I would like to make a film about two college friends who meet after thirty years or so. They hated each other in college, but now they throw themselves into each other's arms. That idea pleases me a lot. And I would like to make a film about a cop in charge of an investigation who comes to realize that the criminal situation is a mirror image of his own personal life. That idea is perfect for me.

DO: Your films have been described often enough as possessed of a Balzacian sensibility. I know you admire Balzac, yet you have never filmed him.

CC: One can't transpose Balzac's time. I broke my back trying to transpose *La Peau de chagrin* to a modern setting, but I couldn't find a way. Anyhow, I would rather take an undeveloped idea—not something so completely developed and filled out. I have been offered big novels. Malcolm Lowry's *Under the Volcano* and Dino Buzzati's *The Tartar Steppe*, for example. As they are already nearly perfect as literature, I don't know how one could impose images on them. It would all be too academic for me. I haven't yet seen Valerio Zurlini's film *Desert of the Tartars*, but I would have had to add lots of flourishes to it since the subject of that book is the absence of something. Of course, critics would say that one had betrayed the book. The answer to that is usually that one has been faithful not to the letter but to the spirit. The problem is that with *The Tartar Steppe* the letter *is* the spirit. No, I prefer either to use an original script or to adapt a thriller.

DO: But neither Simenon nor Chandler?

CC: Simenon, yes, I've tried from time to time, but the rights have always been too expensive. With Chandler one would have to use Los Angeles. You can't change the city. Absolutely not. And I don't want to go to Los Angeles, or reinvent it here.

DO: So that your next project will be either the college friends or the cop?

CC: I don't know, perhaps one of them. I would also like to make a film about the municipal elections, but I can't decide if it would be best to make it during or after them.

DO: Wouldn't you run into the same censorship problems that you encountered when you suggested corruption in high places in *Les Noces rouges*?

CC: I don't think so, because things have changed. The forms of power are growing weaker and they cannot now forbid much because they know it would come right back to slap them in the face.

DO: But they burn films here. Look at the court's decision to burn that pornographic film.

CC: Yes. They burned one. Of course, there are still copies of that film in the producer's office. But all the same it's symbolic. It is lamentable and odious. Oh, the whole story is ridiculous, but dangerous all the same. It is odd. I didn't know that you could burn films any more. I thought that all film was now nonflammable.

Notes

1. A "prostitute film," or more colloquially, a "sellout."

The Magical Mystery World of Claude Chabrol: An Interview

Dan Yakir / 1979

From *Film Quarterly* 32.3 (Spring 1979): 2–14. © 1979 by the Regents of the University of California. Reprinted by permission of University of California Press.

Dan Yakir: Stylistically, what alternative do your films propose to French cinema?
Claude Chabrol: I've always tried to hold on to the cinema of genre, because I think it's the only way to make films. These days in France, but not only there, one veers mostly toward an overly intellectual vision of things, and I think the only solution is to make some good *policiers*, some good soap-operas and comedies. At this moment, there's the disastrous influence of Godard, who is a genius but who is quite alone, and all those who imitate him are really annoying.

DY: What did the New Wave—if one accepts it as an aesthetic and economic movement—give French cinema?
CC: Lots of worries. . . . It was an economic movement, which is always the same: we had no money, so it was an economic problem. There was no unity of inspiration, but rather a unity of rejection of certain things. There was an influence of American cinema, which I find very healthy, but very soon, instead of trying to bring into this existing cinematic structure what they could, they eliminated and betrayed their teacher—they tried to make films which were no longer genre films. I think it's very bad. Fortunately, cinema is still a popular art and we need people to go see films: They'll go to see a *policier*, a love story. Often, people just don't understand the films they are shown.

DY: I've heard the accusation that members of the New Wave, like Truffaut and yourself, are making the same kind of films you used to attack before.
CC: It's not true, of course. It's stupid! If it happens, it is to make, accidentally, a

parody of this kind of film, but that's all. If one doesn't see the parody . . . Frankly, it's not at all possible.

DY: What do you think of the way directors like Rohmer, Resnais, and Godard have developed?

CC: Godard's case is apart, because his is an intolerable cinema—except by himself, because he has genius. When he's in shape, it's superb. It's never great for a long time because it's not the kind of cinema one can sit through for an hour and a half. But for twenty to thirty minutes, it's extraordinary cinema.

As to Rohmer and Resnais, I feel closer to them because I know them better. Let's say . . . *Merde*! I'll say what I think! I reproach them for not trying to make popular films. Yes, even Rohmer. It's not that he doesn't want to—he can't. He just doesn't have the right mind for a large public. The success of his films—and we've spoken about it, the two of us—has always been caused by misunderstanding. The titles of his films—*My Night at Maud's*, *La Collectionneuse*, *Claire's Knee*, *Chloe in the Afternoon*—give the impression of being obscene, and people go to see these obscenities, but they get something else. It's only the titles: *The Marquise of O*—it sounds like a whore.

DY: And Truffaut?

CC: He has no problems. I didn't like *Small Change*. I find the criticism he made about children's films . . . when he made *Forbidden Games*, for example, he was very precise, but I think he fell a bit into the same trap in *Small Change*. Well, he wanted to make a film that would be assured of success in France. It's a cinematic strategy that he has. But I like the fact that although he tries to change, he never does. I say it more as a compliment that as a reproach. He really tries to change his kind of films. He has two lines: the *Jules and Jim* line, and the *400 Blows* line. He also has a less interesting, Hitchcockian line—*The Bride Wore Black*, *Mississippi Mermaid*—because he's enormously influenced by Hitchcock. Even *Small Change* seems to me very influenced by Hitchcock in terms of the way of shooting. It's okay when he doesn't deal with subjects that are *policiers*, but when he does—one gets the impression of a copy of Hitchcock, an almost involuntary copy.

DY: Let's talk about Hitchcock.

CC: He doesn't make films anymore. He's working on a script which takes place in Finland in winter. With his pacemaker, he won't be able to see it through. He'll kill himself, like Molière. It frightens me. I liked *Family Plot* very much, especially when the guy in the garage hides behind the door and finds himself out in the street.

DY: In your book about Hitchcock, you spoke about the transfer of guilt and the reversal of roles, which are present in your films as well.

CC: Yes, I think that they are more present in my films than in Hitchcock's. Of course, it exists in Hitchcock, but we pushed it a bit. I don't think that the core of his films is automatically the transfer of guilt. It must interest him, because he's dealt with the subject several times, but I don't think it interests him above all. And don't ask me what interests him above all, because I couldn't answer.

DY: Why your interest in this principle?

CC: It interests me to the extent that I believe in the revelations of guilt. There is a certain amount of guilt in every individual—it's the real Original Sin—and I noticed that guilt is always transferred from the most guilty to the least guilty. It's never the other way around. So, in a way, the act of the guilty releases him from his culpability: it's enough to commit the act to be able to transmit it to somebody else. In *Violette*, she has practically no remorse. She never regrets her deed and still manages to give a feeling of guilt to her mother and all the people around her—and she's the one who kills!

DY: Do you agree with the view that divides some of your films along the inspiration of Lang and other along that of Hitchcock? In *Que la bête meure* (*This Man Must Die*) there's a very Langian element of fate.

CC: Yes, *Que la bête meure* is mostly Langian.

DY: And *La Femme infidèle* is more Hitchcockian?

CC: I don't think so. I don't consider Lang and Hitchcock from a thematic point of view. I consider them in terms of style, and in this I'm much closer to Lang than to Hitchcock. Hitchcock tries to convey a story subjectively—everything is based on the subjectivity of the character, while Lang seeks the opposite, to objectify all the time. I try to objectify too. It's characteristic of Hitchcock—even the titles of his films always bear on his personal psychology: *Shadow of a Doubt*, *Suspicion*, *Psycho*. They all have to do with personal, individual things. In Lang, it's *Human Desire*— it's never individual. Intellectually—in terms of pleasure derived—I was more influenced by Hitchcock than by Lang. The thing that strikes me enormously—it's a unique case in the history of cinema—is a great filmmaker making a remake of two films by another great filmmaker: it was Lang in relation to Renoir. *La Bête Humaine* became *Human Desire* and *La Chienne* became *Scarlet Street*. At first glance, there is no greater difference between two filmmakers than between Renoir and Lang, but it isn't true. There is a greater difference between Renoir and Hitchcock, and even Hitchcock and Lang, than between Renoir and Lang. One can't imagine Hitchcock making a remake of Renoir. It's unthinkable.

DY: What is the difference between your own scripts and the ones you wrote with Gégauff, or those he wrote himself?

CC: In general, I write for three reasons: 1) I have an idea and I see no reason to give it to someone else, though I don't like writing; it bores me—I detest it. 2) I read a book and decide to adapt it faithfully, with no intention of changing much, so I see no reason to pay—even if it's a friend who may need the money—since I just intend to copy the book. I do this too. 3) For example, *Violette* is a film I wanted to shoot for a long time: about Violette Nozière, the girl who poisoned her father and mother in 1934. Since it deals with what goes on in her mind, I preferred to have a woman do it—Odile Barski. This is a special case.

DY: Do you find in Gégauff something that you want to say, but maybe he can say it better?

CC: That's it. What I like in Paul is that he's quite crazy. I'm crazy too, but it's a *folie sage*, which is not his case. He often has ideas that are extraordinarily courageous. He's one of those people—and I admire it very much—who, when they have a problem of tying up something, they're not taken aback by it. In *Que la bête meure* we had a problem as to how to justify the fact that this guy, by coincidence, tracks down the killer. So, Paul just said it was by coincidence. It was terrific. He's very good at that. He's also good at . . . he says he refuses to write polished dialogue, but as soon as I need dialogue which is a bit polished—I hate it and don't know how to write it—I go to him. I'm good at writing dialogue for fools, and he's good with dialogue for intelligent people. I tell him: "Paul, here they have to be intelligent." So, he does it. If they are fools, I keep them and do it myself—I'm absolutely unbeatable at that.

DY: There's something classical about the scripts you've written—*La Femme infidèle*, *La Rupture*, *Le Boucher*, *Juste avant la nuit*—something very gracious.

CC: It's a matter of construction. I love that. It's my great pleasure. I construct very quickly: I'm good at that. That's why it's classical: because it's constructed.

DY: How did you construct a film like *Le Boucher*?

CC: The construction of *Le Boucher* was based on two ideas: the depth which was in the area, in the earth-bed—the grottos, because they were there—and the sun, the morning sun. From then on, it was very easy—I mixed the two with the characters and it came about all by itself.

The only dramatic element in *Le Boucher* is the cigarette lighter. It's from the lighter that things begin to . . . 1) The lighter is offered. 2) The lighter is found on the cliff-top. 3) No, it's not the one. 4) Yes, it is. So, it's very easy. I adore symmetry, I love symmetrical things.

I think it's an interior need that balances things. Internally, psychologically, I seek to maintain my equilibrium while my natural tendency is toward imbalance. So, the search for symmetry in things helps me in doing that. There's only Hercule Poirot who's like me: he adores symmetry too. But I'm not for simple symmetry. Symmetry doesn't mean putting one chandelier on the right and another on the left.

DY: You have often used the melodrama as a vehicle to express quite a tragic vision of life.

CC: Yes, I adore melodramas. All films are melodramas to the extent that you put some music in. Only Rohmer doesn't use any music in his films. I find melodramas moving. When there are moving elements—like a woman who loses her child—one can take a distance on condition that the film doesn't turn out cold. I prefer this to the other way around. I saw the first film of John Frankenheimer, *The Young Stranger*, which is great, but there's a moment when he returns home, goes up the stairs—and there's this terribly dramatic music—opens up the refrigerator, and takes out an . . . apple! I prefer this to having him find a corpse in the refrigerator: his mother's corpse, for example.

DY: You have also used the *roman policier* as a similar vehicle. Why do you find it useful to express a tragic vision?

CC: Because I've always liked the *roman policier*. I think that practically all *romans policiers* have a metaphysical side to them, to the extent that there's either a mystery with a capital M or a villain who has to be destroyed. This is pure metaphysics. It interests people: to open the fridge door and discover the body of an old woman. It interests them for a while.

DY: Is it mostly as a vehicle to express your vision of life or rather the mechanism of suspense that interests you?

CC: I'm interested in it because the form itself expresses something. Afterwards, you can add all kinds of things to it—tell the history of the world from its origins to our time: this doesn't bother anybody. But what happens to the spectator is that he doesn't fall asleep. It mustn't be too complicated, or else you lose a lot of time trying to unravel it, which is annoying. But when it's not complicated, it's okay, it's a bit like . . . I'm not saying that the message should be bitter, but when you have a bitter pill to swallow, you put some chocolate around it, as you do with children and cats. You can do that in a good *policier*.

DY: You have said you're optimistic, but your vision of the world seems to me quite pessimistic: in your films, evil lurks everywhere while virtue is rare.

CC: Ah, it's very true!

DY: But at the same time, your vision is also curiously humorous.

CC: Virtue is always a bit ridiculous because it's such a rare flower that, first, it has such a hard time surviving, and then, it's rather dull.

DY: *Marie-Chantal contre Docteur Kha* and *La Rupture* are the only films where you have a completely virtuous heroine.

CC: Yes, in *La Rupture*, she's even more virtuous because she has suffered, while Marie-Chantal is an innocent, a *naïve*.

DY: You don't have a male hero who is virtuous in this way.

CC: A virtuous man, no. Not yet. Ah, I have one: Donald Sutherland in *Blood Relatives*. It's really the story of a virtuous man. It's curious: a virtuous cop!

DY: Because he does things for others or for himself?

CC: He tries to do something for others, and a bit for himself. He's a man who tries to understand himself, who tries to behave decently. There is a limit to virtue: to just let things be. The enemy of virtue is preaching, and if you don't agree with the lesson . . . Things aren't as clear-cut as that.

DY: But in a film like *Une partie de plaisir*, I feel that there's a "message"—against self-sacrifice, for healthy self-interest. If everybody took care of his own interest, it would be better for all.

CC: I have an old theory that his thought has to be divided half and half. Half for oneself and half for the others. This is healthy. Otherwise, it's very difficult. One has to be a bit selfish.

DY: In *Que la bête meure*, there is an ambiguous situation (one isn't sure if the hero is going to die at the end) as well as the moral ambiguity (the victim-hero isn't all that pure himself). Is ambiguity an important principle for you?

CC: It's not the ambiguity which is important. It's the . . . I abhor judges. They frighten me. They judge according to what? This is why my "great testament," my "definitive message" is that imported phrase: "Don't judge!" One has to avoid traps, but this is not always easy. One judges in any case, but this judgment shouldn't have too great an import or consequence. Judgments are always made in relation to the self, even with judges and members of the jury. What one demands of jurors is terrible: an intimate conviction. "Beyond a reasonable doubt" is really a phrase that frightens me.

DY: And yet good and evil are often well-defined in your films!

CC: They mix. Laws aren't that simple. If good gains, it doesn't mean that it will also triumph, and if evil sweeps us along, it doesn't imply its victory. The battle between good and evil is more complicated. The principle is: when there's a character who is nice and another who is evil—for example, in *Le Boucher*, which is a limited case and a very simple one: there's the bad butcher and the nice teacher. But you can say that the butcher sometimes has more virtue than the teacher, that he tries to love her but she refuses. He gives her presents. She only gives him a lighter, a kiss—it's not much: he is much more generous than she is. The notion of good and evil is always relative to something.

DY: How about characters who are completely negative, like Michel Bouquet in *La Rupture*, Jean Yanne in *Que la bête meure*, or Akim Tamiroff in *Marie-Chantal contre Docteur Kha*? Is it to caricature?

CC: There, yes. Tamiroff in *Marie-Chantal* is both the good Dr. Lambare and the bad Dr. Kha. He is both, so good and evil are in the same person. The case of Bouquet in *La Rupture* is less about the theory of evil than about the theory of rule: he's a man blinded and misled by his principles. For him, things are no longer within the realm of judgment. He can't be considered evil, because he doesn't reason his evil. He tries to do good—he does evil because he doesn't consider the character of Stephane as a human being, but for his son and grandson he is capable of anything. As to Yanne in *Que la bête meure*, he himself saw the character as very sympathetic and the others as ignoble. Look at his qualities: he's generous, open, a good son to his mother. The only thing that's terrible is his incredible egoism.

DY: But he tortures his wife and son!

CC: Tortures? She writes a stupid poem. And the son doesn't study and gets lousy grades. He spends a fortune on food and his wife doesn't prepare it right because she writes poems! He's right! And he offers a lucrative deal to Duchaussoy.

DY: Still, do you see these characters as caricatures?

CC: Yes, sometimes I make caricatures so the story will be sharper. But at the same time I also notice that one thinks they're caricatures and then one day in the street one sees people who are much worse, who are caricatures of this caricature. Let's say that these are people some of whose traits are more accentuated than others.

DY: You once wrote in *Cahiers du cinéma* that the *film policier* carries the seeds of its own destruction. Can you elaborate?

CC: Yes, because people who wrote *policiers* obeyed the rules of the genre, but these rules are no rules but a mere convenience to keep or reject. The *roman policier* is dying, because they followed the rules to such a point that it's always the same thing: it's like a bridge game where you look at the hand and make a diagnosis—this genre corresponds to this trick and there's never any surprise. Now the *roman policier* is enjoying a new birth, emerging from its ashes, because people have become a bit freer. You have to be flexible with the rules of the genre. When you make a *film policier*, you shouldn't try to find out whether it obeys the rules, whether it's orthodox or not. If you decide in the middle that it won't be a *policier*, you do something else. As was the case with the classical tragedy, the absence of freedom in the *policier* brought about its death. Since there no longer was intelligent material, one invented things just to solicit. There's a guy called Mickey Spillane whom I hate because, in theory, his novels were like those of Chandler and Hammett, and at the same time they were completely disgusting. They're really bad, without interest, stupid. Certainly, one later discovered that it was not the worst. Now they think it's not at all bad—still, it's an example of how decadent the genre can become.

DY: You have often subverted the genre.

CC: Yes, but it's not so much for the subversion. Let's say, I don't want to submit myself to a genre. I use it because it helps me or it seems practical. It's easier for me, but I don't want to become enslaved to it. I don't want to be a priest of the *roman policier*. I think one should be free to do what one wants. I reproach Truffaut for having too great a tendency, when he says, "I'll make a *film policier* based on William Irish," or something like that, to stick to the rules of the genre. Unlike Hitchcock, who has always disregarded them. This is his great strength—he couldn't care less.

DY: How about *Blood Relatives*?

CC: It completely respects the rules of the genre. It's a book by Ed McBain, who is none other than the scriptwriter of *The Birds*: Evan Hunter. When I read the book, it didn't grab me because I realized who was guilty by the second page. And all this, because he obeyed the rules of the genre—I found the trump he was using. But at the same time I thought it was a great subject, so I was quite faithful and simply changed the characters a little bit. But the end result is not the same: it's the same story, but not quite the same subject. I pushed in another direction, which changed the outlook a bit.

DY: What is the subject of the film?

CC: It's the relationship of a forty-year-old cop with his daughter.

DY: Does it develop through an inquiry?

CC: Yes, but it's not even his daughter. We hardly see her. Her presence is there during the inquiry. She is twelve, and there's another young girl in the story.

DY: You seem to be quite interested in the relationship between parents and children. In almost all your films . . .

CC: I'm interested in it to the extent that I'm a father myself. For more than fifteen films, there were no children at all. I started putting children in my films only from the moment when I really felt myself to be a father. My own children grew up and the problem which they represented and which I could not resolve . . . I didn't study the problem and when I did, I had no solution. When I saw them growing up, I noticed that each gesture of your child has a symbolic value vis-à-vis yourself. It's as if it were a projection of yourself doing something. The power—even that of suppression—that a child has over you is superior to that of any other person. This is why I used children as elements representing what one calls "bourgeois stability," and when these element are shattered in some way . . . In my films, one tortures children a lot: in *La Rupture*, he's thrown at the wall right away. In *Une partie de plaisir*, the torture is even more terrifying because Paul Gégauff interrogates his daughter about her mother and gives her messages for her. I find it's an extraordinary representation of the characters themselves—a revelation of sorts. The relations with children and the torture children have to bear—it's violent and it fascinates me. In *La Femme infidèle*, it's double torture: the mother tortures the boy when she throws down his puzzle, and the kid tortures his parents by saying, "I detest you."

DY: Let's talk about Violette's relations with her parents and the shifting system of alliances within that family.

CC: What I tried to show is that she and her mother seek each other. I show it by kisses: either Violette wants to kiss her mother and her mother doesn't want to kiss her, or her mother wants to kiss her and Violette no longer wants to. They have great difficulty getting through to each other. There's a much less difficult rapport between Violette and her father. The scenes where she's alone with him are much calmer and more "normal" than the ones with her mother. And yet, it's her father she kills. This is a great mystery for me: why she kills him rather than the mother. The only thing that made me ask the question is that maybe it's true that he tried to rape her, but I don't believe it. As to the relationship between the Nozière parents, the father always indulges his daughter and the mother is always stern. This is because the father accepts his daughter as she appears to him while the mother wants her daughter to accomplish things she dreams about.

DY: You have often criticized the family and yet you've said you are not against it.

CC: No, I'm for it, but I criticize it because it's lamentable. A family is people you love. I have a family of thirty people and if I add my children . . . It's very pleasant, but I think it's mostly European, or even French. What's frightening is that there's a father, a mother, and children who are all pressed together—it's disgusting. The father keeps an eye on the female next door, the grandmother . . . the children. . . . It's disgusting, frightening! I don't see how people can live this way—and yet it has such strength. It's masochistic; they're unhappy but it endures.

DY: You have made many films where the existence of the couple is invaded by a third person, often the woman's lover. What do you find most interesting in that domain: the power struggle between the three?

CC: No, it's not that. What amuses me is to create an imbalance in a universe that tries hard to stabilize itself. But it's crazy: there can be no equilibrium *à trois*, so it's the suppression of one of the three that causes the imbalance. In fact, I'm not particularly interested in triangles, but this is what people are familiar with most. You can do a lot of things with a sexual triangle and, at the same time, it's very simple—everybody knows what it is: the woman makes a phone call and hastily hangs up when her husband enters. Everyone understands that. No need to add a scene to explain what has happened. It's very practical, which is why I use it. It's also very French.

DY: What do you find interesting in a relationship: the façade, its cracking, or it explosion?

CC: Both interest me. The façade is interesting because it's the social fabric and the cracking is interesting because it's the truth. Maybe it's my pessimistic side, but I can't imagine one without the other.

DY: What is the great evil of bourgeois life? Mediocrity?

CC: It's mostly its extraordinary egoism. Bourgeois life is entirely conceived in egoism, like an old candy that one finds and that is completely . . .

DY: What is the function of the meal scenes in your films?

CC: The meal, for the most part, is the moment when people are united. The father works, the mother is out shopping, the children are at school, but they're united at the dinner table. When a man wants to sleep with a woman, he doesn't say, "Come, sleep with me!" He says, "Let's grab a bite in a restaurant." The meal, then, has a very important function, so I put a lot of meal scenes in my films.

But I noticed that in most of my films—and it irritated me greatly—people never eat, or very little. In *Blood Relatives*, there are small meals—they're not very important, but there are nevertheless six. They gorge themselves all the time.

DY: There are very few such scenes in *La Rupture* or *Juste avant la nuit*. Is it in order to express something?

CC: When there are meals? It depends. For example, the most important one, the one in which there are the most things to see, is in *Que la bête meure*, because it's part of the character—the visceral side of the character.

DY: Do you always intend to make funny films, even when they're serious?
CC: Yes. I always try to make the films funny, with some rare exceptions. *Le Boucher* or even *La Rupture* may have some amusing moments, but they don't try to be funny, while *Juste avant la nuit* is, in fact, a comic film. It's really vaudeville material transformed into tragedy. It's about a character who wants to confess and people say: "Shut up! Shut up!" It's subject matter that could have very well been used in a comedy. But the film is funnier if comic material is treated in an austere way.

DY: What is the role of politics in your films? For example, *Nada* is a critique of the corruption and sadism of the police as well as the brutality of the anarchists.
CC: Yes, but it's not anarchists—it's terrorists. I don't see the difference between terrorists and beasts. They behave in the same way.

DY: Why your interest in the themes of manipulation and the use of power?
CC: It's a will not to let power impose itself. Power is the most twisted, the most evil, the purist. . . . What was misunderstood about *Nada*, which treated that, is that it's not the political stand taken—the extreme left, like the terrorists, or the extreme right, like the policeman or Goemond—in any case, the state crushes. The state is the master of he who destroys it, not of its supporters. Another phrase which applies to *Nada* is: the state prefers its own destruction, and the death of all, to the revolution. It's true.

DY: And in *Les Biches*? What starts as a sexual attraction between two women ends up as a manipulation and power struggle.
CC: Of course, but, alas, if it's a power struggle, I'd be entirely for Why. But it isn't really a power struggle. It's a revolution: the replacement of one class by another—Why replaces Frédérique, but she does it by becoming Frédérique.

DY: But you also show the attraction of fascism in *Les Cousins* and *Une partie de plaisir*.
CC: Yes, but this is Gégauff's side. He loves to pass for a fascist. I call Gégauff. In *Une partie de plaisir*, he plays himself.

DY: You have said: "The real political center could be a form of Marxism for the twentieth century."

CC: Yes, but I speak of Europe, because the US is quite different. In France and the rest of Europe, where the existing social structure is strongly disputed by at least half the individuals, and people think of changing it, I think that the real center is no more right-wing than the left. The center-left is as rightist as . . . I think that the real center will be a sort of modern Marxism. I didn't say it would be the solution. There'll be problems, but it will be the center. The center-right will court the liberals. The left will be leftist anarchists, but it's already like that: terrorists, who are pro-Albanian.

DY: You often use social origins as indicative of victimization: the heroines of *La Rupture* and *Une partie de plaisir*.

CC: Up to a point, yet. If there are men, women are the victims. This I admit quite willingly, given what the poor things have to bear. To the extent that women are victims, it's more certain they'll be victims in a poor milieu than in a rich milieu. The rich are victims of other things, but it's less serious. Women in a modest milieu suffer terribly. It's not amusing at all. It's a cliché, but if they work all day in a factory and at night have to cook and wash—it's terrible! We men are monsters (Chabrol laughs uncontrollably). It's funny. If women don't laugh, I understand, but I find it funny.

DY: How do you see the role of the camera? Does it make a comment on the characters or the situation?

CC: If only I knew. . . . I try to avoid—except when it's the purpose of the film—making the camera subjective in relation to the characters in the film. That is, directly subjective—to make the audience identify with one of the characters by the effect of the camera. Except when I want to play a trick—to make them identify with a character and then make them realize what horrible scoundrels they are. That amuses me. But otherwise, I think that the role of the camera is to give its own point of view on what is happening. Without going so far as to use the "pretty" vehicle of distanciation, which is heavy, let's say that a light step backward in relation to the story allows you to avoid a deterioration into bad taste, into grandiose effects.

With this system, when you use such grandiose effects, it becomes a farce. People laugh. It's very easy to manipulate the spectator. After Hitchcock manipulated the audience so brilliantly in *Psycho*, manipulation was no longer possible.

DY: In the opening sequence of *La Femme infidèle*, the camera encircles the characters who are sitting at a table on the lawn. Why?

CC: It seeks them. The principle of *La Femme infidèle* is that the movement always ends up by returning to its starting point, as if it never moved. At times, it moves to the left but returns to the right: at others, it advances but then recoils. It never returns from the same point, and it's what the character wants, to remain completely . . . He finds himself in his little happiness and he wants least of all to see it move. That's the subject of *La Femme infidèle*—it becomes unbalanced and he pushes like crazy on the unbalanced side to reestablish balance. This movement back and forth was constantly compensated to such an extent that in the last shot I had to use both movements—forward and backward—which is physically impossible. This is why I cheated a bit: I used a zoom forward at the same time that I was moving backward.

DY: And in *A double tour*?

CC: It was the period of madness, because it was the beginning. I had a crane which could go very high up, so I amused myself with it like crazy. But it worked. I like taking a stand. Any scene can be shot in at least two or three different ways. I detest what they do a lot in the U S—the cover shot. Why is it called that? I'm not cold. Even in what is called the master shot, which is sufficient to narrate a film, there are two or three different solutions. What's interesting is to choose a visual point of view which corresponds to the sense of what is to be done and preserve it all along. Contrary to what one believes, it doesn't take your freedom away. With this stand you can do anything: you are not tied to a succession of automatic forms. You can go in whatever direction you want, because you have such a solid structure.

DY: *Violette* has a very complicated system of flashbacks.

CC: It's not very linear, but it's not very complicated. The film can be divided into three parts: the first is the longest, almost half the film—from the introduction of Violette, who comes out of the doorway in the very beginning—up to the fatal dinner. She takes a bus. There, we have a flashback with almost chronological elements of her life, with the exception of childhood memories which take place in the beginning of the third part. It stops the moment she's about to commit the crime. She sees things in their chronology but still doesn't want to accept the deed. The minute it's about to arrive, in her memory, she stops the bus—which represents the line of memory—and walks on foot. From that moment, it's reality—we're in direct reality. She returns home and, of course, finds her parents dead, calls the neighbors, is interrogated by the police, and slips away. She begins to have visions, a kind of depression, and accepts seeing the moment where she prepares the crime. In the first part, the only thing we see of the crime is when she tries to imitate her mother's handwriting, but not the poison. When she sleeps in her hotel room, she sees the preparation of the poison, but she still doesn't accept seeing the crime itself. We return to linearity—she stops it. Then, she's imprisoned and at that moment, when everything is over, she accepts seeing the crime itself. After that, she herself explores her past, the why of things.

DY: Why are there so many closeups in *Violette*?

CC: There are two reasons. First, I didn't have the money to reconstruct the period in a grand manner. So, when I shot outdoors, I was obliged to condense the frames. Had I closed the frame outdoors but let the camera wander indoors, one would have felt I was forced to close the frame. If the frames are closed everywhere, the spectator isn't bothered by the outdoors enclosure. In addition, Isabelle Huppert's acting is extraordinarily internalized, and one can only sense its subtlety when seen from very close. So, I had to use closeups.

DY: And in general, what is the function of the closeup?

CC: To make what's inside pass through the eyes. The human face is a mystery. To pierce this mystery, there are two orifices, which are the eyes. The closeup exists for that.

In *Violette*, I did it more or less systematically. In *Une partie de plaisir*, too, there are lots of closeups, for a much more perverse reason. Since Gégauff himself played the role, I tried while shooting him to find what was real in his performance. He was acting but, still, it was something he knew first hand. I wanted to find out to what extent he wanted to return to Daniele and to what extent she wanted to refuse. It was a bit like a psychodrama but, amusingly, with no results. When we started shooting, Daniele was very afraid of what Paul might do, and Paul had only one idea—to get her back. In the end, they hadn't changed at all: she still didn't want to live with him. Psychodramas can succeed when the individuals are slightly unbalanced, and Paul and Daniele were not unbalanced. So, nothing happened: it's very strange.

DY: Why is *The Third Lover* (*L'Oeil du Malin*) told from the point of view of Jacques Charrier?

CC: It was a film for which we had very little money and since the main character was extremely mean and petty, I told myself that if I made the film subjectively, from his point of view, the meanness of the character would justify the poverty of the means. He is capable of imagining grand things, so he renders everything bitter, with malice, which is why I did it like that. I find it interesting to make a whole film pass . . . In general, it's always the hero who tells the story—or a witness. Here, it's a witness who ends up playing the main role, and who is ignoble, minuscule. It interested me to take the point of view of someone minuscule.

DY: And in *Que la bête meure*?

CC: There it's a trap. The first part is based on the diary of the character, because if the film had to be efficient, it needed an identification of the audience with Duchaussoy. It was very easy—one always identifies with a poor man whose child is dead and who wants revenge. The diary allows augmenting the spectator's identification until the reversal, and the spectator ends up blaming himself: he has identified with the character and thought him good and wonderful, and now he perceives him as full of shadows. This enchants me. In the end of *Que la bête meure*, the construction is as if Duchaussoy kills Yanne. But the spectator completely rejects this idea of a mean and cowardly murder and prefers to accuse Yanne's son, who didn't kill. He makes the spectator create a transfer of guilt.

DY: And the subjective sequences in *A double tour*? The two flashbacks by the father (Jacques Dacqmine) and the son (André Jocelyn)?

CC: There was a problem of symmetry, of construction, with the two flashbacks: to make one flashback and then another, which shows what one doesn't see in the first. There was another thing: I tried—not all that well, I'd do it better now—something quite ambitious: the first flashback was from the point of view of Dacqmine, a man of fifty who lives a love and tries to grasp the beauty that has eluded him till now. I shot it in a certain way. The flashback of Jocelyn was the contrary—a man who can't tolerate the beauty of others. I tried to shoot it in a different way. What justifies the fact that after killing Leda he walks around the room and the camera goes behind perfume bottles and things change their color as he passes behind them is that it's a person who is cornered by, completely imprisoned by, the beauty that surrounds him. He can't escape it.

DY: Do you prefer to work in color or in black and white?

CC: I think the choice no longer exists. Unless you're very rich, you can't work in black and white—you must work in color. But from time to time I do feel like working in black and white. *Blood Relatives* could be shot in black and white: I could have shot it in false colors at the risk of making everything all-black or all-white, or used color and got black and white, but I decided it would be stupid to make an effort to eliminate color, so I shot it in color.

DY: Rohmer told me that everything had already been done in black and white, while there is still a lot to do in color. Franju, on the other hand, told me one could not even get a proper shade in color.

CC: They're both right, but also wrong. It's true that everything has already been done in black and white and there are still things to do in color, but Rohmer was wrong in forgetting that most things in black and white were done using film stock completely different from ours, which enables us to do things we couldn't do before. It also prevents us from doing other things—it's a completely different black and white.

As to color, Franju is wrong in claiming one can't use a shadow. One can, and perfectly well, too. Most cameramen are afraid of black and white. I know only four who accept absolute black. With the others, it's never quite black, and it's a pity because black is very beautiful. There are three Americans and one Frenchman who can do it. Since I couldn't get the Americans, I used the Frenchman.

DY: You often use blue: in *La Rupture*, *La Femme infidèle*, and even the interiors of Gégauff's house in *Une partie de plaisir* were blue. Is it indicative of decadence?
CC: Yes, but blue is above all the color of madness, a form of madness. A psychiatrist once told me that the dominant color in the drawings of the mentally deranged is blue. I thought it was strange: "How could it be blue, which is such a calm color?" And he said: "No, think about it; try to imagine living perpetually in blue." It's the most unbalanced, and unbalancing, color. *Voila!* So, when I wanted to show imbalance, I used blue—to please that psychiatrist, whom I like quite a bit. And it's true that it has a strange effect.

DY: *Les Biches* opened a brilliant period in your career. The six films you made in the period 1968–1971 are among your best. Can you describe the process that led you in that direction?
CC: My first three films (*Le Beau Serge*, *Les Cousins*, *A double tour*) did quite well and then I had four terrible disasters (*Les Bonnes Femmes*, *Les Godelureaux*, *L'Oeil du Malin*, *Ophelia*). I was obliged to make the films that were offered to me.

DY: The *Tiger* films?
CC: Yes, films like that. It was a useful experience, because when I could once more make the films I wanted, I brought with me what I had learned while making those films. I could work faster, making one film after another. It was a good situation which later turned sour because the producer, André Genovès, went crazy with delusions of grandeur. But other than that it was fine. When you're given the possibility to do what you want, it's good; but if you could always do what you want, you could even become lazy.

DY: Why did you decide to shoot *Blood Relatives* in English, with a star like Donald Sutherland? In the past, films like *The Champagne Murders* (*Le Scandale*), *Ten Days' Wonder* (*Le Décade prodigieuse*), *Dirty Hands* (*Les Innocents aux mains sales*), and *The Twist* (*Folies bourgeoises*), which were shot in English, were not very successful.
CC: Yes, it's absolutely true, but those were "bastard films." I shot them in France

with both English and French actors, and the French didn't speak English. There was no real reason. . . . It created complications. *Blood Relatives* takes place in a North American milieu, in Montreal, so there are three French actors—the mother (Stéphane Audran), the son (Laurent Malet), and the daughter (Aude Landry)—who keep their French accent, but the father is English, so they speak English, which is perfectly normal. All the others are Anglo-Saxon.

DY: The language, then, is dictated by the specific reality of the film?

CC: In this case, yes. My first intention was to make it in France, but it couldn't stand on its feet because it's a North American family. And there's another point: the difference between family life and the professional domain—the police—is much greater in North America than in France. In France, there's always the intimate, *soupe au choux* side, while in America it's an enormous machine—those sirens . . . and when a cop returns home, it's different.

I made the other films in English because I was told it would be better commercially, which I never believed. But in *Blood Relatives*, I myself wanted it. I asked to make it in North America. I was a bit afraid it was too much, but it was the ideal thing.

DY: Why did you choose the story of *Folies bourgeoises*?

CC: I didn't choose it.

DY: It's very different from your other films.

CC: Yes. The drama of *Folies bourgeoises* is very easy to understand. A producer called me to make an adaptation of a novel by Lucie Faure, the wife of the president of the National Assembly in France. That very morning I received a belated payment, an absolutely gigantic sum. And these two things together . . . So, I made the film. I made an adaptation for a little film, *comme ça*, and it wasn't all that bad. No, I started by doing something else. I asked the Englishman who wrote *The Ruling Class*, Peter Barnes, to write a kind of frenzied comedy that would bear no resemblance whatsoever to the book. The script was great, but both the producer and Lucie Faure rejected it, because it had nothing to do with her book. So, I made another, very simple adaptation for a minor film, and the producer said it was fine. From that moment on, he lied: "I've never seen it before!" So, from the first estimate of $700,000 for a small French film we found ourselves with a terribly overblown *soufflé au fromage*, with American, Italian, and German actors. I thought of not shooting it, except for the terrible thing that the contract had been signed and the guy had paid me. Three weeks later, he told me: "Let's make the film!" I said: "Fine." I felt dishonest and thought: "*Tant pis*! I'll do it anyway!" It was kind of a mishmash.

DY: The murder scene on the highway in *Les Noces rouges*, was it influenced by the highway scene in Henri Verneuil's *Une Manche et la belle* (*A Kiss for a Killer*), where Henri Vidal tries to kill Isa Miranda?

CC: No, I've never seen it. It's much more curious than that. The topic of *Les Noces rouges*, which is a crime story, is based on a news item. I adapted it scrupulously, making the characters do exactly what they did in life, especially the way the two lovers kill the woman's husband. During the shooting, I realized that it was really *The Postman Always Rings Twice* by Tay Garnett, based on the book by James Cain. What is fantastic is that they found Cain's book by the guy's house. That is, he was really inspired by the book. And since James Hadley Chase borrowed it from Cain and Verneuil adapted Chase's novel, that explains it.

DY: To conclude, how did you construct the streetcar scene in *La Rupture*?

CC: It's for this scene that I made the film, just about. A woman recounts her life—where can she do it? In a streetcar. That is why we had to shoot the film in Brussels, because there are more streetcars there. I was also lucky. The route I chose was ideal, and it was by chance—it was like in Murnau, passing from the city to the country. I was lucky that in a given moment between shots I looked forward and saw the reflection of the conductor's hand in the window, and I thought: "This is too beautiful! I don't believe it!" This is the sort of thing that you don't rationalize at the time—it is based entirely on sensations. Also, you couldn't disturb the actress (Stéphane Audran)—she had changed the text quite a bit, changed the story of her life—but I didn't care because it was good. Stéphane respects the text and the dialogues, but the minute she has a monologue, she changes everything. It's very strange, but not very serious. So, in all my films I put little things like that in order to see what she's going to tell me, because I never know what it will be.

Interview with Claude Chabrol

Philippe Carcassonne and Jacques Fieschi / 1982

From *Cinématographe* 81 (September 1982): 3–15. Translated from the French by CB.

In this long conversation—deliciously interrupted by a salad of pasta with mint—Claude Chabrol shows no deference in discussing the milestones of his prolific production, as he pokes, with ferocious humor, at the bourgeoisie, the confusion of matrimonial and professional roles, the storyboard, and *The French Lieutenant's Woman*, all the while displaying a precise and garrulous cinephilia. This interview is a historical chronicle which illuminates the journey of a generation of filmmakers.

Question: We would like to create a panorama of your twenty-five years of cinematic activity.
Claude Chabrol: There will be gaps in my memory.

Q: How did you meet the other members of the Nouvelle Vague?
CC: I knew them through our shared cinephilia. I had seen *Singin' in the Rain* in La Baule before everyone else saw it. At the time, MGM organized preview screenings, and I wrote the article because no one else had seen it. For a year, I was the messenger boy; I did things at *Cahiers du cinéma* that no one else wanted to do, or almost no one. I had seen *The Sleeping Tiger*, directed by "Victor Hanbury," which I recognized as being by Joseph Losey: suddenly my prestige rose in the eyes of the group! Jacques Doniol-Valcroze was the boss, André Bazin was the conscience, and the others did the work. In fact, there were two groups: the "Hitchcocko-Hawksians"—Truffaut, Rivette, Godard, and me—and those who were against us, led by Pierre Kast, who were promoting John Huston and René Clément. Bazin didn't understand our affection for Hitchcock very well. Doniol-Valcroze played at being Talleyrand.

Q: You wrote a book on Hitchcock in collaboration with Eric Rohmer.
CC: We had done a special edition on him, and then we got this assignment and

we started working on it. I did the British period and Rohmer did the American period, but I did two films from the American period, and no one will ever know which ones!

Q: Do you still recognize yourself in this book?
CC: I recognize what I wanted to do at the time. Hitchcock did not have the keys to the city at that time: we had to impose him on certain cinephiles who disapproved of him. We decided not to discuss the form of the films, and to rave about the content, to see whether it held together. We went to the extreme limits of that argument.

Q: You found a Christian theme in Hitchcock.
CC: That was one of the basic elements. Maybe it took miracles to open people's eyes!

Q: You and Rohmer were very different in your approaches.
CC: That's probably why I've always loved Montaigne and Boethius.

Q: At the time, were you a Catholic?
CC: I was raised in the religion, and I stayed profoundly Christian until after *Le Beau Serge*. And then I let go of all that, with a period of antagonism when I really cut the cord. I really hated the church, but not very sincerely, just in order to put a stop to things.

Q: There is still a Christian theme in some of your later films.
CC: The problem is with God. It's difficult to believe in something that no one can define. At the same time, I don't like chaos. And God is antichaos. My films have a sense of that. From that perspective, they have a Christian resonance.

Q: In the characters, their moral dramas?
CC: No, in that way it's not Christian but almost violently atheist: despite what Dostoevsky says, if God does not exist, nothing is permitted. Without that prop to help us stand up, the moral duty of people toward themselves becomes very important. At the same time, I don't believe very much in certitudes: that is the only certitude I have. When I come on an established truth, I immediately and intuitively adopt the contrary notion.

Q: Did you ever miss your activity as a film critic? Do you still miss it?
CC: No. You practice it when you watch any film. It's the opposite of the creation of a film because it's based on analysis, while making a film is a work of synthesis. If the synthesis becomes perfect, there's a bit of an echo of analysis for the person

making the film. I analyze my own films before making them: I weigh the different elements to make sure they're not too visible. And I hate writing, even screenplays. When I have written a book, it's been a parody of a book. The other members of the Nouvelle Vague liked to write. I don't like solitary work. I prefer company: you don't sweat as much; you don't notice that you're working. The filmmaker can't be a critic: the risks and the questioning of things are very strong for the filmmaker, and they are minimal for the critic. Pierre Billard eviscerated *Lola Montès*, and he later forgot about having done it. At least I think so, because in response to a questionnaire from *Télérama* he said he had no regrets. Normally, he would have had to have regrets about that, so I have to conclude that he forgot.

Q: Do you go to the movies a lot?
CC: I used to see everything. Not anymore: the mind is a box that can't contain everything. But I am a member of committees that conveniently allow me to see a lot of films.

Q: Do you still agree with the tastes you had in the fifties?
CC: There hasn't been any rejection of my tastes. On the other hand, I like certain filmmakers whom I didn't like at the time. In the work of William Wyler, the tie salesman from Mulhouse, I now find that there are good things. Claude Autant-Lara made some very good films, like *Occupe-toi Amélie* (*Keep an Eye on Amelia*, 1949), and *La traversée de Paris* (*Four Bags Full*, 1956). But he had a weakness: since he was such a wild beast on the set, he would speak very loudly when giving the actors their directions. This sometimes becomes difficult to take: in *Vive Henri IV . . . vive l'amour* (1961), for example, everyone shouts! Among the films of René Clément, which we didn't like much at the time, *Monsieur Ripois* (*Knave of Hearts*, 1954), is great. There's that famous "French Quality Production" which was even invoked when talking about *Les Fantômes du chapelier*, proving that we don't know how to define it. Jean Delannoy really embodied it: those antiseptic filmed adaptations written by Jean Aurenche and Pierre Bost. But I was never very harsh as a critic. I only tore apart one film: *Pain Vivant* (*The Living Bread*, 1955) by Jean Mousselle, which was based on a screenplay by Mauriac.

Q: Retrospectively, do you see a common aesthetic in the filmmakers of the Nouvelle Vague?
CC: None. The only thing which would make it seem that way was that we used the same actors, with their recognizable tics. You can't make Bernadette Lafont act in the same way as Madeleine Robinson! Our points in common were in what we refused to do, and in the modesty of our budgets: you know, those scenes where you can see the radiator in the room. We were united by what we liked, and above

all by what we didn't like. Then we noticed that we didn't want to do the same things or do them in the same way. The first of my films that the others started to be unhappy about was *A double tour*: they criticized Henri Decaë for using arc lights in daylight and told him that the photography of *Shoot the Piano Player* was disgusting. That was the end of an era. You have to be obsessed with money, like Lucas and company, to want to keep your little group together at all costs. At that time, we were having fun. Then later, some of us became enemies, and we looked down on others in a pompous and official way. There was the reciprocal indignation of Truffaut and Godard, and even Rivette.

Q: Did you stay above the fighting?
CC: No, not above it, but to the side.

Q: Which films of the Nouvelle Vague do you like best?
CC: I like the ones by Jean-Luc and Rohmer. I love some films by Truffaut, like *The Wild Child* and *The Green Room*, which are very daring, and others like *Pocket Money* not at all. *The Last Metro* is a good film, but it was made in order to comfort the viewer, which isn't good.

Q: Do you still have personal relationships with some members of the Nouvelle Vague?
CC: I feel friendly toward them, but seeing them all the time would be stupid and sterile. I don't believe in groups of filmmakers. It wouldn't do me any good to have doubles of myself. I feel affinities with some of them, but I wouldn't go from there to crying out, "It's another me!"

Q: Have certain recent films changed your attitude as a spectator?
CC: I can still be a very good member of the public. I was completely absorbed by John Boorman's *Exorcist II: The Heretic*. I didn't let myself get analytical, even about the hokiness. *Fat City* by John Huston also captivated me.

Q: What kind of a spectator are you with the films of the "great masters" who are still active, like Buñuel, Fellini, and Bergman?
CC: In my opinion, Bergman made one film that was total stupidity: *The Touch*. I was embarrassed for him: you see Bibi Andersson say to Elliott Gould, "Look, I have short thighs." But I loved *The Serpent's Egg* and *From the Life of Marionettes*. Personally, I am more of a worshipper of the dead, and I prefer the deceased filmmakers. They can't bother us anymore. Today, there are too many good films. Between a good film and a bad one, the difference is negligible. Patent nullity is disappearing: it's a shame.

Q: When you make a film, do you sometimes borrow dramatic situations from other filmmakers?

CC: Obviously, we are penetrated by certain films. But I don't use them directly in that way. The borrowing is on a deeper level than that. You don't have to think about it: the problem is resolved in advance by our memory. When I make films that don't interest me all that much, I sometimes try doing things "in the manner of" someone. In *Les Magiciens*, there is a sequence where Franco Nero, who plays the Arab on duty, goes to see his dying mother. I tried to make the scene like John Ford: it was hard work! And people don't notice it, but there was not a shot in the scene that Ford couldn't have done, or that would have made him blush. In the little twelve-minute sketch I made for television based on Fritz Lang's *M*, only three shots are really Langian. The others are pale imitations. There is no interest in copying someone in an exact way; you have to really succeed in rediscovering someone's visual style. Truffaut, at the beginning of his career, had a personal problem with form, which he resolved in "Hitchcockizing" his form. In the beginning, it wasn't so good, but now it's getting better and better. The osmosis is complete. Francois made a deliberate choice: he wrote a book about a filmmaker who was not his favorite. He preferred Renoir and Rossellini, but they couldn't bring him anything in this respect. *Shoot the Piano Player*, while admirable in other ways, is a film without a form. *Jules et Jim* is still quite badly made. Look at the difference between that and *Les Deux anglaises et le continent*, where the narrative form has been found. He started it with *La Peau douce*, imitating the party of Alicia Huberman (Ingrid Bergman) in *Notorious*. But that was considered aberrant, since it was good old Jean Desailly who got the positive reviews in the provinces.

Q: Your characters often evoke those of Hitchcock: André Jocelyn in *A double tour*, Stéphane Audran in *The Champagne Murders*, and Jacqueline Sassard in *Les Biches* all remind us of characters from *Vertigo* and *Psycho*.

CC: What I really like in Hitchcock is those characters: the crazy ones. I try to deal with them as well, but in a different way.

Q: Your mise en scène doesn't have the same rhythm or the same shot length as Hitchcock's.

CC: Hitchcock has a recurrent stylistic figure: shots which correspond to the point of view of a character who is present, and with whom our gaze must identify. There is a chain of subjectivities. In dialogue scenes, the camera is simply in the place of one character looking at the other. I will gladly admit that this is not at all my way of doing things. I cheat from the very beginning. I don't want the subjectivity of the characters; I don't like subjective shots. For me, the camera has to be an additional character.

Q: Do you consider the shots of the apartment building in *Rear Window* to be purely subjective?

CC: Of course that's not their only purpose. At the beginning of *Vertigo*, when James Stewart goes to see Kim Novak's husband, when the connection isn't there between them and a terrible block establishes itself—which is very well worked out by Hitchcock—a physical distance is established between them, the space of the armchairs, and the feelings of the spectator go far beyond the subjectivity of the characters.

Q: Are you interested in the linear aspect of plot?

CC: No. But I'm not an extremist in this regard. I believe that people have to have a story to follow, whereas Jean-Luc tends to destroy that. I am at a place of contradiction: it would be difficult for me to make a film without a plot, and at the same time plot bores me prodigiously. That is why I am happy to adapt little crime films, in order to remove the problem.

Q: There is a certain slowness in your films up until *Les Fantômes du chapelier*.

CC: I don't agree; I think it's rather the opposite. I am persuaded that my films go faster than others. I try to eliminate everything that is not interesting, though of course I couldn't give a damn about whether the gestures of the characters are fast. The important thing is not the rapidity of movement, but the relationship of spatial volume from one shot to another. One can very easily start with a closeup of a vase, then go to a face, then come back with a little lateral camera move, giving the impression of movement, and during this whole time, the characters don't do anything. It would be an interesting experiment to have two characters face to face, not saying anything, without any particular expression, and to film them in a very fast and a very slow manner. Those are only impressions, which have nothing to do with the profound truth of a scene. But I will persist in saying that my films are fast: the proof is that when they try to cut them, they can't! One day—and perhaps sooner that you might believe—I will have fun making a film that is explicitly fast!

Q: Isn't it true that today we live in a dictatorship of fast movement, which is not your kind of rapidity?

CC: Yes, this frenzy comes from advertising, from the refusal of the continuity of form and of movement. There are fifteen shots and fifteen shocks. The ad has gotten rid of certain relationships of the gaze. It has happened in literature as well: we no longer have the pleasure of the hard little elliptical phrase followed by the long sentence. Today, we confuse speed with hastiness. My rhythm is not slow; it's fast. It's the movement of my *characters* that is slow. In *Les Fantômes du* *chapelier*, we used 162 different locations: that's a lot! And then there are all the scenes in the café where we don't move at all.

Q: Do you consider yourself a shot-centered or a scene-centered director?
CC: I don't care, and I really don't understand the question. Do you mean by that that the shot is everything? Eisenstein, I imagine, comes at it from this approach, but it seems to me that this is also the weakness of his system. It seems equally bizarre to me to consider that the scene is everything, or else one would have to announce one's end with a little squawk.

Q: There are directors who talk about "creating a scene."
CC: They are clumsy.

Q: Someone like Marcel Pagnol, for example.
CC: No, that's something else. He refused to follow any cinematic procedures, except for in *La Femme du boulanger* (*The Baker's Wife*, 1938). He wanted to make his dialogue play as well as possible, almost like an oratorio, and at the same time he wanted to bring out natural elements like the sun, the earth, the water, and sounds. He didn't need the visual except to express the elements of nature. He had the ideas of a genius, worthy of Renoir, but on the level of mise en scène he wanted to shoot in the simplest way, the most basic way. Also, he hardly went onto the set; he was always in the sound truck listening to the actors. Any looping would have been impossible. It was a very particular way of directing: very original, because it was also different from filmed theater.

Q: Do you like to work alone when you write your screenplays?
CC: When I have an idea for a film, I tell myself that I don't need any outside help. Afterwards, I feel the need for a little helping hand, for some polishing, or rather unpolishing. I can't write a script which contains a deletion. I write them longhand in large format Clairefontaine notebooks of small-squared graph paper, using a hard felt pen. I never change. Here is one. (Chabrol shows his pen.) The hard part is having the same one at the end. It really bothers me to change pens: the pen guides the hand if it knows what came before. In the beginning, I wrote on a typewriter, with seven fingers; and then I wrote longhand starting with *Ophelia*. Other than that, I don't have any rules about how I work; I am very lazy, I start and I stop, time passes, I am invaded by anxiety, it steeps inside me, and then I feel shame, shame, shame. I lie to the producer, telling him that I am already two-thirds finished. I am a terrible old cynic, but I make my cinema out of guilt.

Q: Do you enjoy writing dialogue?
CC: I love dialogue. I rewrite it several times, but I hate "brilliant" dialogue.

Q: Still, there are a lot of little comic phrases in your films, like the words of Stéphane Audran in *Les Biches*: "He wanted to take us on safari in Mozambique out of season . . . what nonsense."

CC: Yes, I had heard this pearl in the mouth of a snob who wanted to show off on the day before the shooting began. In *La Muette* also, there are some, like, "I am against the death penalty, except for certain cases." But these are not *bons mots* of the kind Henri Jeanson would write. In *Les Fantômes du chapelier*, one phrase came from the décor: Michel Serrault says to the policemen, talking about the murdered servant, "She never had the pleasure of using the closet."

Q: These are little ridiculous and comic moments, instances of the social grotesque.

CC: I like my films to be funny. Nothing bothers me as much as people who don't dare to laugh. Recently, I hated *The French Lieutenant's Woman*. It's like something by Jean Delannoy, with a hopeless and imperturbable seriousness.

Q: Even the scene of the premature ejaculation? That was quite ironic.

CC: I'm not so sure. I wouldn't want to brag, but I do something much funnier in *Nada*, where an old veteran tries, with little success, to bed a young girl.

Q: In writing the screenplays, what do you expect from your collaborators?

CC: I expect them to add the spice, the extra turns of phrase. I have a tendency to be too explanatory, too much of a notary's clerk. I tend to do that with the actors too. By design, the character played by Michel Duchaussoy never finished any of his sentences in *Que la bête meure*. I also recopy the screenplays that I didn't write. The screenplay for *Violette Nozière* was written by Odile Barski, and I cut fifty pages while recopying it. My pen didn't want to write anymore. But I wouldn't have been able to make the cuts if I hadn't recopied it.

Q: Do you have those ping-pong script meetings, where you argue from 2:00 a.m. to 8:00 a.m. in front of a glass of whisky?

CC: No. A long time ago, with Paul Gégauff, we played pinball all night long in the bar on the Rue Washington. But I have not had a lot of work meetings in the classical sense. For *The Champagne Murders*, the producer had come to me with the title and an idea of his: a murder in a nudist camp. What could the weapon be? We wrote a screenplay which had nothing to do with the final film, and which went through all kinds of upheavals. They foisted a "script doctor" on us, a guy named Jacques Robert who walked back and forth, making a strange noise with a hollow tooth and making comments such as, "Oh, there's a bone in the cheese." Gégauff finally told him to go to the dentist. It was horrible. Paul was finally so disgusted with the work that he wanted to sign the script "Luc Dutourd," an anagram for "trou du cul" (asshole). We had a great idea for the ending, which was taken away by the actors and the censors: the blond secretary turned out to be a bald man wearing a wig! This was even more disturbing because he had come on to the Anthony Perkins character beforehand. Jean-Claude Brialy, who had been proposed for the role, had turned it down, saying, "It's repulsive." So much the better for him.

Q: What is your procedure when adapting a novel?

CC: Once I have chosen it, I recopy it and write it myself. If it's a commission, I find some other poor bastard to take care of the dirty work. I've never read the book by Lucie Faure, *Le Malheur fou*, on which *Folies bourgeoises* (*The Twist*) is based. Or only the first two pages. On that one there was also a procession of people: two Italians who fell into my arms, an Englishman who was rejected by the author, and finally a protégé of the Salkinds (the producers); he was a sexually obsessed hemiplegic who wrote a piece of garbage in which the characters were constantly giving each other blow jobs!

Q: You were extremely faithful to Georges Simenon.

CC: Yes, I had thought about it for a long time, and then I spoke to the Hakims right after making *A double tour*. I had also thought about adapting *Le Fils Cardinaud*, which Gilles Grangier had filmed with the title *Le Sang de la tête*, starring Jean Gabin. Simenon is a writer I adore: I have read all his books, with no exception.

Q: Simenon has done pretty well in the cinema, it would seem: *La Nuit du carrefour* and *La Tête d'un homme*—two Maigret books which are the best films of Jean Delannoy—and *La Verité sur Bébé Donge* (*The Truth of our Marriage*, 1952).

CC: Yes, and the Jean Renoir film (*Maigret at the Crossroads*) is especially admirable, with an absolute fidelity to the novel. But too often, people take the theme of the novel and embroider it. In the case of *Bébé Donge*, which is still a good film, I find that Simenon's dialogue is better than that of the screenwriter Maurice Auberge. The line *"Le bonheur vous va bien"* ("happiness becomes you"), which Gabrielle Dorziat repeats to Danielle Darrieux throughout the film, is a *mot d'auteur*; it comes across as too obviously film dialogue. The dialogue has to earn its cachet. Otherwise, filmmakers are like Audiard, rewriting everything, or sprinkling in a few *bons mots* here and there.[1]

Q: You haven't worked with well-known screenwriters very often.

CC: Yes, I worked with Daniel Boulanger. And with Françoise Sagan on *Landru*: she was even lazier than I am! We had a lot of fun. Originally, the film was going to be about George Sand, but during one day of laughing hysterically we talked about the subject of Landru and started on that.

Q: Do you always write the story chronologically?

CC: Yes, for two or three weeks, every day including Sunday, for five to seven hours a day. I need a lot of noise: music in the morning, and television in the afternoon. I can't stand to be alone. Silence terrifies me.

Q: Isn't it difficult to read a screenplay and judge its quality? How can you know what the interest of the film will be?

CC: All you can read in the screenplay is . . . the screenplay. It has no artistic status. "It is a good screenplay?" is a sentence that doesn't mean anything. At the same time I respect the screenplay; I can't do without it; I require of those who work with me only what is in the screenplay, but *everything* that is in it. The primitive form of the film is there. It's the raw material.

Q: Luc Béraud says that the screenplay is "everything the filmmaker knows about the film at the moment when he writes it."

CC: That's a good definition. Of course, we have to know the most we can, but we also have to know that it is not everything the film will contain.

Q: What do you think about people who do very precise pre-planning?

CC: They're idiots. What if the actor decides to go to the left when you had planned a pan to the right? I can only deal with that at the moment when we are shooting. I might throw a glance at the storyboard if I am making an ad. But a film like *Garde à vue* (*Under Suspicion*, 1981), which was still quite a success, depends too much on storyboards: we feel it, and it's a weakness.

Q: So the screenplay is not a very enjoyable stage of production for you.

CC: Sometimes it's atrocious. The only advantage is that one knows what is not definitive, what one can change later on. The terrible thing is that the production is born there. For a well-known director, it's still negotiable—the producers have confidence in it without reading it—but a new director who goes to see a producer without having gotten financing is immediately jilted. In the old days, when the financing came in after seeing the finished film, that was better.

Q: What are the psychological qualities which make a good director: tenacity?

CC: There are stubborn people who are blocked on a project for years and who, when they finally shoot it, blow it because they have become too soft. Those ones are ripe for suicide. Each film can be the one that prevents you from making another. You have to be able to go to a producer and accept having to make *The Minister in the Nudist Camp*. It's like Sartre's *Dirty Hands*: you have to know how to dirty your hands without dirtying your soul.

Q: Are you still attached to any projects?

CC: No, *Les Fantômes du chapelier* was the last. But today I am too old: I wouldn't make a film like *Les Magiciens* anymore; I only want to make things that I really have the desire to make.

Q: Sometimes they say that the most important quality of a director is sanity.

CC: That's true. He has to have some humility with respect to what he is doing and a strength with respect to what he is. He should never engage in self-censorship, whether it be in ambitious projects or in assignments he accepts as they are. That is my method. You have to maintain your pride, to have enough vanity to withstand blows as hard as *Les Magiciens*, and, if possible, to avoid films whose posters are decorated with angled bars saying "Miou Miou/ Audiard/ Lautner." In that case, none of the three people involved (the actor, writer, or director) is responsible for the life of the enterprise. If you fall into that kind of project, you have to know it clearly; you have to see that whatever happens with the film doesn't come out of any necessity. Lautner knows that, by the way, and he is fine with it.

Q: How do you live through the conflicts and the power struggles that are inherent on certain shoots?

CC: That never happens on my films. The only conflict I ever had was between Romy Schneider and Rod Steiger on *Les Innocents aux mains sales*. I tried to soften it, but he called her "the European star" and she called him "the fat pig." Otherwise, there are problems with money, fights with the producer, which are resolved very quickly. I am loyal to my team, to my crew. I have made all my films with Jean Rabier as cinematographer. With him, it's like a marriage: sometimes we would like to have a little adventure elsewhere, but in reality, not so much. I know exactly how he will respond to my requests, and that is very precious.

Q: How do you go about the eventual directing of actors?

CC: The word "eventual" is not too strong. I am very attentive at the moment of choosing the actors. I don't have a casting director: I see everyone. It is difficult to correct a bad actor. You can only keep an actor who has talent moving in a desired direction. Of course, there are people who like conflict. I imagine that those are people who are fighting against sleep. Often they are alcoholics who snooze a bit during the day, because they are sleeping it off, and then they try to wake themselves up by making noise.

Q: You don't write for particular actors?

CC: In general, no. I knew that Michel Serrault was going to play the hatter in *Les*

Fantômes du chapelier. That helped me, but I didn't write any line saying, "Oh, he's going to say this line well." I try to shoot films with the people I have in mind at the beginning, and not to go from an athletic black man to a sickly intellectual.

Q: In *Ten Days' Wonder*, Marlène Jobert replaced Cathérine Deneuve. Did the role change as a result?
CC: In fact, no. That's one of the reasons why the film fell apart. It was not at all Marlène's fault, but she didn't fit the role. She felt it, and she surely suffered from it. For Orson Welles in that film, you have to see the English-language version, because Pascal Thomas has very cruelly and very justly noted that in the French-language version that character has a stupid voice. In any case, the film was completely botched; it had to rely on the fascination with a period, around 1925. Also, it was very expensive, and the theme only appears in the dialogue. Except for a single sequence involving the robbery of a safe which has a bit of the flavor of the *Le Masque* series from the beginning of the century.

Q: And how do you respond to actors who are imposed on you, parachuted in because of international productions?
CC: I accept them, and I use what I know about them. With Maria Schell in *Folies bourgeoises*, I used the fact that she had made her career on laughing and crying at the same time. That became a parody.

Q: How do you look at your work in rushes?
CC: After a week, you know if you are staying on the rails or not. It's horrible when you have to say to yourself, harshly, "It's a mess." Then you take the beast by the hair by a process of autosuggestion, and you start believing in it again. I don't think that you can straighten it out again once the film starts to go off track, but during the shooting no one can convince me that it isn't the masterpiece of the century! I give myself the illusion that I'm going to salvage it; I hang on to stupid things, to bits of scenes. Then it's time for editing, and the depression sets in. How bad it is really jumps out at you. And then you get used to it again; your fingers uncurl, and you believe it's going better, but it's because you have already been strangled: you don't feel anything anymore. Ten years later, seeing it again, you are suffocated by the horror of it. You have to be able to withstand all of that.

Q: And how do you react to commercial success or failure?
CC: I'm not that preoccupied with money, as long as I am able to shoot again. I really believe in the method of father John Ford, who, after a big popular success, deliberately made a bomb to get to an honest mean.

Q: Let's take up the chronology of your films from the start. You didn't start with making short films, or with being an assistant.

CC: No, I got into it through the cash register. The money was from the old lady. My first wife's grandmother died leaving a small inheritance, and that is how I produced *Le Beau Serge*. Truffaut married the daughter of a distributor. That's the true story: we made our first films because we were able to find the money. Money both makes and destroys cinema in the same movement. At the time, the world of cinema was completely closed: people only got into directing after carrying beers and sandwiches for years. Today, someone who gives himself two, three, or five years to make a film should logically be able to do it, unless he is worthless or feels that way inside. So I made *Le Beau Serge*, which originally lasted two and a half hours, and I showed it to Rivette, who said it was too long: with hindsight, he was right. I cut out the Pagnolesque parts: the breadmaking scenes. The film was at the same time naïf and wily. I was seeking to please certain people with a rural lyricism, with this opposition between positive and negative main characters. And, in fact, it did please people. I made a net profit of thirty-five million francs on a cost of thirty-two million. *Les Cousins* was a more expensive film, with nine weeks of shooting, and terrible financial problems during the sixth week.

Q: With *Les Cousins*, you entered a climate, milieu, and imagery that were more clearly Nouvelle Vague.

CC: I had written it before the other film, but I didn't have enough money to make it. And yes, it was almost parodically Nouvelle Vague: the golden youth of Saint Germain, a world that I knew well personally.

Q: It is sometimes said that there are ambiguous mythologies in *Les Cousins*, and that it is really a right-wing film.

CC: That's because they naively confuse the author with the character. It's true that this corporate, right-wing milieu was the beginning of a certain form of the right wing, of Le Pen and company. It is the story of a character, played by Gérard Blain, who enters into that right-wing milieu. That doesn't mean I shared their opinions.

Q: But the people in the film are seductive.

CC: The right wing *is* seductive! That's what characterizes it: otherwise it would not have had any success. We had come out of an era that was caustic to the soul, rife with a Hussar spirit. The film was dated very precisely: April 13, 1958. It was exactly a month before the arrival of the Fifth Republic. But it is true, during this time, that people like Claude Lanzmann wrote that my characters were Nazified. Many people thought they were on the left, but they were motivated by vague feelings, by a sort of populist generosity. The people on the right are not always fat pigs, or they would have been swept out of office long ago. I had this same problem with *Les Bonnes Femmes*, because of its absence of populism. I tried to suggest that working-class people could also be idiots—which seems obvious to me—and that the influence of large amounts of red wine after work can be a harmful thing. I consider myself to be a centrist, and I believe that the center is infinitely more to the left than this vague swamp of good sentiments.

Q: You often have characters in your films who are amoral and caught up in a moral drama.

CC: Yes, except for *Le Beau Serge*, which is, as I told you, of Christian inspiration. But the Catholic Church put *Les Cousins* on its "proscribed" list, and the Catholic newspaper *La Croix* insulted me because I had shown an actual sign on the door of Saint-Jacques Church, saying, "Closed from 6pm to 7am."

Q: You used the same two actors for the two films: Jean-Claude Brialy and Gérard Blain.

CC: The universe of *Le Beau Serge* is that of a Christian character who arrives in a rural, peasant, socialist-communist world that is anticlerical. The universe of *Les Cousins* is that of a provincial boy who arrives in a right-wing Parisian world. I used the same actors to create a kind of small binary discourse.

Q: *Les Cousins* was an enormous success.

CC: Yes, it did well: it seemed to be in the wind. It was at the time of Marcel Carné's *Les Tricheurs* (*Young Sinners*, 1958) and the intellectuals preferred *Les Cousins*. I was invited everywhere. A Lithuanian named Borcon—born Borcu—asked me to direct a "strip-tease" film, but I held out for *A double tour*, which I wanted to make in color and with flashbacks. They told me: you can do one or the other. Only the Hakims let me do both.

Q: How did you come up with the idea for *A double tour*?

CC: I had met a group of people from the upper levels of Aix-en-Provence society, and I had met one person in particular, who seemed sane, but who had killed his wife and his mistress: he had told his mistress that he wasn't sleeping with his wife anymore, but the mistress wanted to leave him because she found out that the wife was pregnant. I used these story elements in the film. In the beginning, I wanted Charles Boyer to play Dacqmine and Suzy Parker to play the part played by Antonella Lualdi. Belmondo replaced Brialy, who was sick, and who would in any case have been less good in the role. And I put in André Jocelyn, whom I had noticed in a small role in *Les Cousins*, because he cried like a faucet during the speech in German. The reception of the film was tepid: those who had liked the first two films were unhappy, and others liked it fine. But strategically, it was the film I needed to make.

Q: After this period of relative success, you started your first crossing of the desert.
CC: They completely rejected *Les Bonnes Femmes*, and I was surprised because I thought I had made a masterpiece. They accused me of being a misogynist, a Nazi, a bastard! Then I doubled down with *Les Godelureaux*, which was my revenge: purely and simply a provocation. It was also quite a failed film: the premise was so abstract that it was difficult to discern: it was about nothingness, emptiness, pure mockery. The plot was constructed as a series of scenes, which are like random shots of a revolver at anything that moves. The film makes fun of the silliness of its own enterprise: it is a mockery of a mockery of a mockery. There was a Roman orgy where everything gets lacerated, and a charity party in which old whores sang carols. It is my most extreme experiment of the period.

Q: After that, was it difficult to make another film?
CC: No. Afterwards, miraculously, I met the producer Georges de Beauregard, who fell into my arms, and I began to prepare both *L'Oeil du Malin* (*The Third Lover*) and *Ophelia*. For the first of these, we went to shoot exteriors in Germany with one reflector for all the lighting! The film was not very interesting.

Q: But the themes there figure prominently in your later films: these very tightly drawn emotional relations, suspicion, mutual surveillance.
CC: There were a few successful elements. Stéphane Audran had the line, "We aren't like you . . . we don't cry over ourselves." And I loved the last sentence spoken by Jacques Charrier: "I can't help telling this story, and people ask me why a nice boy like me would take pleasure in dirtying himself."

Q: What about *Ophelia*?
CC: It was my biggest bomb: the box-office results were not even reported, which made it even worse. But the producer loved the film: I imagine he still watches it from time to time on cassette tape. In that film, Jocelyn was not up to the task, and neither was Claude Cerval. I liked the character played by Robert Burnier, who was devoted to his daughter.

Q: You then came back to a more classical production, *Landru*, which was in color, with costumes, starring Michèle Morgan and Danielle Darrieux, and with Françoise Sagan as the screenwriter.
CC: Yes, Sagan had liked *Les Bonnes Femmes*, which she had defended in an article in *L'Express*. The figure of the guy who killed women in the midst of a war fascinated

us. The film was well received, but I began to get violently slapped around by the critics. I was said to have betrayed the Nouvelle Vague, and to be preventing others from making their films.

Q: But you had become a star director.
CC: I was attacked for two reasons: first, for my natural extraversion, which was irritating to people, and second, because they recognized my four-eyes face: they could put a name to a face. The drama of someone like Philippe de Broca is that no one knows who he is, and he will never be a star because no one recognizes his face.

Q: After *Landru*, however, it was a journey into the wilderness.
CC: Yes, eighteen months without making a film. Lots of fabulous projects fell apart, among them *Atrox*, in which James Mason was to appear in a kind of ultra-fast *Fantomas*-like serial, where they poured LSD into the water system of Paris. It was after that that Christine Gouze-Rénal pitched me the first of the *Tiger* films, written by Roger Hanin under a pseudonym, and because of which I spent a bit of time with the spies at the Don Camilo cabaret, a hangout for them at the time.

Q: What about the second *Tiger* film?
CC: I didn't want to do it. But Christine convinced me, saying, "We'll have a huge budget, with submarines; you'll see." Actually, instead of the submarines, I had to settle for scuba divers (submarines in a way) who were holding the rubber things you use to clean out toilets, which allowed them to attach themselves to the sides of boats. I thought that was pretty exciting: it was great to play with the chaos of it.

Q: You were interested in the "genre" aspect of it?
CC: I love that. And then, I had the good luck to be making these films right in the era of the spy film. If the porno film had been in vogue, that would have interested me much less.

Q: Between the two *Tiger* films, there was *Marie-Chantal contre Docteur Kha*.
CC: That was a unique film. *Marie-Chantal* was really what I wanted to do with that genre: the commentary on the commentary.

Q: A lot of Chabrolian adages can be found in that film, like when Stéphane Audran says to Marie LaForet, "If you only knew what I have had to to . . ."
CC: " . . . sleeping with men, with women, with animals, with government ministers." And strangely, the people who had torn apart the earlier films started to find something in the parodies, especially *Marie-Chantal* (which is by far the best of the three). After that, Georges de Beauregard had asked Anthony Mann

to make *La Ligne de démarcation*, and Mann, whom I knew a little (having done to him what you are now doing to me), suggested to the producer that he pass the project on to me, though it was a project that didn't interest me at all. Beauregard accepted this, and I found myself face to face with the script by Colonel Rémy, which is something one has to have experienced to understand. I began to recopy the screenplay longhand, changing little things, up until the moment when my pen refused to continue, pure and simple. So I turned in the Colonel's screenplay almost unchanged, except for a few jokes that were hardly visible but gave me pleasure: for example, the World War I veteran limped on the right side, and the World War II veteran limped on the left. And then the last image of the film, which I found quite beautiful: everyone is singing the "Marseillaise," during which the camera moves up to end on the flag with the swastika. The film's premiere was organized by the Rhine and Danube veterans' association: I was quite impressed. There were cohorts of guys with medals up to their nostrils: one would have thought a procession of Russian generals. And at the end of the film, at the moment when they sing the "Marseillaise," the whole room stood up to sing the refrain: they were all standing for inspection in front of a Nazi flag! It made a curious impression. There was one other thing I liked in *La Ligne de démarcation*. Roger Dumas played the role of a complete bastard, a person who pretended to be helping the Jews escape but who denounced his clients to the Germans, keeping the money and the suitcases that they had given him. You saw him conferring with the Jews whom he was sending to their death (Claude Berri played one of them), and then he said, "Excuse me for a moment," and he went into the next room, the kitchen, where his wife and eleven children were crowded in. That was it. I liked that.

Q: The following year, there was *The Champagne Murders*.
CC: Yes. Raymond Eger had told me that by casting Yvonne Furneaux we could get a coproduction with Universal. So why not? In fact, Yvonne Furneaux was the daughter of an important family (Lloyd's) and her husband Jacques Natteau—who was the camera operator on *La Traversée de Paris*—was a producer at Universal. That is how *The Champagne Murders* got made. During the shoot, I suffered a lot because of an aberrant optical process called Techniscope. There were lots of hairs in the camera. And we had to shoot two versions, which is annoying. But there were funny things in the screenplay, and a golden role for Stéphane, even though the role hadn't been intended for her.

Q: We won't talk too much about *Who's Got the Black Box?* (*La Route de Corinthe*).
CC: The film is shitty, but I play a very important role in it: Alcibiade. And I love the shot where the guy washes his hands in the stoup.

Q: Let's talk a bit about your acting performances. Some of them are remarkable, such as the one in *La Muette*.

CC: Yes, it was the main role. I had a good part in the second *Tiger* film as well: the alcoholic—and perhaps homosexual—doctor, who builds a shark. And in *Marie-Chantal*, I play a barman who poisons himself with grapefruit juice. Those are my three most important performances, I would have to say.

Q: You are, undeniably, a specialist in disguises.

CC: For a very simple reason: I noticed that I belong to that category of people who, if they don't really do a lot, will never make an impression on the screen. There are actors like that, even good actors: unless they have a ton of business, you just don't see them. That is the case with me. And then, it seems logical to me that the director should reserve the most caricatural role in the film for himself: that way he doesn't need to worry about his status as an actor. There are thirty-six ways of inventing a mask. Godard chose the black sunglasses; Alain Resnais does the polite coldness; and I put on the clown mask, because I find that to be more fun. Obviously, it is also a question of personal style: I can't see Alain dancing the gigue to amuse the journalists.

Q: After *Who's Got the Black Box?*, it was *Les Biches*. It is often cited as a turning point in your career.

CC: It was a turning point in the sense that it was the first film I had done without someone assigning it to me since *Landru*. After the adventure of *Who's Got the Black Box?* (I would call it "The Greek Evil"), Génovès, with whom I got along well in spite of everything, asked me if I had another subject for a film. And we made *Les Biches*, which was a pure and simple scam, since the screenplay followed that of *Les Cousins*, just changing the sexes and the locations.

Q: Then, from *Les Biches* through *Juste avant la nuit*, there was a series of films which fit together, even more so because they all had Stéphane Audran in them, just as she was becoming a star.

CC: I had always found that Stéphane was a great actress, but our relationship as a married couple didn't make things easy. Sometimes they would ask me, "Whom do you see in that role?" and I would say, "Um . . . Stéphane Audran." "Who is that?" "Um . . . she's a very good actress . . . and my wife." That didn't go over well, obviously. Thanks to *Les Biches*, and to the favor the film brought to us both, I was able to use Stéphane regularly in the character of a woman who I had had in mind for a long time.

Q: Her character in the period from 1967 to 1971 is at once very consistent and quite varied. She is a St. Tropez lesbian in *Les Biches*, a bourgeoise adulteress in

La Femme infidèle, a provincial schoolteacher in *Le Boucher*, a pitiful victim in *La Rupture*, and a vestal virgin of the nouveau riche in *Juste avant la nuit*.
CC: Those were all different facets of the same character, of a woman with a number of successive faces: Hélène (or "Hélènes" since in all these films the main female character is called Hélène).

Q: How did you work around the relationship of husband and wife?
CC: With an extreme severity on my part. The more I was calm and rather accommodating with the other actors, the more I was tough with Stéphane. We knew each other too well, and we could predict each other too much (although Stéphane always managed, in the end, to surprise me), and the tension was too great because of that. Our professional relationship has been much more sympathetic since we are no longer married.

Q: Do you think your collaboration fed your married relationship?
CC: Not the collaboration in itself. But I became more sensitive in having the same face in front of me twenty-four hours a day. With Aurore [Chabrol's third wife and script supervisor], it's completely different: she is at work with me, but off to the side. When I look through the viewfinder, I don't see my wife. Whereas before, when I looked, what did I see? Stéphane Audran.

Q: You ended the Hélène series with *Juste avant la nuit*. Was this a deliberate decision, in the same way that Rohmer created different series of films?
CC: I ended it because I had the feeling that the subject had been treated, that the character of Hélène, like those of Paul and Charles, had come full circle. As for the analogy with Rohmer: I believe that my project was just as precise as his, but more honestly expressed. What he did that was the most astute (other than the films themselves, which are superb), was not to put them in order: Moral Tale 1, Moral Tale 4, Moral Tale 2. . . . That was really strong and was the proof of his "totalizing vision." I would really have believed he had a preestablished plan if he hadn't ended the series with the last one: that makes me skeptical.

Q: So, at the moment of *La Femme infidèle*, you already had the sense of beginning a series?
CC: Yes, but not a series that was attached only to the character of Hélène. Several things were mixed up in it: a certain kind of France under Pompidou, happy and bourgeois, which I found interesting; the relations between men and women (which I had been calling, since *Les Cousins*, the "Charles" and the "Paul"); and finally the woman herself, Hélène. I had this frame, which allowed me to link these films that were apparently fairly similar, but really quite different. Between *La Femme infidèle*

and *Juste avant la nuit*, for example, there is the same relationship as between the right-hand glove and the left-hand glove: an identical subject, but reversed. Usually, I force myself to treat dramatic subjects in a way that makes people laugh; and there, in *Juste avant la nuit*, it seemed to me that the irony would be more pointed in the tragedy, whereas the theme itself was rather funny: the story of a guy who wants to admit something, and no one wants to hear it.

Q: So, the Hélène cycle is completed with *Juste avant la nuit*, and you go on to something else.

CC: All of that was a bit confused in my mind. I wasn't sure of wanting to make *Juste avant la nuit*, which came a bit too much at the end of the convoy, especially since I wanted to make *Ten Days' Wonder* (*La Décade prodigieuse*) at that time. Then Orson Welles got sick, and *Ten Days' Wonder* had to be delayed, but since the crew was already hired and I didn't want to leave the money on the table, we shot *Juste avant la nuit*; the screenplay was already finished. Without that chain of circumstances, I would have no doubt made that film much later, after having kept it on the back burner for a while.

Q: You weren't happy with *Juste avant la nuit*?

CC: Well . . . yes. In fact, I'm never happy with any film. But that one didn't displease me more than any of the others.

Q: What are your favorite films that you have made?

CC: It's difficult to say. I have two weaknesses at this moment: *La Rupture* and *Les Fantômes du chapelier*. But that will certainly change one of these days.

Q: What about *Les Noces rouges*?

CC: That was my favorite a while ago, but not anymore. You know, I had known the characters, or at least two out of the three (the wife and the victim, her husband, who was an ironmonger in Bourganeuf), and the story fascinated me quite a bit. At the same time, I wanted to make something anti-RPR (it was just before the elections), and so I changed the ironmonger into a local government official.[2] But I got myself screwed over, because the trial ended in a mistrial for a technical reason, and the release of the film was pushed back until after the elections. But it was a good fight.

Q: In your films, the victims are always monsters.

CC: Let's say that I begin with the principle that if we kill someone, we should have a good reason for doing it, unless we are completely crazy. And then, I try to avoid hasty judgments, the sort of classification of assassins and victims that are imposed on the public. For example, I was extremely shocked, at the time of the Patrick Henry affair, by the attitude of the justice minister at the time, Jean Lecanuet, who basically called for the head of the accused during his instructions to the jury. For me, in my personal morality, I find the behavior of a minister exercising his power more serious than the act of Patrick Henry itself.[3]

Q: Let's get back to the course of your career. As much as the five films that preceded *Juste avant la nuit* gave an impression of unity, the five films that followed (*Ten Days' Wonder, Docteur Popaul, Les Noces rouges, Nada*, and *Une partie de plaisir*) seem completely different from one another.
CC: That's true. I tried to go a little more into subjects that interested me, being aware that in each case they were in very different areas; and there was no thought of a system as there had been in the earlier films. *Ten Days' Wonder* . . . well, it's a failure. In my opinion, it's my greatest failure, for thirty-six reasons which are not very interesting. The bother is that I really missed something, something that was close to my heart. I wanted to put all the things we were talking about earlier in front of the spectator: God, chaos, nonchaos. And I completely failed, no doubt because of an excess of ambition, given the resources at my disposal, and also because the choice of the book by Ellery Queen, which was very complex, was not the best one.

Q: After *Ten Days' Wonder, Docteur Popaul* seems like the reaction of a scalded cat.
CC: In fact, Génovès had told me, during the shooting of *Ten Days' Wonder*, that Belmondo wanted to do something with me again. That pleased me a lot, especially since I had an excellent memory of working with Jean-Paul. At the beginning, I wasn't sure how to adapt the novel by Hubert Monteilhet. But someone had written a treatment, and it was Gégauff who then took over most of the work. In the end, I like *Docteur Popaul*, at least the villainy of the character, the unclean side of things, like at the end when the guys sing the song "La Famille Tuyau-La-Poele," which I am very proud of having found. The film did well, thanks to Jean-Paul Belmondo, but the reviews were not tender. Patrice Leconte sent me a funny little note that said, "If Louis Lumière had seen *Docteur Popaul*, he wouldn't have invented the cinema." To which I responded later, in the spirit of friendship, that if Louis Lumière had seen Leconte's film *Les Bronzés*, he really would have been in a rush to invent the cinema.

Q: *Docteur Popaul* is, along with *Stavisky*, one of the last films where we see Belmondo take risks in terms of his screen image.
CC: Yes, he made *Stavisky* because *Docteur Popaul* had done well, and since *Stavisky* didn't do well, he then renounced that kind of role. But I don't believe at

all—contrary to what is often said—that Jean-Paul has gotten lost in the fanfare. He really loves his work as an actor; I am convinced of it. One of these days he will turn his ankle or twist a vertebra, and that will give him an occasion for coming back to these kinds of characters. And in any case, even when he doesn't have much to do, he does it well. It's like Sean Connery in the James Bond movies: when you see other actors try to do it, you realize what has been lost.

Q: After *Docteur Popaul*, there was a commercial success but a critical failure in *Les Noces rouges*, which we have already talked about a bit. You go back, in another stylistic register, to the cinema of the Hélène cycle.
CC: It's definitely in another register. The construction is quite different (there are no flashbacks in the Hélène series); also, the relationship of the film to political reality is much more precise, much more direct; I really saw that film as a political tract within an electoral campaign. Let's say that in *Les Noces rouges* there is a sort of recapitulation of what I had done before, but according to a new agency: I tried to superimpose genres as anchor points of the film, and of my own interests, instead of organizing them in a linear fashion as I had done before.

Q: One also has the impression that after making *Les Noces rouges* you realized that you had struck a rich lode but you didn't want to use it again right away; you preferred to explore other domains.
CC: In truth, the film that really followed *Les Noces rouges* was *Violette Nozière*. Between the two, I loitered.

Q: You tend to move forward in a zigzag.
CC: Yes, I am an old crab. It's a way of moving that comes fairly naturally to me: I try to avoid certainties. At the time of *Juste avant la nuit*, I began to pontificate. Aurore said, in a way that was both justified and terrifying, that I was starting to sound like "Saint John Golden Mouth." Then, after *Les Noces rouges*, I wanted to distance myself completely from myself, and I made *Nada*, for what I have to admit was a bad reason: irritation. I was reading everywhere and about everything: "Oh, what a great political film! . . . Oh, what courage it took to denounce war and violence!" This kind of stupidity was burning my ears, and Jean-Patrick Manchette's book seemed to me to be an excellent response. Everything was decided very quickly: we divided up the adaptation between Manchette and me. I did the first 120 pages and he did the next 120 pages. Generally, the film stays quite faithful to the book (Manchette actually changed more things than I did), except for one sentence, which equated anarchism with terrorism, and which I insisted on changing.

Q: Did *Nada* have a directly political function like *Les Noces rouges*?

CC: No, not really. Claire Clouzot said, in a disdainful way, that it was a film with a "communist program." I prefer to make a film with a communist program than one with a Chateau de Blois program! Even so, I still think *Nada* is the only political film made in France and about France, at least to my knowledge. I don't see any others out there.

Q: What about Godard's *La Chinoise*?

CC: There are great things in *La Chinoise*, but it isn't a political film. It is a film about confusion. A film that confuses the spectator cannot be a political film. To make a political film, you have to designate things—and especially the powers that are implicated in the film—in a very clear way.

Q: And *Nada* was intended to be clear?

CC: "Political terrorism and state terrorism are the two jaws of the same trap for stupid people." That is a truth that is enunciated by Fabio Testi in *Nada* (it is also in the book), and which seems very clear to me. My political opinions are extremely simple: I think that political terrorism and state terrorism are two jaws of the same trap for stupid people, and that we have to try to avoid both. And chaos—to come back to ideas we were talking about before—can just as easily come out of the organization of the state as out of its disorganization.

Q: The next film, *Une partie de plaisir*, is once again a complete rupture from the one that preceded it.

CC: It is a film about Gégauff and his wife at the time, a kind of reconstituted documentary. The idea came from Paul: in fact, he wanted to win Danielle back. In the beginning, he was thinking of doing it as fiction, using actors like Trintignant. I told him that I thought it was a great idea, but only if he and Danielle played themselves. We were even able to shoot in their house.

Q: You never felt the temptation, like other directors of the Nouvelle Vague, to use your own experiences?

CC: No, I do not have an autobiographical temperament at all. I force myself to lead the most simple, tranquil, and harmonious life, and thus it's not very interesting. I couldn't tell much about my life, except the story of a guy who tries to avoid conflict. Since autobiography is forbidden to me, under the threat of mortal boredom, I have to lean on the biographies of others.

Q: Now we arrive at *Les Innocents aux mains sales*, which is as different from *Une partie de plaisir* as *Une partie* is from *Nada*.

CC: *Les Innocents* should have been a parody of a film noir, in the same way that

Marie-Chantal is a parody of a spy film. But in fact, I found myself both betrayed and helped by Romy Schneider, who didn't get the parodic side of it at all, and thus her performance gives the film a very hybrid quality. That bothered me for a long time, but in seeing *Les Innocents* again, I found it quite interesting. That said, I don't have a great memory of the shooting. First of all, because the two main actors didn't get along very well, and then because of the mixture of languages, which is always very irritating to me. All in all—Romy's lack of a sense of humor, the fact that the actors played in a completely different way from each other—all of that, in a bizarre sense, helps the film. It gives it a strange *je-ne-sais-quoi*. And then, it seems to me that inside all this smash-up one can still distinguish a real subject, which is to say the relations of a woman with several men. That is why there is only a single woman figure throughout the entire film.

Q: After that, you made *Les Magiciens*. I believe we can pass it by . . .
CC: Completely.

Q: Did you have to make it?
CC: No. What pushed me to do it was a sordid problem with taxes. It's the only thing written by Mr. Asshole I've ever made.

Q: *Folies bourgeoises* was the fifth film after *Les Noces rouges*. By this time, you were no doubt feeling that you had lost your way.
CC: I still hadn't found a means of communication; it was really stupid. But I don't renounce anything: I think that it was interesting to try, even if *Les Magiciens* . . . you never know. You always preserve something of value. In *Les Magiciens*, for example, I really like the line spoken by Gert Froebe ("I can't do it, because I don't have my paraphernalia"), and the speech by Franco Nero on the irrational.

Q: How do you explain the return, every four or five years, to genre films that are treated in a parodic way?
CC: It is, in part, that I love the notion of genre, and also that I would find it dishonest not to try to make people laugh with something that I find funny. Howard Hawks said one thing that really struck me: "Before shooting a scene, see if it is possible to make it funny, and if you can do that it's better, because you avoid having people laugh at it *despite* your intention."

Q: Now we come to *Alice ou la dernière fugue*.
CC: This is a project that I had had for a long time, and that I was able to make because one of my friends wanted to become a producer. In the beginning, the roles were intended for Shirley MacLaine and Laurence Olivier, and then the producers

thought of Sylvia Kristel and Charles Vanel: they thought that would be more commercially viable. And with Sylvia, a whole part of the story disappeared: the part concerning the growth of a metastasized cancer.

Q: You rarely worked with parables, other than in *Alice*.
CC: Never. But when speaking of death, it is difficult to do it any other way. If there is one subject that is a parable by definition it is death. That being the case, I recognize that it is a downer, and would have been even if the film had completely succeeded.

Q: Then you left for Canada, to make *Blood Relatives*.
CC: Yes, based on a crime novel by Ed McBain, which we followed very closely. I had first thought about moving the story to France and making it like *Quai des Orfevres*, with the Noiret-type detective and all the rest, but I realized that in order to remain faithful to McBain and the characters, we would have to shoot it on the American continent. So I found a crew to go to Canada, and I said to Donald Sutherland, "Come on, we're going to make *Inspector Carella*!" He knew the book, he liked it, and *voila*! For me, what was interesting was the fact that the main female character was a growing girl (like my step-daughter Cécile), and also the fact that the inspector was the father of a girl of the same age as the murderess. From this point of view, *Violette Nozière* was the sequel to *Blood Relatives*.

Q: Watching Cécile grow up made you decide to make *Blood Relatives*. Why not make a film like *The Party* or *The Key Is in the Door*?
CC: Because the problems of a girl of fifteen are not those of *The Party*.

Q: So it was more about seeing whether the girl would kill her cousin, as in *Blood Relatives*, or her parents, as in *Violette Nozière*?
CC: Of course. It's interesting in everyone's case, not just in the case of young girls.

Q: We don't see many children in your films.
CC: Yes, that's true. For a long time, there were none at all. And then they started to appear, at the time when mine were beginning to grow up.

Q: With *Violette Nozière*, you seem to have found a new maturity, which is also a synthesis of your previous efforts.
CC: It's hard to say. Things crystallize all of a sudden, and one never knows exactly why. It's like fruit that ripens. I had thought about *Violette* for a long time, and everything came together at the right moment so that I could make it. There are a number of factors—contradictory ones, as well—that allow me to sniff out whether

a film is ripe or not. When I have a lot of trouble finding the financing, for example, it's generally better to abandon the project, or at least to push it back. That said, you can be wrong: *Le Cheval d'orgueil* (*The Proud Ones*) was very easy to make, which didn't prevent it from being a failure for the vast majority of the public. No one understood what it was about. That's when I realized that folklore did not yet have the status of a film genre. When we are in the presence of a western or a crime film, it is so familiar that we instinctively look for the subject beyond the codes of the genre. But when we see Jacques Dufilho with his traditional Breton bagpipe, we can't get past it. On the other hand, the British critics reacted very favorably to the film, because it is not *their* folklore. I was wrong not to realize that certain "exterior" elements of *Le Cheval d'orgueil* completely obscured what I wanted to say in the film. If I had made a film with images that looked like the pictures on post-office wall calendars in any other genre, people would have asked why. In *Le Cheval d'orgueil*, that didn't happen at all: they said, "Well, he made a series of calendar photos about Brittany."

Q: Did the relative failure of *Le Cheval d'orgueil* hold up the production of *Les Fantômes du chapelier*?
CC: It delayed it, but not by much. I had the project in mind for a long time without managing to write the adaptation. What made it click was the involvement of Michel Serrault. After having talked to him about it and realizing that we were on the same wavelength, I found my method. I just had to recopy the book. What I am sure of is that when you want to make a film based on a book by Simenon, it is impossible—whatever certain screenwriters may say—to film anything other than Simenon. I never really got the point of a method that consists, when adapting a book, of changing the characters, the locations, and the time period of the story. Or of using an isolated element of a book in another context. If you do that, it is no longer "adapted from"; it is "with the collaboration of." But in general, if I adapt a book, it is because I want to *adapt* the book, not rewrite it.

Q: *Les Fantômes du chapelier*, and most of your best films (for example, *Violette*, *Les Noces rouges*, *Les Bonnes Femmes*) have a historical context without being historical films or reconstructions of historical events.
CC: To tell the truth, I would like everything I do to have an historical context. But I believe that it is possible to historicize a film without temporalizing it. It seems to me that the historical context has more to do with an *idea* of the era than with the era itself. The difficulty is that—whether you want to or not—you have to show the costumes, the hairstyles, and the décor on the screen. In literature, you can suggest the era by default: if you tell the story of a couple of average French people who knit or read after dinner, we know that it's not happening today, because they're

not watching television! But in the cinema, you have to make things more precise. For *Les Fantômes du chapelier*, I forced myself to set the story in "Simenon time," in other words somewhere between 1930 and 1960.

Q: At the close of this survey of your career, can we ask you how you would define the function of the brand that you have constructed for yourself: the greedy jokester who is both anarchic and very French?
CC: That comes from the fact that I prefer to make people laugh instead of cry, and that, at the same time, what I have to say isn't necessarily funny. I find that we have to involve ourselves a bit in the enormities of life, if only for the sake of honesty towards ourselves. I am not above the fray, seated on my throne watching the people twitching below me. I twitch as much as they do. Let's say that my jokester side is my way of dressing myself, in both a moral and an intellectual sense.

Q: Does Dominique Paini's idea, according to which if you treat other people like pigs you will soon have a snout attached to you, seem true to you?
CC: Completely true. I find that the least we can do is be polite.

Notes

1. Michel Audiard (1920–1985) was a successful French screenwriter known for his colorful, slang-inflected, and often witty dialogue.
2. The RPR (Rassemblement pour la République) was a neo-Gaullist, conservative political party. In Chabrol's film, the hypocrisy and corruption of the political class is satirized within the context of a film noir plot.
3. Patrick Henry (1953–2017) was convicted of the kidnapping and murder of an eight-year-old boy in 1976. His trial was highly controversial, with the prosecution calling for the death penalty and the defense attorneys ultimately convincing the jury to reject capital punishment and impose a sentence of life imprisonment.

Interview with Claude Chabrol

Alain Carbonnier and Joël Magny / 1982

From *Cinéma* 285 (September 1982). Translated from the French by CB.

Question: Your most recent film, *The Hatter's Ghost* (*Les Fantômes du chapelier*) is an old project. Did you do it as it was originally conceived, or did you change it?
Claude Chabrol: It really is an old project; I didn't really know how to do it back then. I tried two or three times. At the beginning of last year, I thought about *The Hatter's Ghost* again, immediately thinking of Michel Serrault for the role. I went to see him, and I made him read the book, and he took the role. Just knowing that it would be him playing the part helped me a lot.

Q: What blocked you in your first attempts?
CC: I don't really know; as is always the case when adapting Simenon, I told myself that I would have to shorten it a bit before rewriting it for the screen. That was stupid. In short, I fumbled it, and then I said: "Let's try to see what happens if we just follow the book." And that was the right idea.

Q: There are a lot of things in common between Chabrol and Simenon.
CC: That's true. But it's also true that I had a bit of trouble in the beginning, because in Simenon there are no real plots; they don't exist, or let's say instead that it is the characters who invent them. In those kinds of cases, it is important to know the people who will be playing the roles; then you know to what extent you can respect the text and to what extent you can change things around.

In *The Hatter's Ghost*, I only changed two elements: 1. In the book, the discovery of the death of the nun is made through a telegram, while in the film the hatter learns about it while on a visit to the archbishopric (which is also in another Simenon novel). 2. Simenon is committed to never having the hatter go inside Kachoudas' house. Of course, in the book he found a solution that is practical in literature but difficult to translate onto the screen: the hatter only dreamed of or imagined his visit to Kachoudas. I tried to see if I could do it in the form of a fantasy, but that didn't pan out because it was too difficult to tell if it was real or not. So I made it as if it was real.

Q: People criticize you for not having taken full advantage of the plot.
CC: There isn't one, and besides, plots don't interest me much, or rather, they interest me in the same way that they interest Simenon: when characters meet each other, their relationships create a plot, rather than the plot coming first. That is why telling a story and sticking characters onto it is less seductive to me than the opposite.

Of course, I have been known to follow a good story, but I prefer to take the characters and see what will happen.

Q: Have you done other projects that were adaptations of Simenon?
CC: I had a project, *Le Fils Cardinaud*, a long, long time ago. It was almost the first project that I had in mind when I decided that I wanted to make films. I had talked to Simenon about it and we had seen things in the same way. And then it turned out that he sold the rights to it for a film with Jean Gabin—*Le Sang à la tête*—that had nothing to do with the novel, which dealt with humility. Just imagine a film about humility with Gabin! It was something else entirely.

Q: In watching your films again, are there things that you have bad memories of making and others you find have become more interesting with time?
CC: When I watch one of my films again, the memory of the shoot comes immediately to mind, and I am very sensitive to that. Was it an agreeable experience? Did everyone have a good time? The bad memories are more often memories of the shoot, and they reverberate on the films themselves; most often, it is also films that were badly received, which confirms me in my own impressions.

I had a pleasant surprise after the death of poor Romy Schneider—who was for me a living Calvary during the shooting of *Les Innocents aux mains sales*—in seeing the film again on television. I found that it wasn't bad; it was certainly better than the mediocre memory that I had of it, even if there are faults, monstrous things, including the outrageous mixture of actors from different nationalities.

Q: Whether your films were received well or badly, it is curious to note that it is often using the same reasons, the same arguments, that both supporters and detractors defend or attack parts or all of your work. One can even see very rapid changes of perspective in the same critic. One year after having torn your work apart, they find it remarkable. What do you think about this?
CC: In general, we are less liable to make mistakes if we don't say too many bad things. Such an attitude may appear fatuous, but, in general, there are a lot of films that improve with age.

You have to be careful about films that you are taken with at the moment when they are made. It's like cheeses: the best ones are not those that one eats when they are fresh.

Certain films where we came out of the theater saying "It's sublime" disappoint us ten years later. You ask yourself, "What was I thinking at the time?" Nothing; you weren't thinking about anything at the time, but it just felt right. Often when a film "just felt right" that is dangerous for the future.

Q: Let's talk about your "flops." The greatest flop was *Ophelia*, with just six thousand viewers in Paris.
CC: Yes, but *Ophelia* is a unique case: it's my only film that was completely financed by a patron. The only issue was whether it pleased the patron; if it did, my contract would be renewed. But still, what a flop!

Q: Why?
CC: For several reasons. The distribution was hobbled, and the patron was no Rothschild. It could have been good and it was not as good as it could have been.

Q: Wasn't there also the effect of the pendulum swinging back from the Nouvelle Vague?
CC: Yes, certainly. Another astonishing thing also happened. *Ophelia* came out at about the same time as *Landru*, and an article by someone I no longer remember—I wonder if it was the admirable Pierre Marcabru, a man who didn't like the special effects in *The Birds*!—said that it was a gimmick releasing an avant-garde film on one side and a commercial film on the other, and that both could be thrown away in the same garbage bag. That made me laugh.

Q: Let's continue with the flops. What about *The Proud Ones* (*Le Cheval d'orgueil*)?
CC: That's a film that was never understood at all, and I am well aware that it is my fault and not that of the people who saw it. The result was that they only paid attention to the Breton hairstyles. When you make a film on a subject that is embellished with a crime story, people will say, "It's really about something else." But when you make a film based on folklore, it's only the folklore that matters. I will know that the next time: I will not put in any folkloric elements so as not to run the risk of troubling people's vision.

Q: What was it about the book by Pierre-Jakez Hélias that originally pleased you?
CC: A very complex notion of resurrection; a renaissance principle of things. But that didn't come through enough.

Q: With *Les Cousins*, one has the impression that you completely got rid of your Christianity; in a general way, you give the impression of being a filmmaker who is calmly and deeply atheistic.

CC: It's true that I hardly have any problems with that side of things. It's somehow difficult for me to attach myself to things that I have a hard time defining. I survived a fairly intense Catholic education which left me with small after-affects, including the after-effect of wanting revenge. From the moment when one tosses one's cossack aside, the desire for revenge begins. That was a bit what was happening with *Les Cousins*, but after that it was over and I don't care about it anymore.

I have one anecdote about the locked church in *Les Cousins*: in the newspaper *La Croix*, they found this scene to be shameful. And I had only filmed the sign that was on the church; I didn't invent anything. It made me laugh that prayer was forbidden between seven in the evening and seven in the morning.

Q: What about the character of Theo van Horn (Orson Welles) in *Ten Days' Wonder*?

CC: The meaning of that was that we don't need those kinds of Jehovahs.

Q: You appear in some of your films: is there a reason for that, other than the fact that it amuses you?

CC: No. In general, it's just for the sake of having fun, or if I think I would be better in the role than someone else, which is rare.

In *The Twist*, I scared the American actor who saw me doing tricks in the background. I am sorry that they cut my appearance in *Les Biches*, because it was important to the film. My most important role is in *An Orchid for the Tiger*, where I play a tropical doctor, and of course my role in *La Muette*.

Q: We know that everything depends on the particular film—the subject of the film, the financing of the film—but in a general way, do you prefer to shoot in studio or on location?

CC: I am not hostile to location shooting, but it's true that I would like to shoot in the studio more often: the only problem is, it's expensive! The apartment in *Les Cousins* was in a studio. The house in *A double tour* also. It was after that that the studios started getting very expensive. At the end of the 1950s and the beginning of the 1960s, the cost was still affordable; I don't know where the enormous increase in cost came from.

For example, in *The Hatter's Ghost*, since I was afraid of not finding the right locations, I thought about using a studio, but it would have cost 1.5 million francs more.

Q: At the risk of shocking you, one might legitimately think that you did shoot parts of it in a studio.
CC: Of course, and in any case, the place looked a lot like a studio. I didn't shoot it on location in order to get the true colors of the stones—I really don't care—but because it was less expensive.

Q: At the center of your work there is what we could call madness, for lack of a better word. Is there, for you, a big difference between the "normal" and the "pathological"?
CC: No, I don't think so. What interests me above all is seeing at what point crazy people are no longer crazy and not-crazy people are crazy. My greatest vice is chipping away at certitudes. It's good to do that with crazy people. People may end up saying that the crazy person is not the most crazy, and that the next guy is maybe even more so; that the first guy is not necessarily the biggest bastard. It modifies preconceived ideas.

Q: In *The Champagne Murders*, we see a character who has just had electroshock treatments, and thus he is a priori a crazy person . . .
CC: He is less crazy than before, but he still believes that he is.

Q: The spectator believes so too, because the treatment also underlines his madness.
CC: In fact, that character is the least crazy of them all; the other characters are much crazier than he is. It's very funny.

Q: Is it only meant to be funny?
CC: I am very shocked by people who judge others: "This guy is a bastard," they say. Also, I don't like the notion of the complete bastard, no doubt because I don't like the notion of the completely admirable person.
   The difference between the admirable person and the complete bastard is absolutely miniscule, and it is along this thin strip of beach between them that I like to walk. It's very narrow.

Q: The father who kills in *This Man Must Die* (*Que la bête meure*), played by Jean Yanne, is really a piece of filth, but maybe . . .
CC: Yes, that is what I deeply admired in Jean's performance: his conviction, his determination to defend the character he was playing. In all our conversations, he explained to me that taken as a whole, the character wasn't as bad as all that.

Q: The most Machiavellian character of all is certainly the one played by Michel Duchaussoy, right?

CC: Definitely! Even more so since he is on the point of making it easier for them to arrest the kid.

Q: Speaking of mean people, here is the topic of your graduation essay: "What do you think of Socrates's formula, 'No one is voluntarily mean.'"
CC: There is no desire in people to be mean, with the exception of very rare cases: of reverse mystics, for example, who think they believe in Satan. In 99 percent of cases, all the dishonorable or mean acts of people are done for excellent reasons which they would be able to explain at great length and in great depth, and which only appear horrible to others.

Q: Aren't the revolutionaries in *The Nada Gang*, fundamentally, people who accept, with certain excuses, being "mean"?
CC: They are not so revolutionary: two of them certainly are, but the others are just regular guys.

Their argument is: if you act like bastards to us, we're going to act like bastards and a half to you. And that is not wrong: the people they are dealing with aren't giving out any presents. The police from the antiterrorist brigade aren't coming to give them presents.

So, it would be interesting to know who engaged in terrorism first: the terrorists or certain governments.

The stupid and childlike question would be: who started it? Kids are very good at that. The one that started it takes responsibility for the whole escalation.

As far as I'm concerned, I have a slight tendency to think that it is the state that started it. I'm not sure about it, but it is the state which would have good reasons for doing things, and from the moment when they have these good reasons, the door is open to bullshit.

One day, I don't know when, there was a moment when we said, "Just because someone doesn't have enough to eat, it doesn't mean he can go steal from his neighbor: we're going to cut off his hands." That phenomenon developed further, to the point where people answered, "You've cut off my hands, so I'm going to kick you with my feet." And so on.

Q: In short, they're acting with a good conscience.
CC: Absolutely, but at the same time with a bad conscience. A good conscience can be horrible!

Q: Isn't the bourgeois class the place where good conscience is the most widespread?
CC: It's where both good and bad conscience are the most widespread. There is a notion of duty which is opposed to the notion of pleasure.

As the bourgeoisie evolves, it also disappears in a certain way. Its primary quality—social propriety—continues to exist, but the secondary qualities are disappearing.

It's funny: I was thinking this morning about the possibility of making a melodrama set at the beginning of the century that would show just that.

In that period, there was on the one hand a social life based on good works and good conscience, and on the other hand the human animal that had to be indulged in a corner. It was a society which stood completely upright but which suggested terrible things, like that a worker was not a full human being, even if he belonged to the realm of humanity. You had to try to protect him, but not beyond what decency permitted.

It was a system that "ran" well and that, at the same time, put those who were exploited on display.

You didn't have to teach the workers to read. Teaching them to read was the beginning of the end for the bourgeoisie: the mandatory secular school system was the worst thing that could have happened! (Laughs.) Look, today, when I see Jean Lecanuet on television, what does he say?[1] "We want a bold politics of social reform." But when you see him, you know that isn't true. But he no doubt believes it. "We have to make it so that these workers get enough to eat, so that this shameful situation disappears, so that everyone has enough to eat. But be careful! Don't give them too much; just enough so that they can hold on, survive." And that's the bold politics of social reform!

Q: Your first films, made in the Nouvelle Vague movement, were aimed at a young audience, which wanted to be, or dreamed of being, at the margins of the bourgeoisie. The other films, it seems, are aimed at a public that is more implicated in the bourgeoisie, more integrated into it.
CC: That's normal. Short of being completely dishonest with oneself, it's clear that we evolve in certain ways. Inside myself I am 60 percent bourgeois, and I have found that it is logical to use things from my interior self.

The audience of cinema is, overall, a bourgeois audience. Of course, there are also young people, but it is very difficult to address them concerning their own problems. They know them better than we do. On the other hand, my films can help show them how things happen on the other side of the fence.

Q: Comparing *Landru* and *The Hatter's Ghost*, while the subjects of the two films are fairly closely related, the tone is different: the first is more humorous, while the second is more grating, more mixed in tone.
CC: The context is different. *Landru* is set during the war: the protagonist is taking

care of women while, on the other hand, the men are being taken care of in another way.

The Hatter's Ghost deals with the problem of an individual, while the problem of *Landru* is also one involving the nonmobilized men who stay behind. Let's say that Landru is a criminal during wartime, and the hatter is a criminal during peacetime. But it is during times of peace that we create, not those who will be criminals during wartime, but war criminals.

Q: For the lack of a helicopter shot, the end of *This Man Must Die* ends with a zoom. In a general way, aside from any concrete material problems, do you prefer, in terms of your own temperament, zooms or tracking shots? And a related question: do we see a reference to *Moonfleet* at the end of *This Man Must Die*?
CC: Yes, yes, we do.

I wanted a helicopter shot because we could have made the boat disappear completely. Oh well.

To come back to the question: I don't like zooms very much. I have been known from time to time to use them, because the zoom brings a change in mood within a single shot; the tracking shot less so. Having said that, if one can do it with a tracking shot, it is purer, because there is no need to use optical effects. The camera movement is not, technically speaking, helping the spectator, whereas the zoom helps him.

Q: Beyond helping the viewer, doesn't the zoom *force* him a bit?
CC: Yes, and I would like people to follow me rather than having to force them.

Q: Are there precise cases where you would use a zoom, other than material contingencies?
CC: I have often used it either to go from a dream to reality, or from reality to a dream.

Q: Are the game of chess and jigsaw puzzles a conception of the world? Are they a playful representation of existence?
CC: Not exactly. There are people who think that chess is an image of life. That isn't true.

It's very important not to confuse representations of things with things themselves.

The beginning of madness can be, precisely, that one starts to identify the world with a game of chess, to identify emotions with a puzzle, etc. And then, suddenly, there is a big blast of wind: the reality of things comes along to sweep all that away and you become aware that you were on the wrong track.

There is a very big temptation to say to oneself: everything is already arranged; we are just pawns on a chess-board. But the queen, when we move her on the board, doesn't care. Of course, when we believe this everything is simplified: we don't need to worry. I believe, on the contrary, that we *should* worry and that, fighting either with or against something, we should take charge of the elements of our own existence, of its destiny.

Words are made for lying, and then there are facts and reality.

Q: In *This Man Must Die*, the chess pieces get knocked over, and in *La Femme infidèle*, the puzzle pieces get dispersed.
CC: They are swept over by the reality of events. In *Ophelia*, there is one poor guy who moves one chess piece each time he goes into his room. He has lost in advance, because he thinks he has the black king, and actually he has the white (or the opposite).

Q: In any case, the presence of these games in some of your films might give the impression that you are playing a game of chess with your characters; it is an impression that perhaps has little foundation, but it is one for which you have been criticized.
CC: There is a problem in the cinema which, to tell the truth, is very disturbing: we make the world exactly as we intend it. Should we bring in chance elements or not? As far as I'm concerned, the answer is no, we shouldn't add more randomness to that which already exists.

In my films, there are no surprises. I don't like, for example, to make shots of two secondary characters who suddenly have such and such a reaction. I don't like extras much and I use them as little as possible. All of that is to avoid having to make the film in the editing, which people can do very, very well, but which, personally, doesn't suit me and, also, would not line up with what I am trying to do.

The other side of the coin is that, even if it is the opposite of what we want to say, we are forced, in a certain way, to use actors as pawns, to treat them in that way.

I hold myself back from bothering them with how I want to see them play their role. I leave them completely free, and it is up to me to make them enter into the preestablished conception of the role. I try as much as possible to avoid saying to them: "You go to the left; you go to the right; you do this thing or that thing. . . ." They do what they want, but I am forced to do what I have to so that things still express what I want to say. That's the game.

According to one's temperament, the director can be tyrannical, debonair, or anarchic.

An anarchic film which I really liked is *Apocalypse Now*: they shot a massive amount of things, and then they organized them as well as they could, putting things in wherever they fit. But the end result is very strong.

For me, shooting like that is not fun, first of all, and second, I would be too afraid of throwing myself into a situation where I don't know how it's going to come out. So, what I gain in clarity, I lose in effects.

Q: In your films, are some shots from the point of view of the characters?
CC: No, never, or very rarely, except in *The Hatter's Ghost*, given the subject matter. If a subjective shot means putting the camera in the place of a character, I try never to do it.

Q: Could one say that they are subjective from your point of view, or simply from that of the spectator?
CC: The spectator or me is the same thing.

Q: Then we could still use the expression "subjective shots."
CC: Yes. Along these lines, in *Le Beau Serge*, the process is reversed: we have the subjective which is objectivized. The film ends with an out-of-focus shot which brought me to notice something quite freaky. As it gets increasingly out of focus, Gerard Blain's face becomes a skull! I found that wonderful: one of them faints and the other becomes a skull, which is generally an objective element rather than a subjective one.

In a general sense, a shot that goes out of focus is subjective in nature, whereas a static shot is a "de-subjectification."

For a long time, out of a worry about objectivity, I started my films with an out-of-focus shot which came into focus: the title sequence was out of focus, and then, wham, it came into focus.

Q: The end of *Le Beau Serge* is an example of what you are seeking in most of your films: an absolute contradiction. For example, the zoom and the reverse tracking shot at the end of *La Femme infidèle*, which are in opposition, much like the skull and the birth in *Le Beau Serge*.
CC: That's right, but the difference is that at the time the skull impressed me, whereas now I would know it's coming and I would use it, and it would no doubt take away from something else.

Cinema is like chemistry: nothing gets lost and nothing gets created. On the one hand, we gain experience; we know things. But on the other hand, we lose a naivete that is impossible to recreate. There is nothing to be done about that: we simply can't discover it again.

In the same way, the absence of financial resources on a film takes away certain things, but it brings you others; and from the opposite perspective, having too many resources—which happens rarely but has happened to me—brings you certain things, often not very important things, but it also takes things away.

When they give you too much money to make a film, most of the time it is not so that you will have more time to make the film, or advantages of that kind, but in order to bring in some coproduction, to impose some actor on you, or to give you a hundred more extras who aren't good for much or for anything. In the end, the money doesn't really matter.

Q: In a very old issue of *Cahiers du cinéma*, you wrote an article on "the evolution of the crime thriller" in which you said, in general, that the genre was exhausted. Nevertheless, you have continued to use it.
CC: The main point of the article was that even though the thriller was exhausted as a genre, it was perfectly usable as a vehicle, if I can put it like that. I still maintain that position, and I insist on it.

The purely *policier* elements of the genre are worn out, whether it is the twelve people and the maître d' in the English manor house, or hot nights in a rainy city with the umbrella and the bowler hat. We know those elements too well for them to have any artistic value. But it is no less true that the crime thriller remains a practical, simple, and unambiguous means of telling a story. You can't say the same about all genres. I don't want to harp on it, but *The Proud Ones* taught me that folklore doesn't work as a genre.

Q: You seem to have abandoned your adaptation of *I Am Legend*.
CC: It has been abandoned to the extent that an amazing thing happened. I got the agreement from Warner, and the coproduction was almost arranged. At that moment, a phone call came from Los Angeles, saying, "We're shooting *I Am Legend* in ten days." So now the film is launched. I actually think it's too late: the film runs the risk of being a retro terror.

Q: What are your current projects?
CC: At the moment, I am adapting Strindberg's *Dance of Death* for television, with Michel Bouquet, his wife, and Niels Arestrup. It's a play that has the reputation of being naturalistic, whereas it's not at all.

In terms of cinema, I am adapting an old detective novel, *Jumping Jenny*, by Anthony Berkley, and I am doing a thing I have never done before: I am changing it completely around. Yes, I have changed it completely, which is something I rarely do. In principle, when I adapt, I am very faithful to the original.

Notes

1. Jean Lacanuet (1920–1993) was a center-right politician who served as the French minister of justice from 1974 to 1976.

On the Flashback

Philippe Le Guay / 1984

From *Cinématographe* 97 (February 1984): 20–23. Translated from the French by CB.

Philippe Le Guay: Do you have a good memory?

Claude Chabrol: I have a selective memory. I remember very precise details from my life, and I completely forget other things. For example, I recognize faces but I have a terribly hard time remembering people's names. I don't have a "flashback"-type memory, if I can put it like that, and I don't like diving back into the past. Sometimes it happens that an event brings up a little flashback, and I meet someone I haven't seen for a long time. When you learn about someone's death, there is a flashback to that person's life.

PLG: You are quite a strong proponent of linear narration.

CC: Yes. I have had to use flashbacks four or five times, not more. The first was in *A double tour*. It was an amusing narrative trick. The film took place in one day, from nine in the morning until six in the evening. The first flashback began at noon and told what one of the characters had done between ten thirty and eleven thirty. The second flashback took place at five in the afternoon and it told what had happened while the guy was having his first flashback! (Laughs). That's why it's called *A double tour*![1]

PLG: It was a nice idea, because we usually consider that the progression of time in a film narrative doesn't count for much.

CC: On the contrary, it counted for a lot in that film! The time of the first part of the narrative was obliterated, and we had to take it up again later. Even more so since the crime was happening at that precise moment! The producers, who were the Hakim brothers, were a bit worried about this construction, and they tried to make the film using a straight narration: but it didn't work and it also cut ten minutes from the film; we never figured out exactly why! It seems to me that there was a chronological overlap: the first flashback came back into the actual time at eleven thirty and went until noon, so there were ten minutes that merged.

PLG: You respect the constraint of the single day, despite the chronological ruptures.

CC: I'm a good player; I play by the rules of the game.

PLG: The easiest way is often to escape from the constraint by having flashbacks to things that happened six months or a year earlier.

CC: That's sleazy! What fascinates me above all is construction, the pleasure of the construction.

PLG: It is the architectural creator who is speaking.

CC: I have to say that it is from that point of view that the flashback interests me. I really don't like the flashback that makes things easier, the kind where there is a voiceover and we see images. Hitchcock had already parodied that in *Stage Fright*, where the words were false and the image was true!

PLG: There was an abuse of the viewer's confidence.

CC: Not at all! The guy was talking over the images. His interpretation of the images was false, but the images were true. Hitchcock did cheat in the sense that the words pronounced by characters are not those that they really say: it is the voiceover that says them for them.

PLG: When a character relates something, you think that it is useless to show the images corresponding to his narration.

CC: That is just a pleonasm! Either we see it, or someone says it. You might notice that most often we do a flashback when we have a strong idea for the first scene. We assault the spectator with violence, and then afterwards we explain how it came to pass. That is not good. The worst example of this I have seen is in Robert Siodmak's *The Killers*. It isn't a bad film. It begins with a short story by Hemingway and then it turns into *Citizen Kane*, where we have the different points of view that are brought out by the investigator. That reminds me of another little-known film, John Brahm's *The Locket*. There is a very curious construction, with a flashback that goes into another flashback, and the second into a third! It was a bit like the narratives within narratives of Scheherazade.

PLG: Are you receptive to the notion that point of view is implicit in the form of the flashback?

CC: The best example of this is *The Grapes of Wrath*. Father Ford was sublime! It's a scene where Henry Fonda finds the old character played by John Qualen, who has become half crazy, in his house, and he tells him how the tractors have come and turned over the fences and taken their land. That is exactly the kind of flashback that I can't stand—it's a way of making the narrative easier and all that—but it's still sublime. Why? Because the narration is not an individual flashback, but rather a flashback of the whole community, of all those who have been dispossessed. The very principle of the psychological flashback is reversed, and it takes on a completely generalized meaning. I even think that it is thanks to that flashback that we have a sense of the whole community in this film.

PLG: Your most recent film, *Le Sang des autres*, also deals with a collective group.
CC: In this film there is a mysterious shot. It serves as the background for the opening titles, and you will know that the entire film is a flashback when you see this same shot at the end.

PLG: What is the shot of?
CC: It's a shot . . .

PLG: From whose memory?
CC: No one's.

PLG: Oh?
CC: It's a still life. We don't know what it is and we notice at the end of the film that the first image was our point of arrival. The novel, by Simone de Beauvoir, is constructed on a system of turning back to the past, but the film is told straight. But I still wanted to evoke this principle of flashbacks in the film.

PLG: Why didn't you keep the book's structure?
CC: It's a book that doesn't have a dramatic form in any real sense, so we had to turn everything upside down while keeping the ideas that are expressed by the characters. With flashbacks, it would have been less strong. What is interesting in the film is the narrative line, a line which doesn't stop, which refuses to stop.

PLG: Literary adaptations usually rely heavily on the structure of the flashback.
CC: You would have to say that in literature there are flashbacks on every page!

PLG: In *Violette Nozière*, you took on a psychoanalytic film.
CC: If you wish. But *Violette* is a straight line, regardless. Its interior movement is perfectly logical: it is tied up in its own torments and it is obliged to follow them. In

Violette, it is less a case of flashbacks than of interior movements within her! It's a fairly frightening construction because she is the one who stops the first flashback, which is represented by a bus. She gets on the bus, she starts to see images from her past, and she yells, "Stop, stop!" The bus stops and she gets off. It is very quick: she refuses to go further into her own memory. In the second flashback, she's the one who forces herself to accept the past, and she makes an attempt to take in the flashback. The line has become completely straight again.

PLG: The images from the past are treated differently from the images from the present.

CC: For a fairly simple reason: I wanted Isabelle Huppert to play the role of the child herself. She is great, but we still had to take away ten years. We had to manipulate the film a bit! The images of syphilitic fantasies make the transition clear. When one has syphilis as she did, one has visions which are fairly often accompanied by fainting spells. We also whitened the images, using a bit of white gel on the lens.

PLG: You assimilate both syphilitic fantasies and images of childhood memory in your imaginary?

CC: Of course. They are the same thing in the sense that they are both profoundly part of her. The childhood images are not whitened; they are overexposed. Only the fantasy sequences allow the spectator to accept the change in cinematography.

PLG: Why was it important to you to keep the same actress for the childhood scenes?

CC: It is the dream of every filmmaker to have the same actor play a role throughout an entire life. Obviously, this isn't possible. If you had Gérard Depardieu in short pants playing marbles in school, people would laugh out loud.

PLG: In your opinion, where does this desire come from?

CC: If you could establish a maximum of continuity by using the same actor to play the character at different stages, it would be ideal! Truffaut did this over the course of several films with Jean-Pierre Léaud. It was great, because it really was the same person, just as in real life. A novelist doesn't have this problem, naturally.

PLG: Speaking of *Violette Nozière*: we could imagine that she always has an image of herself at the age of ten.

CC: That's possible, yes. We have that in a very astute way in Robert Aldrich's *Whatever Happened to Baby Jane*, where the regression of the Bette Davis character ends up being expressed by Bette Davis herself, looking ridiculous in her little white dress asking for an ice cream on the beach. It's certainly a continuity of narration: it respects the real passage of time but it's seen as if it's a flashback!

PLG: Your approach in *Violette* is one of sympathy and understanding of the character: is the flashback necessary for this kind of perspective?
CC: I think so. I say to the spectator: "If you know more than I do, you have to tell me." You have to do it in such a way that the character is accepted as quickly as possible, and the return to the past is an immediate means of doing that. Because, after all, Violette is a character who is a bit scandalous; don't forget that she murdered her father, and it's not a very good thing to kill your parents. The real Violette's children were there on the day of the first screening, which was a special screening that had been organized for them. It was very sad, because we were showing them their mother from a time when they didn't know her, which has nothing to do with what she became later on. She really wasn't the same person anymore! And that was a flashback for *them*, which must have really shaken them up! Strangely, they all became educators. They understood very quickly that I like Violette, that I had tried to understand her, and I do say "tried." Deep inside, she had to kill in order to become herself: at least to kill her father, who was like a cancer. It's bizarre . . . and fortunately they didn't cut off her head, or it would have been over!

PLG: On the other hand, in a film like *Le Boucher*, the character remains opaque.
CC: It's in letting him stay opaque that he becomes touching. The frightening moment is the sacrifice: he sticks the knife into his stomach, whereas ten minutes earlier the spectators, even though they liked him, were sure that he was going to butcher the schoolteacher! (Laughs). The minds of people, for sure . . .

PLG: Usually, you are more of a proponent of linear narrative. *Que la bête meure* is perhaps the most striking example.
CC: In that film we begin with a very strong scene, which puts everything into play: the death of the little boy. With a flashback, we would have ruined the effect of the opening scene. That said, there is a little one which comes in the form of a little amateur film that the Michel Duchaussoy character watches of his son playing. One could say that it's a flashback.

PLG: Do you consider that the cinema is itself a flashback?
CC: In a certain sense, yes. When we watch a film on a screen, we are absolutely not conscious of what is happening around us. If you show your friends a film of your trip to East Indies on Super 8, it is really obvious that during the projection

you will find yourself back in the East Indies, and you will forget the reality of the present. The problem is there because it is a game of memory.

PLG: And in both cases it is the materiality of the film that makes it possible. In our lives, we know perfectly well that our memories and the images that are projected of them are substantively different, but in the cinema everything is confused.

CC: The cinema is also a use of memory.

PLG: We could imagine narrating *Que la bête meure* in a completely different way: Duchaussoy's character has lost his son, who was mowed down by a reckless driver, but we don't know that. The character arrives at the home of the murderer and we learn only at the mid-point of the film what his secret is.

CC: That would be possible, but it would have taken away a part of the meaning of the film. What I wanted was the easy identification of the spectator with Duchaussoy's character and the spectator's terrible trouble from the moment when the character no longer does what we expect: in other words, when he renounces getting his revenge. It is a film that is against justifiable self-defense! (Laughs).

PLG: Jean Yanne comes into the second third of the film as a kind of Tartuffe character; you play on the desire of the spectator to discover who he really is.

CC: And to kill him!

PLG: It reminds us of another filmmaker whose vision of the world doesn't allow turnings and backwards movements: Fritz Lang.

CC: *Que la bête meure* is deliberately Langian. For Lang, the flashback is unthinkable. There could have been a terrible one in *The Secret Beyond the Door*, but there was no question of doing it! When you can have a beautiful straight line, it's great. If we look to do something other than that, it's because the dynamic of the story we have to tell is not sufficient for it not to require a few arabesques. But when we feel that we have the strength to go straight ahead, it's still the best thing!

PLG: You speak in aesthetic terms, but your preoccupations are above all moral ones.

CC: That's complicated, because theoretically the straight line would imply a certainty. And as far as I'm concerned, as much as I like the straight line, as much as I dream of being able to have it, I have absolutely no sense of certainty! That is a little interior contradiction, which is perhaps what makes for my charm. . . . In any case, the straight line requires a certain honesty.

PLG: You can lead the spectator to one point, but you have to *drive* him to another.
CC: Yes, and you try not to rattle him too much!

PLG: If we place things in their historical context, the filmmakers of the Nouvelle Vague—Godard, Truffaut, Rivette, and Rohmer—were marked by their desire to capture the present moment. At that time, you were the heirs of Lumière.
CC: Absolutely! When you put the camera on the railway platform, it is important for the train to arrive! That was anti-Méliès. We were on the side of Lumière, and we talked about that a lot. I pulled away quite quickly because I adore construction; it's a thing that fascinates me and entertains me.

PLG: What about Truffaut?
CC: François did flashbacks starting with his second film, *Shoot the Piano Player*. They were well done: like refrains, like songs. There was something in them that corresponded to his character: he lives a lot in the past; he worships the dead; he has all kinds of aspects that are not at all the same as mine. But Godard, on the other hand: it would be unthinkable to imagine flashbacks in one of his films!

PLG: Rohmer also never uses them, curiously, in spite of his literary tastes.
CC: We never talked about it, but he must have purely aesthetic reasons for refusing to use the flashback. And he's right! I'm also against the flashback! Because it's dangerous. It is easy to be sleazy in the cinema, and especially when you use flashbacks! Most of the time flashbacks are a way of delivering certainty. What was great in *Citizen Kane* was that all the certainties came from different characters and they contradicted one another! Most of the time the flashback is a vile procedure: it's an easy way of imposing a point of view, a sort of "dialing it in." It's not good.

PLG: We find in certain recent films that revenge is the principal motivator for the character: Jean Becker's *One Deadly Summer*, or Jean-Claude Missiaen's *Tir groupé*.
CC: In all these films, flashbacks are there to justify the unjustifiable. Instead of illuminating something and improving the film, they make it worse.

PLG: Are you against obscurantism?
CC: Oh, yes! I'm a champion of lucidity! We have to try to find the "why" of things, don't we? It's difficult—it's even impossible—and therefore it's a marvelous thing to attempt. The attempts by films to oversimplify things make me sick: they are always rubbing up against dishonesty. But if you tell the story of a guy whose friend or whose wife has been killed, and he wants to get revenge and he isn't able to do so because he is not one of those who are able to be vengeful: that interests me. When people asked Lang which is more responsible, the individual

or society, he answered "Fifty fifty," which is marvelous because then you can never condemn anyone! Everything is complicated . . . but also very simple. Once you have understood that it is complicated, it becomes something of great simplicity! It's complicated, and that's that!

Notes

1. Chabrol plays with the meaning of the film's title, which can refer to the "double turn" of the key when locking a door, but here can also refer to the form of narration, in which flashbacks create a kind of turning back of the narrative on itself.

A Lesson on the Cinema

Michel Cieutat and Ambroise Perrin / 1992

From *Positif* 605–6 (July–August 2011): 21–25. Reprinted by permission; translated from the French by CB.

Question: Everyone knows that you read a lot before choosing the book to adapt for your next film. What are the criteria you use in deciding whether to adapt a novel?

CC: That can be purely a matter of chance. A good example is *Betty*. I wanted to make another film with Michel Serrault. He is an actor whom I like a lot. After *The Hatter's Ghost* (*Les Fantômes du chapelier*), I had at first thought of giving him the role of Monsieur Homais in *Madame Bovary*. I proposed it to him, and he told me: "I have to admit something: I hate Flaubert!" So I made an effort to find something else for him. I looked in Georges Simenon's books and I recalled *Les Quatre Jours du pauvre homme*, a very beautiful book. I won't rule out directing it one day. Simenon is pretty fast reading—each book averages about 160 pages—so as soon as you finish one, you immediately start reading another. I had therefore read three or four in a row. I fell upon *Betty*, which I had read in the past. I heard about the book again when, coincidentally, I met Marc, Simenon's oldest son, who recommended that I read it, not knowing that I had already read it. Rereading it, I literally fell in love with the girl. I immediately wanted to live with that girl for two or three months. That is how I decided to make the film. Next, I spoke to the producer, who was Marin Karmitz, and with whom I have a close relationship. I asked him which of my two projects—*Betty*, or another one that interested me—he preferred. He answered: "Do the more impossible one: *Betty*." I informed him that the rights were available, and he asked me when I wanted to start shooting. He came up with a generous budget, and *voila!*, we were on the road. It was as banal and simple as that!

Q: What is your working method when you are adapting a novel?
CC: I read a book once or twice, and then I try to see what I can remember and I write it down immediately. Next, I buy a Clairefontaine notebook and I write

the title at the top of the page. I put a "1" on the first line, and then I stop. Then I have to think for three or four days! This is a difficult moment. Everything is moving around in my head, and then the four or five first sentences (descriptions of situation or setting, or even dialogue) start to become obvious to me. I start writing those sentences down right away, and then I go on from there. It's the principle of ripening fruit. I go slowly, thinking about it more, and going less on natural instinct. In fact, I use the same system that Georges Simenon did when he wrote. He would just stay there, stupefied, for several days, and then he would write. Except that, in his case, it's amazing, because he would write a whole novel in ten days! He worked nonstop from nine o'clock in the morning until ten o'clock at night. I can't work more than four and a half hours a day, for a really stupid reason: since I played a lot of tennis when I was young and I had a very heavy racquet, I paid for it with a terrible case of tennis elbow. Ever since then, when I write for more than four hours a day, it comes back and I can't write anymore! So I am forced to stop, because I write by hand and the pain is too great.

Q: How do you work? Do you start with descriptions and then add the dialogue later?
CC: No, I write everything at the same time, in chronological sequence.

Q: Do you write several drafts, or several different versions?
CC: I don't do drafts. I can't stand having to erase things. On the other hand, it doesn't bother me to rip out a page if I don't like what I wrote. As soon as I have to erase something, I rip out the whole page and start over, like the Jean-Pierre Léaud character in *The 400 Blows*! It's a very good system, because it allows me to have very clear ideas; also, it is easier to type up for the person who has to do it.

Q: Do you work at home or at the office or studio?
CC: I work at home, in Anjou. I work at my home because I have to work with the television on. It doesn't matter what program, even if it's the most idiotic one; I don't care, because I don't pay any attention to it. I can't write in silence. It's very convenient because that way I have peace and I work faster than I used to in Paris. It's more difficult to get started because it's the country, and the rhythm is different, but once I start it goes very fast, perhaps because I want to finish sooner.

Q: Do you write out precise directions for the shots?
CC: I think of them at the same time as I write, but I don't put them in my screenplay. And if I don't remember, it's because they sucked.

Q: Do you ever improvise the shots?

CC: No, I don't improvise. You can't call that improvisation, because it's all clear in my mind.

Q: Do you shoot in chronological sequence?
CC: As much as possible, because it helps the actors. Personally, I don't care, but it helps them so much to work in continuity that I try to satisfy them on that level.

Q: Who prepares the shooting plan, you or the producer?
CC: The producer doesn't have a clue. He foots the bill, and that's all! No, he also reads the screenplay and he often has smart ideas about how to find money . . . unless he doesn't know how to read! He also manages to find the right distributor. And he contributes to putting together the crew by choosing the most appropriate technical people, so that everyone will be happy and work well together. As far as the shooting plan: I never go over time or budget. People often ask for more than what they need in order to get enough, but that is not my style. I ask for the time that I need and I stick to it.

Q: When do you start casting? When the screenplay is finished?
CC: Yes, as far as I'm concerned.

Q: You don't have particular actors in mind when you write?
CC: No, because if I have an actor in mind when I write and that actor or actress gets injured, then I have to find someone else. If the screenplay isn't written for someone in particular, it's easier to find someone else for the role. The choice is more open.

Q: Do you have a particular way of directing your actors?
CC: Directing them doesn't mean much. It is giving a direction to indicate that they have to go over here or over there. If the actors have been cast correctly, they will astonish you with what they do. They will give you more than you had in mind when you were writing.

Q: Do you assign much importance to the position of actors in space?
CC: Yes, I often have fun with the right/left symbolism that is so precious to Hollywood cinema. That consists in putting the actor who is playing the good person to the right of the frame, and the person playing the bad person to the left. One good example of this is in *Les Noces rouges*: in a scene that has the husband (Claude Piéplu), the wife (Stéphane Audran), and the lover (Michel Piccoli) in the shot together, we see them taking turns occupying the good and the bad places. This symbolism comes from the very natural principle of writing in the West, where

we write from left to right. In the cinema, what is important is what comes after. So, if we put the bad guy to the left and the good guy to the right, it allows the spectator to begin with the bad person and then come to the good person! That reassures them. Then we can intervene to worry them again.

Q: That is what William Wyler was surely doing in *Ben-Hur*: in the scene where Messala (Stephen Boyd) is ideologically opposed to Ben-Hur (Charlton Heston), he framed Messala to the right and Ben-Hur to the left, which troubles the spectator. If Ben-Hur remains the good guy in the scene, then Messala, who has been a very sympathetic character to that point, starts to become the bad guy.
CC: Wyler, who was known for having multiple shooting angles and viewpoints, must have shot that scene in every possible way. As he realized that it worked better when the rule wasn't respected, he kept those frames in the editing. I have an interesting and true story about Wyler. It was during the shoot of *The Heiress*. There was a scene in which the character played by Ralph Richardson has to go home, put down his fur-lined cloak and hat, and then go toward the living room. In the first take, Richardson goes home, puts down his cloak and hat, and goes toward the living room. Wyler doesn't say anything. They do a second take: Richardson goes home, puts down his cloak and hat, and then goes toward the living room. There is the same silence from Wyler, so they decide to do a third take. Richardson comes home, etc. They get to the ninth take . . . the fourteenth take. Still not a word from Wyler. The twentieth take: Richardson goes home, puts down his cloak and hat, and goes toward the living room. The twenty-first . . . the thirty-first. At the end of that take, Wyler finally says to Richardson: "My dear friend, it would be ideal if you could put down the cloak as you did in the seventh take and the hat as you did in the thirty-first." Richardson answers: "I absolutely agree. All right, let's do it again." Richardson does it again, and Wyler, now satisfied, hears Richardson say to him with a big laugh: "Actually, I put down the cloak like the thirtieth take and the hat like the twelfth!" This is the true story. It was an absolutely insane duel of two bluffers!

Q: When you direct Stéphane Audran, how do you proceed? She knows all your tricks and your bluffs!
CC: I don't bluff; I just don't say anything! I sleep! On the shoot for *Betty*, something extraordinary happened. Everyone noticed that Marie Trintignant was great, and that created a somewhat unusual atmosphere of complicity. Sometimes that happens. If it happened with Isabelle Adjani, people would think it was normal. But in this case, we were discovering a very impressive new talent, and everyone was under her spell. That really helped me to bring the other actors up to her level. They all realized that we were in the presence of something exceptional, even those

who had already seen a thousand exceptional things. And, since they were now sitting in the expensive seats, everyone had to outdo themselves. Which naturally made Stéphane Audran step on the gas in order to stay in the race. So I didn't have to do anything!

Q: In scenes that involve complex relationships or situations, you must have to give more precise directions. What did you say to Marie Trintignant for her nude scene?
CC: She admitted to me that she was bothered by it, because she doesn't like to be naked in public. In that scene, after having had sex with her saxophone player, she had to open the door, but she said that she didn't know how to do the scene. She couldn't just walk toward the door in a normal way, because it's never a nice thing to see a nude woman just take off like that. She added that she couldn't wiggle her ass, because that would really be unacceptable. So I suggested that we play some music during the rehearsal, which would perhaps allow her to find the right behavior for the scene, with a swaying of the hips that was appropriate or even funny. So we did that: I put on some kind of music, and she enjoyed that a lot, and it gave her the idea of doing what you see on the screen. We get the sense that she is making fun of herself. It was a good idea, stolen from the silent era, that made her feel comfortable!

Q: Do you do the casting for the supporting roles yourself? For example, what would be your basis for casting someone who had to play a very old person?
CC: I would look at their teeth, like you do with horses!

Q: Do you do your own framing of the images?
CC: I'm the one who looks through the camera first to make sure of the framing, and, if necessary, to ask for it to be moved a bit to the right or a bit to the left. But I'm not the one who keeps the shot in frame during the takes. That is the camera operator, because, on a technical level, it depends on him. But, since I have my little monitor, my "combo," I can see if a pan is done too quickly, and I can correct it right away.

Q: Do you ever reshoot a scene after seeing the rushes?
CC: I don't look at the rushes since I have my little monitor, and I can see what they are doing in real time. Nowadays, seeing the rushes is pointless.

Q: Do you choose the costumes of your actresses yourself?
CC: That was the case for the white suit that Marie wears, because it is a Chanel white that suits her very well. I don't think that it was an imitation Chanel suit, but on that level I don't have the competence of the costume designer. I also chose

this suit in the context of the possible deterioration of the outfit, because we didn't want it to be completely destroyed by the end. It had to be able to get dirty and be resistant to being worn in the rain.

Q: Let's assume that it really was a Chanel. There is another well-known brand in *Betty*: that of the pack of Marlboro Light cigarettes, which we see very clearly. How comfortably do you accept this kind of indirect advertising, which certainly profits the production company?

CC: I know that we didn't get any money from J & B scotch or Eau Ecarlate laundry detergent, and Marin Karmitz, the producer, was furious. In the case of Marlboro, I don't know, but I think that in general they do pay something. In the case of the whisky, the people who make it know that we're cheating, that we're not really serving it to the actors. For this film, we encountered another problem. We couldn't get the right color of the J & B with the tea or the apple juice that are usually used in place of small quantities of whisky. In that case, we had to reproduce the color and also the texture. We got that effect with water and a food coloring that the prop manager found.

Q: Do you wait until the end of the shoot to start editing?

CC: No, not at all. On *Betty*, principal photography was finished on December 10, and Marin—for mysterious reasons—wanted the film to come out on February 19, which gave us a very limited time for the editing. When I arrived at the editing room, my editor had already cut the whole film. We just had to make the final adjustments, which is what takes the longest. And, of course, do the sound.

Q: Do you spend a lot of time on the soundtrack?

CC: Oh yes! I don't do the work myself, but I ask the technicians to do exactly what I want. Then I listen to the result.

Q: Could you edit your own films?

CC: Yes, but it's really boring!

Q: Do you use a lot of film?

CC: Not really. On *Betty*, we shot about twenty thousand meters.

Q: That's about a ten to one shooting ratio?

CC: Not even that, since the film runs for an hour and forty-three minutes.

Q: Do you expect to retire one day, or will you keep shooting until your last breath?

CC: I will shoot films as long as I still want to. One of these days, it's possible that making films will start to bother me, but that is still not the case. . . . I don't have any preconceived ideas on the subject. What I would like is to produce my last two films, to be able to make a perfect circle: to end my career in the same way I started it when I produced *Le Beau Serge* and *Les Cousins*. We'll see.

Q: These days, are you still relying on the success of your last film to allow you to make the next one?

CC: It's a privilege to do this line of work: as opposed to the functionary who has to stop at the age of sixty, the filmmaker can stop at thirty-five or go beyond his sixties. We have no job security, but we can continue for as long as we want. In fact, we end up having more job security at the *end* of our careers. If my last film wasn't a success, I don't really care: it doesn't prevent me from making another. Of course, if I have five films in a row that get smashed like watermelons, then everyone will say that I am being self-indulgent. In that case, I think that I would have a hard time continuing. When I started, it was different, as it is for all beginners. I had some very hard times. And even quite late in my career—during the years from 1975 to 1976—when I was forced to find really crazy gimmicks to shoot because of guys who made me go shoot in Canada to avoid taxes. Those were demented films, but they allowed me to continue working.

Q: Does it bother you to have to look for money to make films?

CC: Yes! It annoys me because it doesn't interest me. But in general my films are not very expensive. *Betty*, for example, must have cost around fourteen or fifteen million francs. *Madame Bovary* had a larger budget: around fifty million.

Q: Are there certain of your films that you like the most?

CC: That depends on the moment. If there are ones that I haven't seen for a long time, I feel a desire to see them again. It's a bit like your kids: if you don't see them for a while, you suddenly want to see them right away. It's terrible, because it ends up equalizing everything. Someone who has just seen one of my old films tells me that it's great. When I see it, it seems all right but nothing more. And there are others where I say, "My God, those films are pieces of shit!"; but when I see them again, I tell myself they're not as bad as all that.

On *La Cérémonie*

Pierre Berthomieu, Jean-Pierre Jeancolas, and Claire Vassé / 1995

From *Positif* 415 (September 1995): 8–14. Reprinted by permission; translated from the French by CB.

Question: The origin of your film *La Cérémonie* is the novel by Ruth Rendell.
Claude Chabrol: Yes, it's her fifth or sixth book; I think it's the first one that doesn't follow the normal investigative process, with a recurring police character, which is interesting. Here, it's a crime thriller only because she wanted it to be: she could have easily considered it not to be. I found it great at the time—fifteen or twenty years ago—but I didn't think about adapting it in the way it was presented in the book. There are two characters: the maid who is named Eunice in the book—a large girl with a gelatinous quality that is disagreeable to imagine—and the female postal worker, who was also very different in the book. Both of them were fairly typically British. So I let some time go by, and I read other books by Ruth Rendell. I noticed that she was evolving, that her work was changing, and she was the one who gave me the idea to change the book. It was just a matter of reading her more recent books, which pointed out the way in which I could adapt the book.

Q: What was the contribution of Caroline Eliacheff?
CC: I was helped by Caroline Eliacheff, who first of all stripped away—with a wave of her hand—the psychological and psychoanalytic origins of the book. Then we were able to move ahead in a way that was a bit different, but which still corresponded, in my opinion, with Ruth Rendell's vision. Rendell has still not seen the film. It was be interesting to me to have her point of view. I tried to be faithful to her current state of mind.

I asked Caroline to make me a fairly succinct tidying-up of the book, and she did a much deeper job for me. When I started working on the book, I already had whole parts of the dialogue ready, which assured the psychiatric authenticity of the characters' actions, so as not to go off into complete madness. Very often, I see films that put psychopaths on the screen. After one or two scenes, you forget that they are psychopaths, and then it comes back, while generally there would be more of an unbroken line of development. Here, on the contrary, Sophie is always illiterate, and Jeanne is always a psychopath.

Q: We discover both the illiteracy and the psychopathic character gradually. And then we notice that we have been given hints since the beginning.
CC: Of course. I told them both—the two actresses—to really hold their characters on a straight line. For Sandrine Bonnaire, the key was the astonished look when she sees symbols she doesn't recognize. Isabelle Huppert had a really good idea: she would say her lines without thinking, without giving the impression of thinking, which produces a real sense of logorrhea. The two of them work really well together. It was the same thing for the family: they needed to have a certainty that they were behaving perfectly. Someone even said to me that they were really a wonderful family, that this butchery was scandalous, and that it had been done by two pieces of trash!

Q: What did you tell the actresses about the characters' pasts?
CC: Not a lot. I made them read the book so that they would have some basic elements about the past. They both had a lot of fun talking about it, seeing if one had really burned her father and the other killed her daughter. They came to the conclusion—which was mine as well—that Jeanne hadn't done it on purpose, but that Sophie *had* done it on purpose.

Q: The character played by Sandrine Bonnaire (Sophie) is more determined, and she becomes the motivating force of the pair.
CC: She does become that, but mysteriously. A moment comes when she is the one who does things. Their positions change. Sophie comes to a place of total submission in the scene where she serves coffee to Jeanne, just before going to the Lilièvres' house; she then takes the upper hand again when she shoots. She comes up, goes from the background to the foreground, and dominates Jeanne.

Q: The line "We did a good thing" is the admission that the postal worker, Jeanne, is much more uncertain about the legitimacy of the killing. She even says it in the voice of a little girl, a bit different from the voice that she has used up to that point.
CC: Yes, above all because she delivers the line in a great way, with a vaguely suggested question mark. Just the fact that she asks the question horrifies people! After all, they are saying that they might have done a good thing by killing the family!

Q: The novel is entitled *A Judgement in Stone*. Why did you give the film the title *La Cérémonie*?

CC: I tried to find something equivalent to the original title, but it was quite complicated: the English title is clear but difficult to translate; it also makes a reference to the stone statue at the feast in *Don Giovanni*. I didn't want to let the cat out of the bag from the first scene on by calling it *The Illiterate Woman*.[1] I came up with *La Cérémonie*: they really act as if they are carrying out a formal execution, and the Lilièvres are dressed up as if they were going to the opera. There are two other films called *The Ceremony*: Nagisa Oshima's film, and the only film directed by Laurence Harvey, both of which deal with an execution. In the end, the title works well, because it's a ceremony on both sides. And it's a lot more appealing than *The Massacre*!

Q: And what about the fact that, as in *Betty*, you adapted a book without staying in the same time period?
CC: The reason was the same as it was for *Betty*: the time period didn't have much of an influence on the story. You're not going to put money into reconstructing a period that is not that far away from the present, and not that extraordinary. When I see my films from the 1960s, they could—aside from a few details—have been made more recently. There isn't a big difference. Not changing the time period just makes it a little less picturesque.

Q: Was the setting of the film in Saint-Malo significant?
CC: The book was of English origin, so I tried to set it as close as possible within France to England! I love Brittany, and there is a great restaurant in Cancale. The place worked perfectly. And the proximity of the gulf stream tempers the climate in winter. Saint-Malo is one of the best places to shoot a film!

Q: One has the impression, even if the expression of it is a bit restrained, that the film marks a return to politics.
CC: In a more direct way, yes. I noticed that the last of my films that had an important political element was *Poulet au vinaigre*. What interested me in *La Cérémonie* was to show the provincial bourgeoisie in a light but important way, without pushing too hard. In these past years, I hadn't seen any particularly stimulating social developments. But for the last two years, I have changed my opinion a bit. In discussing things one day with a young working-class guy, I got the impression that society was about to explode, or rather implode, and not only on the periphery. Then I decided to deal with this subject, but not in a precise, documentary way. That was smart, because I would have been smashed flat by Matthieu Kassovitz's film *La Haine*. Our films are similar, I believe, in their movement toward the start of the explosion. He sees the possibility of an explosion,

while I see an implosion. The young guy in question thought that things could not last for more than three or four years. So we still have two years to go!

Q: The film suggests a real blueprint for class warfare.
CC: Yes. I remember an article, I don't know by whom, that was written after the fall of the Berlin wall, and which said that class warfare ended with the fall of the wall. Only a yuppie could write such a thing: you have to ask people from the lower classes if class warfare can end! *La Cérémonie* gave me the opportunity to deal with the subject. Once the screenplay is ready, I always try to see if I can stick in some of my little personal preoccupations. Here, it worked really well: it was really based on the principle of class warfare.

Q: Was this social vision already contained in Ruth Rendell's book?
CC: Rendell's books have a social significance. She is proworker, unlike P. D. James, who is conservative.

Q: Isn't P. D. James also proworker?
CC: Perhaps. But her books are more conservative than those of Rendell, even if they contain some fairly hard portraits of the bourgeoisie. P. D. James is still very squishy. Let's say that she is on the left wing of the conservative party. Ruth Rendell writes in a more impious, atheistic vein: for that reason, she is more interesting to study. I was thinking about a book by P. D. James, *Innocent Blood*, where the problem is posed in such a quirky way that I found the blueprint had too much flesh, too much complexity. *La Cérémonie* is very simple, very obvious. After a quarter of an hour of the film, the spectators are already spotting moments of humiliation.

Q: Is the second appearance of Bonnaire in the train station an homage to Hitchcock?
CC: First of all, it's a clue about her illiteracy. There is one clue even before that. One of the rare precise instructions I gave to Sandrine in the scene before the credit sequence, in the café, was to press on her thigh when Jacqueline Bisset asks her, "Does Tuesday work for you?" Other than that, Sandrine found everything on her own, which is pretty great. But to come back to your question: no, it's not really an homage to Hitchcock. First there is the gag of having Jacqueline dressed almost as a little girl who is waiting for something which is not coming. That is very funny. And another thing: the film started ten minutes ago and we still haven't heard about Isabelle's character. I said to myself: "People will be waiting for that." Then you see Isabelle. Jacqueline waiting and the spectator waiting are happening at the same time.

Q: The form of the scene seemed to give a supernatural quality to Sandrine Bonnaire's appearance.

CC: Yes, that's why I made all the other people in the scene disappear very quickly: it's a trick that Hitchcock may have invented. Otherwise, the effect would not have worked. I had to make the train arrive on a platform which wasn't the right one, and have half the people leave through a place that is not the real exit. I really love that waiting effect.

Q: Speaking of opacity and strangeness: there is a constant use of windowpanes and mirrors in the film.

CC: Especially the oval mirror in the hallway that leads to the other world, the kitchen. I like mirrors, because they are a way of crossing through appearances. I am always careful not to put in too many of them; I often say to the set designer: "Don't put in too many mirrors!" I also love bells, and I always saying to my sound editor: "Not too many bells!" I know that I would not be able to reject them on my own! This particular mirror seemed to me to be really indispensable: it was a simple and obvious way of making the viewer aware of the two universes.

Q: And what about the glass wall of the café at the beginning?

CC: In the first shot? Oh yes, that is a very interesting shot. I hope that you saw Jacqueline's face when the truck went past. I wanted the film to be really well constructed without it being too visible. I decided to make the first shot in such a way that people wouldn't see everything, so that they wouldn't say, "Well that's really quite complicated." In reality, the shot *was* quite complicated. The truck going by had to happen at just the right moment. Jacqueline couldn't be in the field of view at the time of the turning camera movement when Sandrine passes by on the sidewalk. And how were we going to balance the lighting between exterior and interior? We couldn't use scrims as we normally would: there would have had to be a lot of them, and they would have changed the real relationship of exterior and interior while also creating a difficulty in terms of showing Jacqueline's face. So we decided to overexpose the exterior shots very slightly. The results were disappointing. So we overexposed more, changing the aperture at the moment when Sandrine enters. That change could be seen as clearly as the nose on your face, so we tried another solution: we very slightly overexposed everything, which you can't see.

Q: We feel it a bit at the beginning of the shot: it's very bold.

CC: Yes, the shot is very disturbing. We pulled back the effect a bit when we made the prints. We had a margin to take it up or down a bit. When the rushes came in, we got an urgent call: "The image is overexposed!" "Yes, yes, we know." I always try, in general, to shoot films in chronological sequence, in order to help the actors.

Here, it was really important to me to start with the first scene, so that Sandrine would really give the impression of arriving.

Q: Was it shot with a handheld camera?
CC: No, it was on a little track about fifty centimeters high. I don't really like handheld cameras. The track gives us freedom without the effect being too visible. I also used other special effects. At the moment when the two men are in the car, when the kid starts acting out, hoping that the new maid will not be too ugly, there is a build-up of tension. We did it with a tracking shot, going backwards with the car, and I did a very slight forward zoom. You have the feeling of a sauce that's beginning to thicken. At least I have that feeling. You really feel it; at least I do.

Q: Wasn't there a rupture in tone between the ending and the rest of the film?
CC: Things had to be triggered at a given moment. Just as in my thought about society, the dominant feeling of the ending is that of implosion. It's amusing to have it start with watching television, where the very notion of implosion is embodied. At the moment when the opera starts, the work begins.

Q: The way the film is made changes at that moment. For example, there are some uses of classic parallel editing.
CC: I wanted to avoid any particular effects at that moment. You can certainly imagine slow-motion effects with the bodies falling, the blood. Here, that would have been catastrophic. I tried to make the filmmaking as straight and dry as possible, accompanied by the music of Mozart's *Don Giovanni*, which is the least dry music in the world. When I write a screenplay, I pose all the possible problems to myself and try to resolve them. That made the shoot easier: I had anticipated all the glitches! I had asked, even though Rendell had chosen *Don Giovanni*—with the paradoxical relationship between the plot of *Don Giovanni* and that of the "ceremony"—whether it wouldn't work better visually with *The Marriage of Figaro*. I tried it, in vain. I would have had to change the progression of the killings completely. Rendell worked like a dog to write her book, so she must have had her reasons for choosing *Don Giovanni*. She must have also thought about *The Marriage of Figaro*. I kept her reasons a secret. I worked to create a lot of connections to the opera. We even included a sequence from it inside a shot: the two girls drinking tea. So the connection had been made, and then we said, "Okay, now let's go for it." And ten minutes of opera had already gone by. That was quite an invention: we're going to patent it!

Q: And what about the final ironies of the film: the car accident and the recording?
CC: In Ruth Rendell's novel, the girl gets arrested, is sentenced, and refuses to

learn to read. The book ends with a litany of words—"crime, murder, blood, horror
. . ."—which occur in a very powerful way. I wanted a different ending, where the
girl leaves the house earlier than in the book, while it is the other character who
turns the tape recorder on. The whole difficulty was in finding an ending that was
not completely realistic, but still plausible, and to end the film with the line "We
did a good thing." We came across a little problem: when the end titles start to
roll, what do we do so that people don't start to get up from their seats? If they get
up, I'm not going to kill myself over it, but I would like them to stay until the end
to hear the "We did a good thing." By making the titles start a bit sooner, at the
moment when we go to the closeup of Sandrine, I gained about fifteen seconds.
People didn't realize it until afterwards, and they got up fifteen seconds later.
Those fifteen seconds are the seconds of silence between the end of the musical
track and the final line.

Q: Repeating the sentence at the end is a great idea.
CC: Yes, it works well. It locks the dramaturgy of the film into place. People
criticized the ending of *L'Enfer*, which they thought was too simple. But a film called
L'Enfer which ends with the word "Fin" (The End) would have been impossible, so . . .

Q: Doesn't the fact that it was the tape recording that incriminates them go back
to the problematizing of the image, of television, which already started with *L'Oeil
de Vichy* and *L'Enfer*?
CC: Yes. It incriminates them, but someone would still have to hear it. You see
Bonnaire leave. She disappears into the night. Maybe they won't arrest her! The
police have to put together what happened.

Q: You are settling scores with both kinds of television: the "bad" one and the
high-cultural one, right?
CC: I'm not settling scores. But the dumbing down of the television does, after all,
have a part to play in the . . . enemy's plans. We have to denounce it. I had some
great luck. I wanted to have Dorothée be in the televised sequences.[2] She didn't
want to do it. Her handlers must have understood what it was about and said no:
this story was too sordid for Dorothée to appear. Very smart of them! So I used
another television presenter, Maureen Dor, who is no doubt less malignant. I found
a wonderful moment when she is talking about a dictionary. "Dictionaries are
usually really boring, so I have found a way of adding images," she says. And the way
of doing that was the television. It's crazy! All the televised sequences in the film
really existed. We looked for them, and I watch a lot of television, so I found some
terrible things. I also used parts of the children's television program *Minikeums*
to add to the sense of the grinding noise in Sandrine's head. She plays the show

really loud. I also took a bit of *Les Noces rouges*, because it was less expensive to use. Without exaggerating too much, I wanted a scene which would be a little "hot," so that, when the mother asks the kid to go get cigarettes, he tries to hang back a bit.

Q: And what about the choice of the actresses?

CC: In the beginning, I wanted to make another film with Isabelle. I decided that she should choose which role she wanted. I wanted to give her the role of Jeanne, but I wanted her to choose, because she could easily have played the other role. I had Sandrine in mind for the other character: she could also have played the postal worker, though obviously in a different way. To my great delight, Isabelle didn't hesitate for a second. "I already played the other character twenty years ago," she told me. The way the two actresses complement each other is very strong, very tight.

Q: Their geometries are very different: Sandrine is all lines and angles, and Isabelle is rounder, more than she is in reality.

CC: Oh, the roundness of Isabelle . . . On *Madame Bovary*, I had told her that she was as thin as a nail. The costume designer told me not to be so sure. In fact, she can do both! What she wears can change everything. Her shoulders are not round. Sandrine was thinner than usual after giving birth. She was perfect.

Q: What about the choice of Jacqueline Bisset?

CC: I wanted a beautiful woman, but I hadn't thought about making it an Englishwoman. Looking back, it was an amusing and interesting idea. I had first though of Caroline Cellier, but she didn't feel ready to do it. Dominique Sanda wasn't available. I was still looking, and my agent, who is also Jacqueline Bisset's agent, suggested her to me. I went to see her and, *voila*! She was also superb in the role. The fact that she has a slight accent, that French is not her native language, and that she has some differences in intonation from a French speaker, gives her a kind of fragility or uncertainness which I like. It was one of my pleasant surprises. Her opacity is necessary: the opposite would have been too easy. Each member of the family has little secrets. Two of them—Jacqueline's character and her son—don't reveal theirs, while the others reveal more: they don't really have any mystery; they feel at home. There are no mysteries in your own home. Jacqueline's character is an "immigrant," yet perfectly integrated.

Q: What is it about her that fascinates the postal worker?

CC: The postal worker finds her beautiful. She represents everything that Jeanne would have liked to be: the wife of a rich businessman. She has a fixation, concentrating all her anxieties on one person. That is something that needs to be treated, I think!

Q: In your cinema, we are immediately interested in the characters. Do you start with situations or characters?

CC: I start with a relationship between the plot I have to relate and the characters themselves. In this film, no one notices that there is no plot. Little by little, the characters reveal themselves, their relationships change, but without creating any real plot. Like Simenon, I believe strongly in constructions that are built out of confrontations between different characters. I take an important aspect of the character which defines him or her, whatever that may be (for example, sex in the case of Betty), and I try to see its evolution in terms of relationships with others. It's a kind of chemistry of affinities! Even though I make a lot of crime films, I don't like plot. What fascinates me the most is the mystery itself, the mystery that is inherent in characters. The best Agatha Christie book is *Hickory Dickory Dock*. Hercule Poirot is investigating in a student dormitory, and he finds the culprit: a young man who has killed twice. No one suspects the monster inside him. The idea is magnificent. The fifteen last pages are an accumulation of horrors.

Q: Are there actresses who particularly inspire you?

CC: I'm not like Bergman: I don't need to have intimate relationships with my actresses. But I do need good relations in terms of communication and mutual appreciation. It's also important that what I see pleases me. And I say to myself, "Well, it's possible that I will get along well with her." It can also be a case where someone I have worked with says "you should see this person," or my daughter, who goes to see almost everything that comes out, suggests someone. She's the one who advised me to cast Virginie Ledoyen, telling me that she would work well in the role. And she did. With Isabelle and Sandrine, I get along well with both of them even though they are very different.

Q: Can you shoot a film with an actress you don't get along with?

CC: I have had that experience. I don't make scenes, and I hate tension, whereas Maurice Pialat can't work *without* having tension around him. There are also people with whom I had a hard time getting along: dear Romy Schneider, for example. "I warn you, I don't have any sense of humor," she told me. It's great to have a girl tell you that! Oh well, it was true. Everything happened very correctly, but she did as much acting between takes as during them. We even ended up arguing about the voice looping.

Q: How did Marie Trintignant enter your acting troupe?

CC: I used to make her jump onto my knees. When she was bigger, she told me, "I would like to make a film with you." It was terrible, because I had never thought about casting her. After reading *Une affaire de femmes* (*Story of Women*), she decided she wanted to play the prostitute! Jean-Pierre Kalfon was making a video for a song, and he asked me to make him a pimp. And Marie arranged it so that she played a prostitute! She told me, "There, you see!" And so she was in *Une affaire de femmes*. For *Betty*, I didn't think of her at first. Fortunately, my first idea didn't work out, and I said to myself, like at the end of one of the episodes of *Les Cinq Dernières Minutes*: "But of course: it's her!" There are people like that, with whom I know I am going to work. Now I have all the women I need: I'm going to be able to close up shop soon!

Q: Do you write your characters with an actress in mind?
CC: No. Writing for actors is often a mistake, because you use whatever is the least good part of them: their tics, their habits. I prefer not to write for particular people.

Q: Let's come back to *Betty* and *L'Enfer*. The construction of *Betty* is very different from that of *La Cérémonie*. The character is explained through flashbacks, while the characters of Sophie and Jeanne remain mysterious.
CC: With *Betty*, I stayed completely faithful to Simenon's book. Contrary to what people think, when you adapt Simenon you can't try to reconstruct it. Given his way of writing, if you move away from the spontaneity of his construction you completely distort the story. That is where the labyrinthine construction of *Betty* comes from, with, at one point, a flashback within a flashback within a flashback, which is a lot of flashbacks! People have to be able to follow. *Betty* tries to explain a character—a bit like in *Violette*—which ultimately fails because any attempt to explain a person fails. You send in a laser beam, but the opacity of a person is so great that it can't cut through. *Betty* and *Violette* are two films that are fairly similar: they both tell almost the same story. In *La Cérémonie*, on the other hand, any flashback would have been unseemly. It would have privileged a character, and the film is not called either "Jeanne" or "Sophie." Instead, it is a process, a ritual that is being studied.

Also, I don't like having too many flashbacks, for the simple reason that I can't understand anything. I put myself through a hell of a time so that people will understand my films. Among my projects, there is only one where I try to exploit the future perfect tense, which requires flashbacks. I didn't use Clouzot's ideas about flashbacks for *L'Enfer*. I just used the idea of a variable treatment of time: the rapid passage through time in the first few minutes of the film, and then the expansion of time as the story advances.

Q: Talking about *Betty*, you said something quite surprising: "It's a reflection of nature. Only the strongest survive."
CC: That's my pessimism. Not in all my films, but certainly in *Betty*, yes. My

characters are not strong, and they don't survive, except for the strong ones; but you don't find a lot of those in my films. Having strong people as characters suggests that I am giving them as a positive example. It's almost a fascist, or at least a fascist-leaning, way of operating. The notion of fascism is both strong and dangerous. A strong character almost necessarily becomes a model for people. From that point on, he becomes a worry.

Q: For example, the character played by Orson Welles in *Ten Days' Wonder*?
CC: Yes, there is one example. We don't need people like that. And he himself said that! Providential men, national heroes—they always scare me a lot. The world is such that it is better to be strong than weak. You can almost explain the totality of the world's evolution through this notion, which I did not invent: "Might makes right"!

Q: In your mind, is Betty a strong character who pumps the substance of the character played by Stéphane Audran into herself?
CC: Yes, she says it herself. But Betty is a strong *woman*, and there is a difference between men and women. Our world is masculinized and macho. In the context of that world, a woman has the right to be strong. If not, she is liable to become just anything. A woman who wants to find her way has to pump where she can. Betty has her faults, but she is not responsible for the people around her. In Simenon, there is a powerful vision, which I also used: he considers the female sex organ to be a wound.

Q: You draw a distinction between strong men and strong women.
CC: I make this distinction because man is a priori stronger, and he uses an organization of the world that is made for him, that calls him the strong sex. The woman came out of his rib. He has to be able to find his way without any problem, whereas for women the problems are always more complicated. We can forgive them more readily for having to show their teeth.

Q: In your films, taken as a whole, we can distinguish three periods: one dominated by male protagonists, another split between Michel Bouquet and Stéphane Audran, and a third, today, when you are a women's filmmaker.
CC: Yes, that's fairly accurate. I have always had a weakness for the company of women. A woman is a real subject for a film. A living woman, a woman who survives. We talk about the labors of Hercules, and not the labors of Hercula. Compared to men, she is a real subject, an inexhaustible subject. I am also fascinated by homosexuals, who are a very interesting subject. I had even written a project about two guys who wanted to have a child together. I must have talked

about it one night when I was drunk! The film was going to show the inanity of it, in relation to humanity. Someone made the movie with Alain Souchon, and completely ruined it.

Q: Without going into the history of the screenplay for *L'Enfer*, what is your relationship with Henri-Georges Clouzot?
CC: Clouzot was, along with Jacques Becker, one of the two men who, when I was starting out, really wanted to be nice to me. We played bridge together while we were preparing the script of *L'Enfer*. I saw him afterwards, with his wife at the time, Vera, with whom I have remained good friends. I almost made a film with her, but the poor woman didn't have time. *L'Enfer* was an interesting experience, a pleasant experience. I tried to bring a subject that was not at all meant for me, and that I hadn't even chosen, closer to myself.

Q: Which gives the film a fairly original style: it's deliberately very stylized.
CC: It was difficult to make it in any other way. One thing really amused me: seeing how many angles I could find in one room. Nearly half the film takes place in this one room. I was especially delighted with François Cluzet, who is superb in the film. I didn't want the actors to hate each other too soon! They got along very well. Emmanuelle Béart has a tremendous energy; she is very strong. And that gave François the possibility of going off-track at times. We ended the shoot in this cursed room, after shooting all the exteriors. They were both there for three weeks, cutting each other to pieces, and they ended up detesting each other. Which was perfectly logical! Neither of them gave up. I suppose that things are back to normal again now.

Q: And what are your projects for future films?
CC: There is one tricky comedy which will be called *Trompe-l'oeil*, and which will be about appearances. I would like to make it in a hotel, during a thalassotherapy cure. People taking care of their bodies are always amusing. I also have an old project that I hope to bring to fruition: an adaptation of William O'Farrell's *Les Carottes sont cuites*, with William Hurt, and probably Sandrine in a small role. When I announce my projects, I always make another film first. I was also thinking about a very free adaptation of an old book by Philip McDonald, *Murder Gone Mad*, which was translated, I think, as *Le Vampire*. It's the story of an anarchic crime, with people getting killed for no obvious reason and according to no logic. It's a very difficult subject. That said, anything can happen. Maybe I will take the luxury of making a television film and showing what one can do with it. There is a conspiracy in the television journals: I get anxious when I see three stars for *Navarro* and two for *Night of the Hunter*. There is no paranoia in that worry. It can't just be chance:

there must be a political motivation for ranking television films in such a bizarre way. I don't care whether I have one, two, three, or four stars, as long as I have as many as *Navarro*.

Notes

1. The novel was titled *L'Analphabete* in its French translation, published in 1978.
2. Dorothée, the stage name of Frédérique Hoschedé (b. 1953) is a singer and television presenter, known in particular for presenting popular television programs for children.

Time Doesn't Exist: An Interview

Philippe Rouyer and Claire Vassé / 2003

From *Positif* 504 (February 2003): 34–37. Reprinted by permission; translated from the French by CB.

Question: What is the point of departure for the screenplay of *The Flower of Evil*?
Claude Chabrol: It began with my telling the screenwriters Caroline Eliacheff and Louise L. Lambrichs the story of Lizzie Borden. This young American woman, accused of having killed her father and mother, was acquitted and lived for sixty more years. That story fascinated me. Where did she live? How? As time went on, I gave some other directions to Caroline and Louise: a family, marriages between cousins . . .

Q: After *La Cérémonie* and *Merci pour le chocolat*, this was your third collaboration with Caroline Eliacheff. How do you work with her?
CC: The first two films were adaptations. I gave her the novel and she took a kind of psychological skeleton from it. In the case of *La Cérémonie*, she wrote an adaptation that was almost ready to film. I just made a few changes. In the case of *Merci pour le chocolat*, she deliberately left some holes. On this third film, it was something else entirely. I gave her a vague idea, and she, with Louise L. Lambrichs, constructed the screenplay. She brought in two important elements. First, the circular construction: going from the house to the pharmacy to the city hall and campaign center. It was a circle that I broke—I don't like constructions that are too set in stone—by introducing the vacation house, which is itself the equivalent of a flashback. To tell the truth, I could have put that sequence in the main house, but it wouldn't have been as good. Second, the political aspect of the film came from Caroline, who had followed electoral campaigns in which her friends were involved. That provided an added clarification about what these people are like, and the desire on the part of Anne (Nathalie Baye) to direct others, to bring them around to her way of seeing things. I chose the setting in the Bordeaux region because of the character of Aunt Line's father, who was a kind of Maurice Papon character.[1] It was as if Papon's daughter had killed him.

Q: Did having a psychoanalyst as your screenwriter bring you to a new awareness?
CC: Let's just say that it prevented me from saying too many stupid things. Above all for the women characters. Men have a very theoretical idea about female psychology, and it is not a bad thing to have a woman there to correct us.

Q: "Time does not exist: it is a perpetual present." In what way did this sentence, which occurs in *The Flower of Evil*, inspire you?
CC: I am very interested in the relationship between sensations, feelings, and the passage of time. It was while I was reflecting on this question that I noticed that time does not exist as we conceive of it. We are in a perpetual present. And it is even more true when you are shooting a film. In *The Flower of Evil*, the character of Aunt Line has an immediacy in her relations with others. The origin of those relations is all in the past, but it only appears in time as the present unfolds. We only go into the past in order to look for what can be used to clarify things in the present. That is why I used the staircase as a symbol of time. You can go up or down, but it is always there. That's what I was interested in doing: making a film where everything evolves in the present.

Q: Did this conception of time affect your choice of mise en scène?
CC: Yes, because that sense of time couldn't be indicated by the dialogue. One sentence is all right. But to spend time philosophizing about time?! That's why I filmed the titles in that way. When you come into the house for the first time, the camera pans toward the dining room, where the maid is setting the table. When you come in for the second time, in the company of François and his father, several minutes later, you find this same movement of the camera, which is useless in itself but which helps the spectator to understand that the film is constructed on the principle of reminiscences.

Q: By putting the original murder at the beginning of the film, you avoid the classical use of the flashback.
CC: Yes, there is a linear progression. What is amusing (it was my wife who pointed it out to me) is that this sequence connects with the image of the jet plane that brings François to France. In a casual way, there is a movement in time, and this movement helps us to say that time doesn't exist, because we just need this connection between two images to move forward by fifty years.

Q: And what about the auditory flashbacks? The first takes place within the same shot. We are looking at Aunt Line's face, and then the camera moves toward the voice in the past which she hears, and then we find ourselves in the same place, but fifty years earlier.

CC: One has the impression that everything happens in the same shot, but that is actually not true. In reality, there are several pans which make the camera movement feel habitual to the spectator. Except that we cut the last of them in order to come back to something natural: Anne's face while she is reading the letter. Afterwards, we go back to the end of the pan, but there, it is in order to go back to the past. That only works if you have planned for it in the shooting: you can't do it in the editing. This first flashback, using images, allows us to bring in the principle of the voice of the past. When those voices reappear, the spectator is accustomed to it; he understands the system. Even if it is only one sentence, he knows where the voice is coming from.

Q: How did the shooting go?

CC: This happens very rarely to me, but I didn't have any difficulties with this film. Things seemed obvious to me, and I was sure of my ideas about camera movement. Above all, I wanted the spectator to realize very early on that he had to pay attention to details, that it was the little things that form the subject of the film. I'll give you an example. At the beginning of the film, when François and his father have been reunited, they seem to get along like thieves at a fair. In the car, I made the relations between them move ahead by moving the camera. When the father and son are dealing with each other on an exterior level, the camera stays outside the car. Then they start establishing deeper relations, relations that are returning to what they once were—in other words intolerable—but this happens without the spectator being completely aware of it. The viewer knows that there's no question of a great love between them, but that's all. Then we start to move gradually in. First we are in front of the windshield, and then we go into the car's interior. Finally, in a single move, we find ourselves behind the car. And that feels like a mismatch. The spectator doesn't analyze it in that way, but he feels something; he is brought into the form of the film.

Q: The complexity of the plot, especially with the reading of the tract which tells us about family relations, contrasts with the clarity of the mise en scène.

CC: When I had finished *Merci pour le chocolat*, I said to myself that we were going to get slammed by the critics, that it was going to be a flop. And in fact, there weren't many people who understood it! But even so, it did well. And that is where I noticed that you have to give just enough reference points: it isn't a serious problem if people don't grasp it on every level. Here, I wanted to push that idea even further, to refine what I had done. What is interesting is to see how far you can go in leaving the spectator behind. If it's too complicated, if it goes by too fast, the spectator gives up on you. At the same time, it is interesting that he is afraid to give up. It's a question of dose, of a tension between the two poles. I think that it was in this film that I succeeded the most in finding that tension. The situation is very complicated. I had to make a genealogical tree in order to follow it! But you can understand it without too much trouble, even if certain details escape you. There is the mind-blowing bit of sophistry on the part of François when Michèle tells him that she might not be the daughter of his father. When he says to her, "If that is the case, we're not even related," one could reply, "Even if that is the case, you are still brother and sister."

Q: Just as in *Merci pour le chocolat*, the question of incest is at the heart of the film.
CC: Yes, and there is also Aunt Line and her brother. It is obvious that she was in love with him. I even wonder if they didn't have sexual relations! Incest is one of the rare taboos which have lasted into our time, and we denied the existence of it until not too long ago. It's like pedophilia. I thought it was a good thing not to deny it; to see its contours, the why and the how. This kind of thing happens in all families, and not only poor families, not only in subsidized housing. In the film, it should be noted, there isn't any incest in the subsidized housing. I thought about putting it in, but that was not the subject of the film.

Q: There are other connections with your previous film: the use of repetition, the sense of guilt. There is also a way in which one film is the negative print of the other: the Isabelle Huppert character in *Merci pour le chocolat* is the negative of Suzanne Flon's character in *The Flower of Evil*.
CC: Absolutely. Aunt Line has been in an incestuous relationship and killed her father, but she had her reasons. That is really interesting! We want to know her. She has a large life force which makes her think that only the present matters. So, we want to taste that!

Q: The figure of repetition brings us back to psychoanalysis.
CC: Of course, but it is a reorganized repetition. Part of it is natural, and the other part is intentional. The past becomes the present for Aunt Line; it erases the past. That is taken from psychoanalysis: the principle of catharsis. But that doesn't erase anything for the young girl, Michèle. There is a transmission of the flame and I don't think it corresponds that much to any of the discoveries of psychoanalysis. I am under the impression that it is a much older notion, an idea that asks the following question: "Is a human being unique, or are there thousands of roots or leaves that connect us?" Both answers are valuable, which is what makes it interesting.

Q: Just as in *La Cérémonie*, there is no story in the end. The film relies on the opacity of the characters.
CC: Yes. The only "story," the only troubling question, is that of knowing who

wrote the tract. But it's really a MacGuffin. The spectator has theories, but there is a moment where he no longer cares if he knows the truth. I think that no spectator is going to leave the movie theater asking who wrote the tract. In any case, it would not be their first reaction. Which doesn't stop me from having my own theory about the identity of the author of the tract. For me, it's the awful Matthieu. Look at who would profit from the crime: it's Matthieu who comes into the house at the end. You might think it was Gérard, but he never admits to doing it. He only says to Michèle, "It excites you to think that."

Q: This "iceberg" quality, where the bulk of things is hidden from view, has been part of your cinema from the start.
CC: Yes. What complicates everything and what makes stories is the fact that people like to hide things. This behavior is definitely both useful and interesting. In society, modesty is rather a hindrance. Not that you should take off your pants at dinner, but a modesty in terms of emotions can make you lose some of your understanding of others. If you hide part of what you are or what you would like to be from your cousin, or if your cousin does the same thing, the relations that you can have with him or her are purely superficial. And this kind of relationship creates families like the Charpin-Vasseurs. They marry their cousins in order to be sure of remaining within the family. I saw that in my family. It isn't pretty!

Q: Your gaze on the bourgeoisie seems less cynical and acerbic than before. We feel quite strongly the pleasure that there is in living a bourgeois lifestyle.
CC: Yes, that pleasure exists. It's true that we have to look harder for the ways in which the bourgeois people in *The Flower of Evil* are despicable or antipathetic. Even in the sequence that takes place at the subsidized housing apartments, Anne finds the right words: "*Bonne continuation.*"[2] But she is still not a heroine. I don't believe in bourgeois heroes.

Q: Why?
CC: Because the bourgeoisie is the enemy of transgression, and heroism is almost by necessity transgressive. Even if it is only a transgression against caution. And the bourgeois are cautious. At the time of the resistance, it was in the bourgeois class that there was the highest proportion of both members of the resistance and collaborationist bastards. In the working class, there were a lot less bastards, but there were also a lot less resistants. But if the bourgeois were to become heroic, it would only be because they had lost their inherited advantages. That would be the only thing that could lead them to transgress. The only heroine of the film is Aunt Line. Why is she heroic? Because she transgressed. It is for the same reason that Michèle also becomes a heroine at the end.

Q: In terms of actors, you have completely updated your team.

CC: I said to myself that I would cast people I had never worked with and with whom I wanted to work. At least, that was the case for four out of the five main roles. In the case of Mélanie Doutey, it was different. I wanted to work with her after seeing her screen tests. She is the daughter of Alain Doutey, an actor with whom I worked a while ago, but I had never made the connection. At the end of the casting process, she was in competition with Laura Smet, the daughter of Johnny Halliday and Nathalie Baye, and I hesitated for a long time between the two. I chose the one whose physical presence corresponded the best with the character of the young girl from a good family who is pursuing her studies and wants to succeed.

Q: And what about the four others?

CC: Suzanne Flon has long been a fascination of mine. About fifteen years ago, I had a project to make an adaptation of Simenon's *November* with her, but it didn't work out. I saw her a lot in the theater, and she fascinated me. She projected a kind of force that I discovered as soon as we began to work. Strangely, she was able to give an intensity to things without apparent effort, without my being able to see her work hard. On top of that, she was a bit like Isabelle Huppert, and, in another way, like Nathalie Baye, who excels in bringing out details. Nathalie delighted me when, after she reads the tract, they ask her what she is going to do and she replies, "I am going to fight, my dear!" There is a formidable truth there, and at the same time, there is a slight quiver in her voice which allows us to think that she is strong but perhaps not strong enough. All of the actors were able to make it so that their characters were not detestable. That was an old trick of Jean Yanne, to whom I said, when making *Que la bête meure*, that he was going to play the worst of bastards, and he replied, "I will justify your guy when I choose to." That is how an actor should play the part, except, of course, if he is playing a character who hates himself. For that kind of role, Bernard Le Coq was great. Because I find the character of Gérard to be someone you feel sorry for.

Q: You have the reputation of being very discreet in your direction of actors.

CC: When they tell me that some directors show actors what they should do, I don't understand. What is interesting—if you have a precise idea—is to let them find it themselves.

Q: How do you work? With rehearsals? Doing a lot of takes?

CC: This time, I might have done one or two more takes than usual. When you have four actors in the scene, you have to make sure that they are really working in the same rhythm. But everything happens before the take. We had discussed their roles with them, or we had even done a little scene where we could see pretty quickly if they were really in character. Afterwards, you have to push them to enter completely into your vision of the character, just as you have to come into theirs, and since they have to be aware of the other actors as well, it quickly becomes quite complicated.

In this film, I had made the choice of actors in order to be sure that they would be able to work well together. For the first two days I was content just to watch them. After that, I only had to work out some points of detail. The only one who had a bit of a problem was Benoît Magimel. He wanted to know to what extent his character had become Americanized. So we figured that out together. I noticed that he wanted to look like Sean Penn and that corresponded well with his character. From the moment when they feel that you are on the same wavelength as them, actors become freer and start inventing things. In general, it's always a good thing. Which is to be expected, since you have given them the character so that they will do something with it.

Q: Could you give an example?

CC: At the end of the film, when François learns what happened in the election hall, he makes a little movement which causes him to tilt forward into the backdrop of the night. I thought that this was much better than a facial expression. Benoît understood this without my having to explain it to him. At the moment when he arrives at the place where there is a night backdrop, he slows down slightly to emphasize the idea that he is going into the darkness.

Q: For the cinematography, you used Eduardo Serra, who was also your cinematographer on both *The Swindle* (*Rien ne va plus*) and *The Color of Lies* (*Au coeur du mensonge*).

CC: On *Merci pour le chocolat*, I have no regrets about using Renato Berta, who did good work. But Renato, who has shot a lot of directors' first films, has a tendency to suggest that other camera placements would be better, and I don't have the time to explain to him why that isn't the case. Our first two or three days on *Merci pour le chocolat* were hard, but after that things went well. With Eduardo, I felt much better. And in terms of the actresses, who are always very anxious about their images on the screen, there is no worry with him. They trust him and he doesn't have to put up a weave every time I ask for a closeup of their face. I find the cinematography of *The Flower of Evil* particularly impressive. The way it goes really dark in the night sequences is very successful.

Q: Did you give him any points at the start of the shooting?

CC: He knows that I hate it when the cinematography is dominated by browns. We had already done some shots in *The Color of Lies* where blue was dominant. In a general way, I don't like filters, and he knows that he has to make do without them. Moving toward what we might call more rarified air, I told him that I wanted to go more toward narrow apertures. He understood right away; he's not stupid. Also, he has the Atanassian brothers as his gaffers; their father was the gaffer when I worked with Jean Rabier. So there is a family side to it. At the end of the shoot, he informed me: "I always speak both for myself and for the Atanassians: you need to know that we only did a third of what we could have done on the film!" In other words, what I asked him to do did not require the kinds of acrobatics he was prepared to do. I don't know if he regretted that or not, but I don't see why I should have to do things that I don't need. As Billy Wilder said, "No helicopter shots, except in dining room scenes."

Q: What do the two films you made between *La Cérémonie* and *Merci pour le chocolat* mean to you?

CC: In the case of *The Swindle*, the idea was to make an amusing film about the circulation of money. Since I had had the idea of making a film about a couple of grifters for a long time, I mixed that in. The idea of the circulation of money worked well, since more than half of the spectators didn't see the sleight of hand at the moment when there was the non-transfer of the suitcase in the plane. Which means that more than half of the spectators get scammed their whole lives and don't realize it! It's a film that I really like, but which got a mixed reception. Probably because it's a bit broad in its comedy.

Q: And what about *The Color of Lies*?

CC: One of my motivating principles was to come back to the Cancale area in Brittany where I had shot *La Cérémonie*, but without using all the same settings that I had found for that film. And then, it was pleasant to be able to capture the moving sands. I remembered that I loved a little detective novel that I had tried to buy the rights to adapt. It wasn't possible because the widow of the novelist said that her husband, an old British soldier, would never have allowed his book to be adapted by the vandals of the cinema. There was a tasty story there, which would have made a good subject for a film. Well, I kept just the idea of the moving sands, as an homage to this man, and I imagined a film about a guy who was in the process of dying inside. I had named him René so that Sandrine Bonnaire could say the line at the end, "*René, René, renaît*" ("Rene, Rene, born again"). The line fell flat everywhere except in the countries where there were subtitles, and in those places they lost the phonic rhyme! So it was a very bad idea.

Q: People don't talk much about Monique Fardoulis, your editor, but she has been with you for a long time.

CC: I have had very few cinematographers in my career, but even fewer editors. Only four in total for my full-length films. The first was Jacques Gaillard: he had married Monique Fardoulis, who worked with him as his sound editor. When they separated and Jacques stopped working as an editor to try to become a director, he suggested—gentleman that he was—that I hire Monique to replace him. That is how she started editing my films, beginning with my second worst film, *Les Magiciens*. From then on, she worked on almost all my films. She starts editing during the shoot, but I have to say that I don't give her thirty-six different solutions, just a few possibilities of refinement. I never shoot more than what is strictly necessary. For *The Flower of Evil*, I set a new record: there was not a single shot that did not end up in the film. Occasionally, you have to take out the beginning or the end of a scene. But that hardly ever happens, except in *The Color of Lies*, where I took out things about the family of Sandrine's character's friend, and where I almost completely cut out one character: the brother who was a masseur. He was not indispensable to the film, and no one ever knew he had been cut.

Q: Your last two films have ended in a similar way, with the action continuing over the titles.

CC: First of all, I did it to add a point of connection between the two films. And I have always been irritated when I see spectators—even cinema people—who don't watch the titles to the end. I find that very impolite. I had already had the action continuing during the titles in *La Cérémonie*, where it worked very well. It didn't work as well for *Merci pour le chocolat*, where people thought that the story was over. Here, I tried something different. I give the impression of ending the film abruptly, and then I have it go on in such a way that it reinforces the idea that Matthieu (Thomas Chabrol) has taken over. And we end with the primordial image of the staircase.

Notes

1. Maurice Papon was convicted of crimes against humanity for his role in deporting sixteen hundred Jews during World War II.
2. This expression is difficult to translate, but it means roughly "Enjoy the rest of your day," or "I wish you well."

The Flower of Evil: An Interview

Yves Alion / 2003

From *L'Avant-Scène Cinéma* 519 (February 2003): 69–73. Reprinted by permission; translated from the French by CB.

The Flower of Evil. Under this Baudelairian title, Claude Chabrol offers us a new opus with a heady fragrance. And the rather cheerful, sometimes violent trial that he has been conducting for more than forty years against the French bourgeoisie has been supplemented by a beautiful new film. It provides us with an opportunity to return with him to view the spectacle of the world, which he first learned to observe as a child during the dark hours of the Occupation.

Yves Alion: You have made more than fifty films. A number of them, including *The Flower of Evil*, seem to be digging in the same patch of ground to make us experience the "discreet charm" of the provincial bourgeoisie. Is it fair to say that it's an obsession of yours?

Claude Chabrol: Clearly, *The Flower of Evil* is not avoiding the subject: the Charpin-Vasseur family belongs without any doubt to the bourgeoisie as it occurs in the provinces. I have counted, and I would say that half of my films deal with this social category. Others take place in an urban bourgeois milieu. Which doesn't mean that the bourgeoisie is the theme of the films. *La Cérémonie*, for example, is not a film *about* the bourgeoisie, or at least not directly. So what conclusion should we draw? That I am still persuaded that the bourgeoisie is the dominant class in our society. And that the shift in focus from the political to the economic is not going to change that. And we need to be interested in the dominant group.

YA: It's as if nothing has changed since the nineteenth century, since *Madame Bovary*, which you have also adapted.

CC: What has changed is that the aristocracy has disappeared. It still existed at the time of *Madame Bovary*. Then it declined, until it disappeared completely. What remains of it today has no other function than that of interesting ordinary people. It's picturesque, rather pleasant, but totally anecdotal. What remains is the bourgeoisie. Because it's forbidden to treat the proletariat: we can't do it. We can only describe it, which for me is insufficient.

YA: What about *Modern Times*?
CC: *Modern Times* isn't a film about the proletariat. It's a film about industrialization, which doesn't present things from a social point of view. On the other hand, it is true that *City Lights*, which came right before it in Chaplin's work, *is* a proletarian film.

YA: The difference between treatment and description is not always very clear. Should we understand you to mean that the cinema is a key which permits us to open certain locks and put things in perspective?
CC: The cinema allows us both to underline the faults and to glimpse the good qualities of the upper-class people portrayed in the film. They are not absolute monsters. The bourgeoisie has its charm, which is not all that discreet. And that's why it's so dangerous. The members of the upper class do not always accept the consequences of their power, and that is the most serious problem. In most cases, they have not understood that they have certain duties, while even the most broken-down members of the nobility of the previous century had this awareness. The bourgeois have only one ambition: to possess. Their favorite game is *Monopoly*.

YA: But at the same time, they try to preserve appearances: the appearance still trumps the actuality.
CC: I'm not sure that that is only true of the bourgeois class. Given human nature—the relative power of the human being and the complications generated by the world which he has in part created—it is clear that mankind has to burn whatever wood is available to survive. Appearance is a question of survival.

YA: Why did you choose the Bordeaux region?
CC: There are two reasons. First, it is true that there are quite a lot of examples of close blood ties between families in the region. Families unite with each other. When you have vines that resemble each other—when you have the same earth, the same grapes—you will make almost the same wine, as long as it stays within the same family. The second reason is a more precise one. Given that we don't see the father of Aunt Line, played by Suzanne Flon, I wanted people to understand what kind of guy we were talking about. It makes things easier to suggest that he could have been someone like Maurice Papon.[1]

YA: This isn't the first time that you have shown an interest in the period of the Nazi occupation. Is it because it was a moment when false pretenses were even more hidden than they normally are?

CC: I was between ten and fourteen during the occupation. At that age, if you don't keep your head too much in the sand, it is interesting to observe what is happening. I noticed that people had a tendency to let themselves be manipulated. At the beginning of 1941, my father came for the first time to see us in the Creuse region, where we were living as refugees while he continued to work in Paris. Until that day, the images I had of the world which surrounded me corresponded to what we heard on the radio. But my father explained to me that everything we were being told was false, and my whole perspective changed. That is why I made *L'Oeil de Vichy*, a critical compilation of news reports of the time. Because those reports were how the world was presented to us. But I had a key to better understanding that had been given to me by my father.

Also, because it was a very tense time, it was very easy to reveal oneself. The bastards were really bastards and the good guys were really good guys, and a lot of people were in between. That is when I realized that the principle of survival is the most important one for human beings. All of that influenced me a lot. In a curious way, that vision of the world brought me closer to religion at first, and then pulled me away from it later on. I saw that the reaction of human beings to a given problem depends on their age, their culture, their temperament, and thirty-six other factors.

YA: Is *The Flower of Evil* a film about memory, about the passage of time?

CC: The idea of the film is that in order to survive with memory, you have to abolish time. But at the same time, memory plays an enormous role. For Aunt Line, everything happens in the present, which allows her both to be very appealing and to have a deep cynicism.

YA: The scenes from 1944 are empty of characters. Only the voices appear. Did you know from the beginning how you were going to present those memories on the screen?

CC: I wanted to eliminate flashbacks, because they are a somewhat crude materialization of the past, as opposed to the memory of voices. I didn't want the past to be materialized in any ostensible way. It is memory that has to be on the screen, not the past. I had to take precautions to avoid that becoming superficial or boring.

YA: One has the feeling that the political domain is treated with a more obvious irony than the knots of family relations, especially in the scene of the visit to the inhabitants of the low-rent apartment building.

CC: I wasn't going to tell the story of the electoral campaign in a serious way, because it isn't a serious thing. It's completely ridiculous. It is one of the elements in the film that explain how the grandfather could have made lists of Jewish children. What Anne (Nathalie Baye) displays in terms of her political engagement is rather hollow. But at the same time, this waste is not necessary: the politics that we get are nothing more than what the politicians do with them. And what the citizens want to hear.

YA: That's very pessimistic.

CC: No, it's really optimistic, because you only need to know that in order to be lucid about it. There is an obvious laziness in people, which is compounded by a fear of change, because on those occasions, there are opportunities that get lost. Many things don't get done because the fear of a major upheaval is omnipresent. People were very marked by the experience of May 1968.

YA: Has the state of politics changed since you presented Claude Piéplu as a right-wing member of parliament in *Les Noces rouges*?

CC: It's been thirty years. Politicians are used to things going back and forth. They are at the same time less sure of themselves than before and more determined to stay in place, whatever the political tides may be. I also didn't want people to be able to identify the candidates in the film. We had a lot of fun making up the candidates' posters for the film. And it was my wife who was the one running "With the workers."

YA: In order to be delicious, irony can sometimes be dangerous. Doesn't it risk turning into cynicism? Is the filmmaker not tempted to play God the Father watching the poor creatures below twitch around?

CC: That's a real problem. But the dividing line is fairly simple: you have to love your characters. I love them all, even Gérard (Bernard Le Coq), who displays character traits that are not very appealing. We can hit our characters as hard as possible, but only on the condition that we preserve a certain tenderness for them. You can't make a film like this one with hatred. But you also have to be careful not to go too far to the other side and become sentimental.

YA: Last month, we met with Lucas Belvaux, who was struck during the shooting of *Poulet au vinaigre* by your desire not to use a shot/reverse shot structure. *The Flower of Evil* is equally devoid of that technique. Is this a way of reinforcing a certain softness, a sensuality that is underlined by movements of the camera that take place without jolts?

CC: Given the fact that my problem is not with advancing the plot, I have no reason to use shot/reverse shot, which is the more utilitarian method. The worst are shot/reverse shots where you're primed in advance. That is the most heavy-handed thing they do: it's a way of underling the monotony and lack of imagination of the filmmaker, of showing that he has nothing in his head. That said, it would be interesting one day to make a film that is composed *only* of shot/reverse shots.

YA: Does that mean you like stylistic exercises, that nothing is more interesting to you than giving yourself constraints in the way the writers of the Oulipo group did?
CC: The playful side of things is not enough. Constraints, it seems to me, come out of the necessities of the story I want to tell. These are more interesting constraints than the one which consists of only shooting actors on their best profile.

YA: Your formal biases make the camera feel very present. The characters often seem like they are being caressed by the camera.
CC: I tried to think about each shot. The first time there is a sensual lure for the viewer, it has to be very strong. When François (Benoît Magimel) and Michèle (Mélanie Doutey) rediscover each other after several years of separation, the shot is a little bit closer than the one before, and made with a slightly shorter lens. Their cheeks and lips are very noticeable. I wanted the viewer to really be with them.

YA: We have the feeling that the anonymous letter that pulls the family through the mud belongs with the famous Hitchcockian MacGuffins; it is the bait which allows the action to continue while the director offers us something more substantial from under his coat. Is *The Flower of Evil* a Hitchcockian film?
CC: This letter is, in fact, a true MacGuffin. I knew that there had been a tract of this ilk during the Frédérique Bredin campaign: it was completely crazy.[2] That gave me the idea for this epistolary delirium. They rejected my first version of the letter on the pretext that it was much worse than that in reality, though I had not held myself back. Having said that, it is interesting to know who the author of the letter was. No one says it clearly, and it is necessary that it not be known to the viewer, but I will give you the key to the enigma. The first time that Anne's assistant goes to the home of the Charpin-Vasseurs, he walks in first in a very brusque way. Then there is another shot which resembles this one, when Bernard goes to vote; we see him tear up the ballot papers, and he enters the voting booth in much the same way. Thus, his behavior unconsciously reminds us of that of the assistant. I won't say anything more.

YA: Since we brought in Hitchcock, it is difficult not to invite Fritz Lang. Isn't this fascination with badly hidden secrets, with things behind things, a way of rendering homage to the director of *Secret Beyond the Door* and *Beyond a Reasonable Doubt*?

CC: We don't have the same style—alas for me—but I have the same method as Lang in that when I am shooting I really think about how to make the scene. I think I have figured out both my Langian side and my Hitchcockian side. My Hitchcockian side is a certain pleasure in defining secondary roles, such as the inhabitants of the low-rent apartments. Hitchcock was great at that.

Notes

1. Maurice Papon (1910–2007), a former official of the Vichy government, was accused of war crimes involving the deportation of sixteen hundred Jews to concentration camps.
2. Frédérique Bredin (b. 1956) is a French female politician who served as a cabinet minister in the government of François Mitterand.

Concerning *Comedy of Power*: An Interview

Yves Alion / 2006

From *L'Avant-Scène Cinéma* 548 (January 2006): 76–80. Reprinted by permission; translated from the French by CB.

We don't know where Claude Chabrol's reputation for being lazy came from, but it is in fact something of a joke since the auteur of *Le Boucher* is, quite to the contrary, the most prolific of contemporary directors. In all of Europe, we tried in vain to find a longer filmography. Even if not all the films are masterpieces (the interested party would himself agree), the number of successes is still undeniably high. *Comedy of Power* is incontestably one of them. The film stays within the straight furrow that Chabrol has never tired of plowing, film after film, for fifty years. The film is a portrait of French society that is acidic in tone, with a subtle aggressivity. This is how Balzac would make cinema if he were here today.

The film has another point of fascination, which is its multiple allusions to recent judicial cases, as Chabrol molts into a wily tomcat who plays with the little mice who have made the headlines in these last years. He doesn't turn himself into an avenger, as Yves Boisset would have done (with talent) in earlier times, and still less into a muddle-headed Don Quixote (which Jean-Pierre Mocky did so marvelously). Instead, he is content—if we dare say it—to shine a harsh light on our political-industrial mores. With his usual verve and with the talents of Isabelle Huppert—who gives one of her most beautiful performances—the result is beyond our hopes.

Yves Alion: When we watch *Comedy of Power*, it is difficult not to be tempted to recognize the real figures from the political and the business worlds that the film has taken as its target.

Claude Chabrol: To be honest, that would be quite fruitless.

YA: We feel that you have nonetheless taken a jubilatory pleasure in putting up signposts as soon as the occasion presented itself. Eva Joly becomes Jeanne

Charmant-Killman (a "killer of men" who moreover is one); Roland Dumas is played by Roger Dumas.

CC: I admit that I had fun doing it.

YA: We also remember that, just like the character played by François Berléand, Loik Le Floch-Prigent had a problem with eczema.

CC: This problem of eczema worked well in the film, because it is obvious that the lies in which the character is imprisoned are itching at him. It is true that the relations between Humeau and the judge were inspired, in a very loose sense, by those that were established between Eva Joly and Loik Le Floch-Prigent.[1] Their relations were not good, but they both ended up regretting that. Especially Eva Joly, who became aware that what he was saying was true, and that he was far from being the primary culprit in the story. Instead, he was the first fuse. And on the other side, Le Floch-Prigent came to recognize that the judge was not the most inhuman member of her profession.

YA: Beyond this question of "who's who," what would be interesting to know is how you were able to maintain a line between being too close to reality—which could have given the film a militant feeling—and being too distanced, which would have deprived the film of part of its impertinence.

CC: To be honest, I never asked myself this question. Given that we know only a small part of the reality, it would have been fruitless to try to render it in a faithful way. I made the story move forward in the way I needed it to move forward. I asked Odile Barski, my coscreenwriter, to gather documentation so that the foundations of the story would be as solid as possible. But since no one was mentioned by name, there was no reason for the film to depart from the real events. We started with the principle that if someone recognized himself in the film, he would at the same time be admitting what he was being accused of. Obviously, it is tempting to make a connection with the Elf-Aquitaine affair, but I will remind you that in the film it is never a question of oil.

YA: I would be tempted to say that the film presents a mixture of things that somewhat resembles you: the presentation is quite acidic, but it never goes to the limit of meanness. There is a bantering tone. In the end, you are far from detesting these people.

CC: There is, in fact, one character I detest, but I won't say which one. It's true that I find all the characters fairly interesting, so the one I detest is the one who interests me the least. He's the one whom I would have the greatest tendency to distrust; in my opinion, he is capable of anything. We will see if he recognizes himself.

YA: So you would agree with me if I said that you regard this little world with malice.

CC: Certainly, these people have made me indignant, but the issues are above all issues of money. In France, at any rate. In America, it's different: these kinds of affairs have caused quite a bit of damage. But one has to recognize that this whole circus is extremely funny. The convictions of these classic hypocrites didn't move me to sadness.

YA: The political world has always inspired you. We haven't forgotten that the female protagonist of *The Flower of Evil* was trying to get elected, or that the deceived husband in *Les Noces rouges* was a member of parliament.

CC: They say that people are less and less interested in politics. That isn't true: they are very interested. And in a healthy way, because they are beginning to laugh at it. I push them in that direction. I sincerely believe that the renewed prevalence of racism in France was born out of the stupid formula of the "right to difference." Instead, we should have highlighted the "right to similarity." There are definitely more similarities than differences between people! We often become attached to laughable differences. You're not going to tell me that the color of our skin is an important factor!

YA: Do you never regret the ironic distance that is characteristic of your films?

CC: Why would I? I have never seen a film change anything. On the other hand, I have seen an eruption of laughter change things. But the cinema can help us to develop our thoughts, which is not a bad thing. That is the whole difference from television, which doesn't have the function of waking people up.

YA: You connect the love of power with the love of money, but we have to recognize that for some people power can above all induce a kind of erotic intoxication which transforms them in a profound way.

CC: That's true. What is terrible about power is really the intoxication that comes with it. Which means that it very quickly becomes impossible to see things as they really are. The mechanism is quite childish. But this isn't the first time I've found people to be childish.

YA: Each person has power over others in a particular way. When making a film, you have to share your desires and your fantasies with a certain number of people: first of all, with the technical crew and actors, and then with the public.

CC: I try to do that without abusing my power. Power allows us to use our position to impose things on others that they cannot accept. When I make a film I don't impose anything, because no one is forced to go see the film. In a film there isn't the same use of power; instead, there is a respect for the rules of the game that everyone knows and that no one has invented.

YA: As an admirer of Fritz Lang, these are questions that must strike you quite often. The creator of *Dr. Mabuse* is—based on all the evidence—fascinated by power and the abuses that one can engage in by using it.

CC: That is really the kind of cinema I love. I love that mode of reflection about the world that Lang offers us in his films. Many recent films irritate me a bit, because they privilege sensation over reflection. But the truly beautiful cinema invites thought before it provides sensation. That is why good cinema is usually encoded.

YA: Do your films all fall into that category?

CC: No, of course not. My films have pushed toward reflection when it was possible. I am well aware that when I made *Marie-Chantal contre Docteur Kha* it wasn't Schopenhauer. I let the spectator know that in that case it was a simple piece of entertainment. But at the same time I invited the spectator to ask himself why. And that has worked pretty well for me. When it didn't work, it was because I failed in my attempt. Why do people love horror films? Because they are films which function on the level of pure sensation.

YA: Is the dividing line the same as that between films that tell us things and those that—beneath brilliant exteriors—reveal themselves to be completely hollow?

CC: I don't think so. Perhaps because I don't think much about these brilliant films that are about their own form and that tell us nothing. Most often they aren't brilliant at all. Most of current Hollywood cinema is quite appalling on that level. The films are imbecilic, and when they try not to be they are often worse.

YA: To come back to your film: everyone has noted that it is the seventh time you have worked with Isabelle Huppert. How would you evaluate her development, and the image that she has presented since *Violette Nozière*?

CC: She has stayed perfectly adequate to what I would call her work as an actor. Because she is one of those actors who do nothing by accident and who contribute to each film an element that supplements the overall construction. She is very conscious of her image. Right now she is very thin, simply because she sees herself like that. But since that works perfectly for the character of the judge, there is no problem.

YA: For a long time, Isabelle Huppert projected an introverted and suffering image, starting with *The Lacemaker*. Then she developed a more whimsical, rounder side, which bursts out in *Coup de Torchon* and *La Cérémonie*. This side of her is, paradoxically, not a small part of her performance in *Comedy of Power*.

CC: Without that whimsical part of her, the nephew's philosophy would have nothing to hook on to. For this philosophy to speak to her, part of her has to be nostalgic for it, for that kind of model. She tells him that he is the only person she can talk to. He is the only one who can take a little distance, and she feels that she needs to begin to understand that distance. She is too deeply involved in her work not to lose her sense of balance. After all, she ends up going to the office in her pajamas.

YA: The character of the husband is indispensable for showing to what extent her private sphere has exploded. His malaise is abysmal.

CC: The character of the husband is also indispensable for underlining another aspect of the character of the judge: her desire for social climbing. At the beginning, this marriage was a bad match for the husband. But the judge has been able to catch up to him and pass him. Now he only exists through the gaze of other people on *her*. From that point on, it's over; he crumbles. But he doesn't want to die. Which was not the case with Eva Joly's husband, who did not mess up his suicide attempt.

YA: The power of the judge appears to be very great, but we see that in reality it's just a lure. The judge in the film is subject to pressures that put her power in perspective.

CC: Her power is real until the moment when it is taken away from her. And in a completely legal way. But the law ends up being lawless. There are her superiors who are watching out so that we don't notice that the world is not perfectly fair. Since she doesn't think in that way, they take the case away from her. And this is the question about judges that the film asks. And God knows that it's still a burning question today, at a time when Judge Burgaud—who presided over the Outreau trial—is the subject of so many conversations.[2] Personally, I have a hard time understanding how he was not made to wince by the fact that, according to his conclusions, in a world which still operates by the rules of physics and mathematics, where the notion of statistics still means something, twenty-three pedophiles could have been living in a single apartment building. It's outrageous.

In my view, a judge is always going to be led toward becoming schizophrenic, because the same person, with the same evidence, has to find both reasons to convict and reasons to acquit. He has to split himself in two. This exercise is infernal for the human mind. Burgaud appears to have felt this intoxication of power. One has to admit that he had bad luck. He had done well in school and had been named to the court of northern France, which was still under the shock of the Dutroux case. He thought he had the case of the century.

YA: There are a number of scenes in the film involving legal hearings. How did you deal with the fairly nonspectacular aspect of those scenes?
CC: It's true that they would seem not to be very spectacular, but our interest in them comes from wanting to know what gets said behind the closed doors of a judge's chambers. I wanted to watch Raymond Depardon's documentary *Délits flagrants* (*Caught in the Acts*) again so as not to get too far away from reality, and I had a dean of the academy for judges watch the film. But I had to make some choices in the mise en scène to emphasize the face-to-face encounters of the accused and the judge, whereas in reality they are not alone in the room, since the clerk is also present, even when they're in a very cramped office.

YA: To many, you are the filmmaker who best described society in the Pompidou era. But Pompidou has been dead for twenty-five years and the bourgeoisie as you like to depict it doesn't seem to have changed much.
CC: That's exactly what defines it. I think that there is a certain consistency in the films I make. Because I continue to observe what is being done and to listen to what people are saying—and even what people *aren't* saying—in order to nourish my imagination.

YA: And on the level of your directing style, isn't there also a clear consistency?
CC: Sure. But with the desire not to put that directing style at the forefront with the air of saying, "Watch me shoot a film!"

YA: Which doesn't prevent you from beginning *Comedy of Power* with a signature sequence shot.
CC: That is one of the rare shots in the history of cinema to go up thirty floors! The shot isn't all that complicated: the Steadicam allows for a fluidity that wouldn't have been possible before. The real difficulty in a shot like that is more with the lighting. But Eduardo Serra is a cinematographer for whom nothing is impossible. It was the sound that did us in: the elevator made noise, and we had to do a bit of postsynchronization, which I usually never use.

YA: How do you deal with all these technical developments that have affected the cinema in recent years?
CC: By taking a lot of distance. I'm not a lover of digital—even though I recognize that in time it will only get better from a technical point of view—and I still make my films in the traditional way. The technique of digital allows wild things to be done which, on the other hand, bring absolutely nothing to the film. When I saw Robin Hood pull back an arrow in Kevin Reynolds's film, and the arrow crossing

space from the subjective viewpoint of the camera, I said to myself that the film was off to a bad start, and I was right. But as you may have realized, the stories I tell have no need of special effects.

Notes

1. The film is loosely based on a case in which the magistrate Eva Joly investigated the Elf Aquitaine corporation and its CEO Loik Le Floch-Prigent.
2. The Outreau trial was a much-publicized criminal trial in northern France in which it was revealed that a number of innocent people in Outreau, a working-class town in the Pas-de-Calais region, had been unjustly accused of child sexual abuse and had been held in custody for between one and three years.

The Girl Cut in Two: An Interview

Pierre Eisenreich and Grégory Valens / 2007

From *Positif* 559 (September 2007): 9–13. Reprinted by permission; translated from the French by CB.

Question: What led you to make *The Girl Cut in Two*?

Claude Chabrol: I had wanted to make a film about a young woman who propels herself into a semipublic existence and who has to create, in some sense, her own identity. From there, I wanted to see how she would deal with all the traps that were placed for her. I chose Cécile Maistre to write the screenplay. I shared these thoughts with her, but we still didn't have a plot. I suddenly remembered *The Girl in the Red Velvet Swing* by Richard Fleisher, which, by good fortune, was shown on the Ciné Classics television program right after that. There was also *Ragtime* by Milos Forman, a magnificent film which was, alas, underestimated in its day. Milos Forman had borrowed the same news story that inspired *Girl on the Red Velvet Swing*. It was the story of the assassination of the great American architect Stanford White, who was killed by the husband of his mistress Evelyn Nesbit. She wrote a book of memoirs that I consulted. I asked Cécile Maistre to develop the story of this affair, and she gave me a first draft of the screenplay that I thought was very successful. I was even a bit frustrated, because I saw that there weren't a lot of changes I could bring to it. The dialogue already worked really well. However, I wasn't able to figure out how to end it. It was the choice of the title, *The Girl Cut in Two*, that allowed me to create the ending. We just added the character of the uncle who is a magician and we had him literally cut the heroine in two.

Q: This method of writing the screenplay is somewhat new for you.

CC: Not really, because I very often let a woman begin the first draft of the writing. Women are good at that. For example, when I work with Odile Barski, she brings almost all the different possibilities into the story, and I have to do a triage of the four hundred pages she gives me. With Caroline Eliacheff, the method is different in another way, but I still have to play my role as coscreenwriter. So, with Cécile Maistre, my participation was less needed, and I almost felt frustrated by that.

Q: In *The Girl Cut in Two*, you go back to a tradition of the woman's drama, where we watch a woman who is manipulated by men, and whom the world of the spectacle destroys. That was the case for *The Girl in the Red Velvet Swing*, and more recently *Mulholland Drive*.

CC: David Lynch's film really impressed me. But I don't feel guilty, because it is not my temperament to be a wizard of the screenplay like he is. The beginning of *The Girl Cut in Two* is, let us say, realistic, and the arrival of the magician brings in a coda which helps us to understand the rest of the film.

Q: That is why we made the comparison with *Mulholland Drive*; the last shot of your film reminds us of the Hollywood image of the smiling, ethereal, and airy face of Naomi Watts. And Richard Fleischer ended *The Girl on the Red Velvet Swing* by showing Evelyn Nesbit (Joan Collins) in the air, balancing above her masculine public.

CC: I would explain those endings by the fact that we can't imagine the failure of young women. No one wants to deal with the cruelty of that. For my part, I cut her in two, it's true, but Gabrielle (Ludivine Sagnier) appears at the end, complete and triumphant, even if it is in a more limited domain than the one in which she started the film. Of course, she never becomes a television star.

Q: Gabrielle is not careerist. She doesn't run after either money or celebrity. She does, however, want a romantic life.

CC: She needs, in effect, to fill her heart with a certain number of feelings. She misses the large presence that was her father, and she goes in search of an older man who can replace him. Which is perfectly normal. And her mother tells her that she suspected that she would bring home a "papa."

Q: We really only come to understand the extent of the perversion and manipulation by this "papa," Charles Saint-Denis, who is played by François Berléand, when he is killed.

CC: He's an infernal character because his arguments are foolproof. He doesn't want to leave his wife, Dona (Valeria Cavalli), because he has nothing to reproach her for. He is right: she represents an attentive but not completely submissive slave. She is the ideal wife. She's a dream come true! His relationship with Capucine (Mathilda May), his editor, is clear enough to make us understand the duplicity of Charles Saint-Denis. Any normal spectator should recognize, when he sees the writer between the two pairs of thighs by the swimming pool, that he is an "old pig."

Q: There are several signs before that which reveal the obsessive character of Charles Saint-Denis.

CC: The first hint comes when Capucine, who arrives at the writer's home, opens the trunk of her car; he holds her hand in a rather suave fashion.

Q: The other hints in the set—such as the obelisques in front of nude portraits— are just as clear. This can destabilize the spectator if he notices them and interprets them, because his own fantasies become as twisted as those of Saint-Denis.

CC: We had a lot of fun with that. We put the décor to good use to make the public more complicit. I also have another anecdote: a twelve-year-old child, who was the son of one of the members of the crew, asked me what that special establishment was where Saint-Denis went every evening. Just before I could explain it to him, he added: "Am I stupid, or is it a swingers' club?" To play the role of the manager of the club, I wanted a real porno actor who actually owns a swingers' club. He wasn't able to be in the film, because he was in the process of opening another club in Corsica! His name was Alban, just like the character who appears in *The Girl Cut in Two*. He had a club behind Saint-Sulpice church in Paris; that wasn't invented!

Q: In the swingers' club, we see a version of the cultural bourgeoisie that you contrast, later on, with a moneyed bourgeoisie that feels like a bit of an anachronism.

CC: The cultural bourgeoisie is on the left politically, while the moneyed bourgeoisie is on the right. There are practically no exceptions to this. At the same time, the famous swinging of the swingers is also connected to this fact. These two social classes diverge on large political and moral questions, but they both accept the swinging of the older men. I found this thought delicious. I am still impressed by the way Gabrielle asks Charles Saint-Denis, when they are in the club, if he will introduce her to his friends. Gabrielle accepts all the social rules right away.

Q: Ludivine Sagnier told us that she was a bit intimidated at the beginning of making the film with you, because you give very few directions, while she needs to be directed with precision.

CC: In fact, I do give very few directions, because I'm not the one who is playing the roles; it's the actors. I do direct the actors, but you won't ever hear me tell them: "Don't forget that your mother's grandfather was a cobbler." There's no reason to do that. I have noticed that when actors are intelligent the system functions with efficiency. They have the feeling of being free, and at the same time they realize that my way of shooting doesn't leave them many options for how to play the role. Ludivine Sagnier was very quickly reassured. I was even impressed by how fast she adapted, because some actors take four or five days to understand my method. That method was formulated in reaction to a film by Claude Autant-Lara: *Vive Henri IV*

. . . *vive l'amour!* The filmmaker gave all the vocal intonations to the actors, which brought about a terrible result: everyone spoke in the same way! I avoid giving directions about vocal intonation. One day, I heard a director ask one of his actors for more interiority! That is really unbelievable!

Q: Ludivine Sagnier also confided to us that she auditioned for *Merci pour le chocolat.*
CC: That's true, but I didn't think she had the right face for the young pianist, while Anna Mouglalis did. This phenomenon happens fairly often, and it is why I do auditions for one out of two of my films. For *The Flower of Evil*, I had a choice between Mélanie Doutey and Laura Smet. I was torn, because they were both very good; then I asked myself which of them looked more like a law student from Bordeaux. It was Mélanie Doutey, and I was able to use Laura Smet for the next film, *The Bridesmaid*, without having to audition her.

Q: Knowing your admiration for Fritz Lang, the character of Paul Gaudens (played by Benoît Magimel) reminded us of the characters of the eccentric singer played by Dan Duryea in *The Woman in the Window* and *Scarlet Street*.
CC: Yes, it's the same kind of schizophrenic individual. Benoît Magimel had to give a real performance, because his character was very difficult to put together. He worked really hard. Working with the costume designer Mic Cheminal, we tried to give Paul Gaudens the look of sartorial extravagance. I asked him to go to the boutiques where the animator Ariel Wiseman buys his clothes. It was Benoît Magimel himself who had the idea of the hairstyle, to add even more extravagance to his look. I was afraid that it would seem exaggerated, but he was right: it didn't. The characterization of the character came from the line: "No, *I'm* the one who is rich."

Q: You reverse the convention: he is the one who is a puritan, while the old, respectable writer is decadent.
CC: Of course: the real pigs are the old guys!

Q: The casting of François Berléand seems obvious.
CC: Although I took a long time deciding on him. Cécile Maistre tried to convince me; she said he would be believable as a seducer of women because he seduces beautiful women in real life. It was when I saw a photo of him where he looked like the writer Romain Gary that it started to seem obvious to me: if he looked like a writer to me, then he would be believable as one! I have a tendency to not write for particular actors, and when I know that an actor is going to play a role, I intentionally add things that will seem difficult to him, to make it a bit tougher. I admire the work of Audiard enormously, but when he is not as good, it's when

things are written for the tics of actors. For *La Cérémonie*, I asked Isabelle Huppert, who as an old member of the troupe had the right to have a say in the matter, which of the two girls she wanted to play. She told me, "I don't want to play the illiterate one; I already did that." I was delighted, because I had dreamed that she would play the postal worker. Sandrine Bonnaire was extraordinary in the role of the illiterate woman. She told me, "I've got it: I'm a leek!" Once that word had been spoken, whenever I saw her I saw a leek. She plays it like a leek. I admire actors who are capable of concretizing abstractions.

Q: There is a similarity between the murder of Saint-Denis in *The Girl Cut in Two* and the murders in *La Cérémonie*.

CC: Yes: pow! In both cases, it's sudden. Jacqueline Bisset had a nervous crisis while we were shooting *La Cérémonie*, because her character dies from a gunshot and then the scene goes on for a long time afterwards.

Q: That's where the reality of the narrative bursts forth. In both films, we only have clues about the event until it happens. Then the reality is exposed.

CC: It's at that moment that we understand that there was no other solution. The fact that he makes her put on the red dress is great: we have the impression that he *wants* to be arrested.

Q: The color red is very present throughout the film.

CC: Yes, it is something we worked on a lot. We looked for a long time to find the bistro where Gabrielle and Capucine have their conversation, and we fell upon it right near where we were shooting. That was good luck!

Q: How did you work with Eduardo Serra?

CC: It was very simple. I said to him: "You understand that it's a smutty film? Shoot it that way." And he did.

Q: Saint-Denis's house reveals the ambivalent quality of the character: it is transparent, and has nothing to hide, yet at the same time there are hints of something hidden.

CC: In fact, he has nothing to hide, because he doesn't need to hide anything. I intentionally put in two bathtubs: in the smaller one, he is listening to music by Julien Clerc, and he seems inoffensive. In the big bathtub, he is simply disgusting.

Q: Did you get involved in decisions about the décor, or did you leave it in the hands of your set designer?

CC: I have noticed that in order to get what I want, the best solution is not to get involved! If I give my opinion about the décor, I am content with what I come up with and I say to myself: "I can get along fine with that." Whereas if I explain what I want, people will work overtime to find what is needed. That's what is great in this line of work as a filmmaker: you are surrounded by forty people who will do everything to help you realize what you have in your head. That isn't even true for a government minister!

Q: After the first lie is told by Saint-Denis, when he is sitting between the two women at the restaurant, there is an acceleration of the narrative: the dialogue in the next sequence is very fast.
CC: Yes. I wanted to have ruptures. And there also had to be harmonies. So I chose to have an alternation between scherzo and moderato tempos. I took this idea so far that I cut a scene that I liked, at the end, when she goes to see her uncle. He says to her, "I like the fact that you aren't crying over yourself." We didn't need that scene, because as soon as she opens the door to her uncle's room we can see her rebirth happening. And you might have noticed that the scene takes place at the Hotel Renaissance.

Q: Was that rhythm created in the editing, or was it already there in the screenplay?
CC: It's in the screenplay. People who are used to reading screenplays noticed right away that I wanted it to accelerate. There are suddenly more commas.

Q: You have had an affection for abrupt endings in your last few films, as well as for title sequences that are on the screen while the action of the film continues.
CC: I did that for *Merci pour le chocolat* and *The Flower of Evil*, because I noticed that in film festivals and in certain movie theaters, people are used to turning on the lights at the beginning of the end titles. With my films, you can't do that! There are even people who leave the theater. Well, too bad for them!

Q: But that isn't the real reason why you like doing this.
CC: The goal is to give an extra breath to the film. It is a matter of saying to the spectator: "You have understood everything; now let's see if you feel good at the end or not. . . ." Generally, I am against the idea of end titles in films: I would like films to end abruptly with the words "The End."

Q: In *L'Enfer*, you ended the film with the words "Without End."
CC: Yes, that was one of the ideas that I kept from Clouzot's unfinished screenplay, which I adapted. It is an endless hell, so there is nothing else one can say!

Q: The character of Gabrielle's mother in *The Girl Cut in Two* is very restrained.

CC: It's a terrible thing: if you try to make an objective judgment about the events of the film, you see that she is responsible for everything! She's the one who engenders chaos. She wants to create happiness, and it is in fact hell. I love Marie Bunel: she is a restrained and very accurate actress.

Q: The television chain for which Gabrielle works is regional, but she could almost be on national television.

CC: Yes, it's right on the border between the two. We are in Lyon, after all. One of the people who play the anchors is a real professional from the regional television news, and he gave me a lot of advice and helpful hints, like for example the play on words, *"une consoeur que l'on croyait blanche comme Deneige."*[1] That's really the kind of thing they say!

Q: Did the fact that you shot it in Lyon come from a desire to give more amplitude to the narrative?

CC: I wanted a city that has a certain reputation. Lyon has a reputation: in the past, there was the Lyon silk industry, and now there are pharmaceutical products. That makes what happens in the film more believable. Since I wanted to play with the difference between appearances and reality, I chose not to have people actually eating in the scenes involving meals. That really mattered to me. In the same way, there's the swinger's club, but you never actually see them having sex!

Q: The film always stays within a realist mode, but you play with the theatricality of certain characters.

CC: Yes, because they are living in a world of theatricality. There is nothing more theatrical than the people who work in television, except for the people who are in politics, as we saw in *Comedy of Power*, where each one of them does his "bit." That's why it is more difficult for me to make a film about suburbanites: they also have their form of theatricality, but you can't laugh about it because it wouldn't be fair to them.

Q: The male characters in *The Girl Cut in Two* are more troubled, and the female characters are more serene. The character played by Caroline Silhol is marked by her frankness.

CC: She doesn't wear a mask; she doesn't need one. Women are so much more used to the materiality of things that they end up being able to understand the world better than us men.

Q: The character of Capucine is wonderful. We always have the impression that she knows more than she wants to admit.

CC: Mathilda May is an exceptional actress! And she can be so smutty! I wanted a really sensual girl for that role, and I thought of her right away. She blew me away in the sequence at the little television party. I had asked her to kiss Berléand on the cheek, but in a way that was just a bit suggestive. We feel like she practically licks his cheek! She is an actress whom I love, and it is too bad that she has handled her career in the particular way she has.

Q: She is also great in another troubled role in Michel Deville's *Toutes peines confondues*. In a general way, do you follow the careers of the actors in your films? **CC:** Yes, absolutely! Benoît Magimel also has a small role in *Toutes peines confondues*. He has completely accepted his double career: on the one hand, he does films like *Sky Fighters*, and in another vein he does more risky things. As for Isabelle Huppert, I am starting to be able to see when she uses actors' tricks. I sometimes say to myself: "Well, you already did that one for me." And I have to say that she was great with Benoît in Michael Haneke's *The Pianist*. She recommended it to me.

Q: Do you consider *The Girl Cut in Two* to be a remake? **CC:** Not at all! If I hadn't talked about it, most people would never have made the connection with *Girl on a Red Velvet Swing*.

Q: Have you seen the remake of *La Femme infidèle*: Adrian Lyne's *Unfaithful*? **CC:** Yes, and I was very surprised, because his film lasts twenty minutes longer than mine, and I felt like it was ten minutes shorter!

Q: Did the television chains take issue with the content of *The Girl Cut in Two*? **CC:** No, because I have been selling them my films for a long time. And since I am almost an old man, the owners are nice to me: they open the door for me.

Q: What is your next film? **CC:** It will not be a sad one. Odile Barski has finished the second draft of the screenplay. It's about a fake Simenon novel. You might think it's an adaptation of Simenon, but it's really an original screenplay. One of the characters is inspired by a guy who made people think he was dead so that he could collect the insurance. But it's not pastiche: instead of adapting a Simenon novel, we wrote a story about a cop who could have been Inspector Maigret, who is on vacation with his wife. And Gérard Depardieu is supposed to play the role. It will be our first collaboration together, because all our previous projects fell apart.

Q: Who had the idea of giving the very beautiful poster campaign to the artist Miss.Tic?

CC: That was an idea of my producer Patrick Godeau, who wanted a campaign that would last for several weeks, because of the vacation starting in early August. He knows Miss.Tic and asked me if I knew her work. I told him I did, and that I thought it was a great idea. The poster is magnificent: it is Ludivine without being Ludivine. It's a girl. It's all girls.

Notes

1. This is a play on words based on the last name of Gabrielle's character, Deneige. The line can be translated as "a female colleague who we thought was as white as Snow."

On the Release of *Inspector Bellamy*

Yves Alion / 2008

From *L'Avant-Scène Cinéma* 574 (September 2008): 101–4. Reprinted by permission; translated from the French by CB.

A lover of the cinema of Hitchcock, that great master of manipulation, Claude Chabrol takes fairly regular pleasure in creating "MacGuffins," those famous ruses in Uncle Alfred's films which held the spectator in suspense while the master was knitting together a more secret film in the dark. Chabrol has always cherished the crime genre, but only for the purpose of diverting it to his own ends, because in the end he is more interested in the malfunctions of his characters than in the crime-driven, often mechanical structure of his films. It is no coincidence that he is more influenced by the sadness of Georges Simenon's novels (which he has adapted several times) than by the very sophisticated clockwork of Agatha Christie. *Inspector Bellamy* does not escape from this rule, as it throws us into a story of an insurance scam (a wonderful MacGuffin) in order to plunge its characters (and us) into what we might call, for want of a better word, the sufferings of the human condition. Nothing more than that . . .

Yves Alion: The film is dedicated to two Georges. The first is implicit, since the film begins on the tomb of Georges Brassens in the town of Sète. The second is less so. We understand that it is Georges Simenon. What is a Simenonian film?

Claude Chabrol: Simenon said that he was looking for the "naked man." *Inspector Bellamy* is an attempt to strip a man naked. Thus for me it is a purely Simenonian film. On another level, and in a more anecdotal way, I had fun presenting a contemporary portrait of Inspector Maigret and his wife, just as Simenon's novels presented them. I didn't ask them to prepare a veal cutlet with sorrel, so as not to be too explicit, but I wasn't far away from that.

YA: In a certain way, if the criterion of the "naked man" announces Simenon, all your films refer to it. Are the characters of this film just more open about it than usual?

CC: I think so. Bellamy is the subject of the film. And all the elements which are exterior to him are still part of him. I also played with the fact that it would be interesting to reverse the perception of the real and the imaginary. What people consider to be the element of truth in the film (the relationship of the couple) is completely imaginary, while the plot (the insurance scam), which seems to be a flight of imagination, is based on a real news story. We hesitated before putting in one detail, which was when the young lawyer of the character played by Jacques Gamblin started singing Brassens in the middle of the trial. The funniest part is that it was true, even if in reality the lawyer didn't do his whole summation in the form of the song. To make a bit more trouble, I chose a posthumous song that Brassens himself never sang. It is on the record that was recorded a few years later by Jean Berthola. But Brassens had composed it in his youth, and he must have put it aside because he didn't think it was very good. We snacked on it all the more easily, without any shame, and took from it what worked for us.

YA: This improbable pleasure in making true things crazy and inventing everyday things is an added delicacy, but it isn't the heart of the project.
CC: Of course not. I think it's the first time that I have taken so much care to make sure that a film is not transparent. The main plot, that of the insurance scam, fairly quickly becomes of secondary importance. At a given moment, Bellamy comes down the stairs, almost walks out of the frame, and declares: "I think I've had the wool pulled over my eyes." That is almost the subject of the film. Because he is in the same situation as the spectator.

YA: In that way, you diverge from Hitchcock, who liked to give the spectator information that the characters did not have. The suspense came in the divide between the two.
CC: I didn't try to create suspense. On the other hand, what is interesting, given the implosion of the plot, is that the flashbacks are not there for that reason. They are images that reflect what Bellamy understands from what people tell him.

YA: They are a bit like the mental images of the character played by Mathieu Amalric in *Un secret*, which are presented to us as real while they're really not.
CC: Exactly. I think Claude Miller's film is great. It's because I wanted to film mental images that the character of Gamblin is divided into three parts. It's because he obsesses Bellamy that Bellamy has the impression of seeing him on the street corner. And it's a way of showing the duality of people, their Jekyll and Hyde aspect.

YA: It's a kind of homage to Lang, decidedly your favorite filmmaker, who spent his life questioning good and evil.

CC: In a certain way. I wanted the film to give the impression of getting lost in a sort of fog which gets thicker as the action of the film evolves.

YA: One prominent aspect of *Inspector Bellamy* is that you cast Gérard Depardieu. In nearly sixty films, you had never worked with him.
CC: It wasn't that we never had projects. But malicious bad luck made them all fell apart. Before *Inspector Bellamy*, the most serious project we had had was an adaptation of Stefan Zweig's *Balzac*. But Gérard wasn't free on the right dates, and he had already agreed to play Balzac for a telefilm by Josée Dayan. We found each other again two years ago in Nimes for a film festival and we decided it was time that we finally make a film together. I told him: "In two years, we will shoot a film in Nimes. You will get the screenplay at the end of next year." He said yes, but it was obvious that he didn't believe me. He was wrong. What interested me was mixing two levels of representation by also making—in a certain way—a portrait of Gérard, or at least of Gérard as I perceived him.

YA: It is not usual for you to create a character knowing in advance who will play him.
CC: I think it was the first time.

YA: You can't get me to believe that you didn't know that Stéphane Audran would play the female character in your films of the 1960s and '70s.
CC: I didn't write them thinking of her, and I didn't try to use what I knew about her to write her characters. I hope, on the other hand, that I was able to trace some traits that are unique to Gérard through the character of Bellamy.

YA: Depardieu is a myth, a monument. And an actor who regularly admits to being tired of acting.
CC: In this case he was not tired. He didn't drink a drop during the whole shoot, and he didn't turn on his cell phone. He was completely involved. It's true—and he would be the first to recognize it—that he doesn't really invest himself in all the films he makes, and some of his choices are purely nutritional. But when he's at his best, he's an extremely agreeable guy. I was very happy to work with him and I think that the opposite is also true. It's true that I don't often have problems with my shoots. Harmony is essential for me. If by bad luck I have happened to make a mistake and chosen an actor who is not always agreeable, that actor was making two films at the same time: his first and his last.

YA: What is it that you wanted to reveal in your portrait of Depardieu?
CC: I would say that what I wanted from him is well said in one of the lines I had

him say: "I found some dignity in despising myself." Physically, he is quite massive in the film. Since then he has lost almost thirty kilos. But this physical aspect worked well for me, because I liked having an elephant in a china shop. We played with that, and he was game. When his wife climbs on top of him on the bed, he says to her: "I thought I saw Sir Richard Hillary climbing Everest."

YA: The choice of his acting partner in the film was much more difficult.
CC: I asked Gérard whom he saw for his wife in the film. He made two or three suggestions, which I rejected, because I wanted a woman who had not had plastic surgery, whose face was natural. So I put forward the idea of Marie Bunel, which Gérard thought was excellent. But I have to say that on the first day he put her through her paces with bawdy allusions, etc. It was a kind of hazing. But she took it very well and played the game. Which served the film well and delighted Gérard.

YA: A number of journalists have written on the duality of Depardieu, who balances a certain brutality with very feminine aspects.
CC: No doubt. It's true that there is a certain fragility in Gérard. But he plays with it; he remains an actor. Everything is about the proper dosage.

YA: The Bellamys make a splendid couple. They are always simpering; one never knows when they are sincere, which is part of the game.
CC: Their married life is a kind of comedy for two which goes on forever. There is a real emotional connection between them. But at the same time there are cracks in the surface. When the character played by Clovis Cornillac asks, "What's going on between you two?" she replies, "When?" That chills the spine a little. Especially since Clovis's character advertises a certain virility. And it is for that reason, for the sake of contrast, that I created the homosexual couple.

YA: We know that for you directing actors is mainly a matter of not making a mistake in the casting. But in terms of the relationship of the Bellamy couple, which is in large part based on the unsaid, one might ask if you didn't intervene more often than you usually do in the performances of the actors.
CC: No more than usual. I had intelligent actors. When I said to Gérard that I wanted his partner not to have had work done, he understood what I meant. When I said to Marie, "It is completely normal for you to love this big elephant," that was enough for her to enter into her character. They both found the right tone very quickly.

YA: In terms of the character of the brother, the least that we can say is that there are many areas of shadow.

CC: That is, in fact, the least that one can say. Because the brother is not his brother, but his son. A son he didn't want and toward whom he forbids himself to show affection. But the border between the two men is not very clear. At one moment someone says to Bellamy that the other man looks like him. He answers: "Worse than that, he *is* me." The character played by Cornillac has a certain fascination, especially since he is trouble—a bit of a hoodlum—while Bellamy is a cop. A troubled cop who is fascinated by the disorder that he is supposed to be fighting against. But during this time, the fake brother is under the impression that Bellamy has stolen his luck. At any rate, that is how he tries to justify his failures.

YA: It seems to me that the film resembles you, in that it gives the feeling of a certain lightness which then evolves without our being aware of it into a bad feeling, or at least a certain anger toward the spectacle of the world.

CC: I don't know if I give off that, but it is true that I am often angry, even if I don't express it in a direct way. And beyond that, it doesn't displease me if the spectator takes part in that feeling. At worst, if he experiences a certain confusion, he will have the idea of going back and seeing the film again.

Looking Back on *La Cérémonie*

Yves Alion / 2009

From *L'Avant-Scène Cinéma* 578 (December 2010): 4–7. Interview conducted in 2009. Reprinted by permission; translated from the French by CB.

Yves Alion: There is a saying that filmmakers make films in reaction to the films that preceded them. And the film that came before *La Cérémonie* was *L'Enfer*. Is the maxim true?

Claude Chabrol: Not really. It hasn't often been the case that I told myself I should make a blue film after making a pink one. That said, I do try to guard myself against dealing with the same subject twice. If we are really going to talk about *La Cérémonie* in connection with *L'Enfer*, I would say that the societal aspect is not developed very much in *L'Enfer*, which deals exclusively with the madness of love.

YA: On the other hand, some of your films, like *The Proud Ones* (*Le Cheval d'orgueil*) and *Quiet Days in Clichy* (*Jours tranquilles à Clichy*), seem to be far outside of the norm, or at least far from your usual world.

CC: Definitely. But it is easy to find good reasons for having made those films and even for recognizing them as mine. What is interesting in *Le Cheval d'orgueil*, for example, is to think about the naiveté of folklore. I like to make films in which the real subject is hidden, films which give the feeling that they are talking about something other than the subject that really interests me.

YA: Could we say that if we had to define your work in one sentence, it would be that of a painter from the French bourgeoisie who winks at his audience?

CC: I prefer to be more general and say that I am particularly interested in people who privilege the exterior of things rather than their deeper meaning. To take up an old and fairly explicit formula, those who prefer appearances to reality.

YA: That is the case of the Lilièvre family in *La Cérémonie*.

CC: Yes. They live in a certain kind of very bourgeois harmony. What is terrible in their case is that you can't blame them for very much, except for the fact that each member of the family performs one disgusting act at a certain moment, which they do without being aware of it. And each time they do it to the poor maid, played by Sandrine Bonnaire.

YA: We tell ourselves that they are sympathetic because they make an effort to be. But it isn't natural for them.
CC: Absolutely. The necessity of appearances requires that they project a certain kindness, a certain beauty. But what is repressed comes galloping back with certain phrases or gestures. For example, I love the way in which the father plays the enlightened despot. He chooses television programs for the whole family, which has to pretend to enjoy them. But it is clear that the son, for example, is bored, which is not allowed when listening to Mozart. Which does not at all excuse it when he declares that the maid smells bad.

YA: The way in which bad behavior is combined with false good manners is delightful. You just have to hear the father say to the maid: "It's not completely your fault that you are illiterate."
CC: That is really a way of suggesting that in a similar situation *he* would have found a way out of it. He would not have remained illiterate.

YA: Opposed to this bourgeois family are the two girls, whose madness is gradually revealed.
CC: What is interesting is that they are only crazy when they are together. Separately, they are harmless, but when they are together they feel they can do anything. But that is a well-known phenomenon that has been identified by psychiatry. It is really a case of shared madness (*folie à deux*). In fact, they are both looking for ways to shock each other.

YA: Did you and Caroline Eliacheff, your coscreenwriter, study this phenomenon in a scientific way?
CC: Caroline is a psychiatrist. She has studied the subject in detail. We had to avoid writing things that were inaccurate. I can't help thinking that the film is plausible from one end to the other. In any case, no one came looking to pick a fight with us on the level of the clinical description of the case. On the contrary, several specialists came to tell us that they found the film very accurate.

YA: What is interesting is that the girls are complete opposites: one is an introvert, and the other displays a certain larger-than-life extrovert quality. The maid only starts opening up to her friend halfway through the film, whereas the postal worker almost bares her soul at the very beginning.

CC: In reality, they use very different methods to reach the same goal: that of hiding their secret, which is the same secret for both. What is interesting is that when they get into talking about serious things, even about killing, it is the maid—seemingly the more reticent of the two—who shoots first. That said, the sounding of the starter's bugle comes in a state of total confusion. But once blood has been shed, they become aware of their power. They don't kill a whole family in order to have witnesses, but simply because they have entered a state of war and they are trying to conquer territory. Revenge is in the air. It is not by chance that the maid also shoots at the books. She only goes into the library very reluctantly. She has to vacuum in that room with her eyes closed.

YA: The whole film is also constructed around her secret, which isn't revealed to us in an explicit way until fairly late. Everything she does is tied to her fear of being discovered.
CC: It is at the moment when she is discovered that everything goes off the rails. And we see her hatred for the daughter of the house when she asks her if she is dyslexic, a word that she doesn't even understand. She answers immediately, spitting out her venom. Because she is forced, in that moment, to recognize herself as an inferior being.

YA: There is a permanent state of tension, which allows us to experience the suspense when she is forced to read and has to use subterfuge so that she won't have to do it.
CC: That tension is not an artificial one. I can put myself in her place: she must be living a horror. It should be said in passing that illiteracy is much more prevalent in French society than we think: the character played by Sandrine is not so extraordinary on this level.

YA: Your field of action in the film is in a general sense the domain of culture. And the film puts culture in question in a violent way. What function does culture serve? What are we to think about it?
CC: Culture is not knowledge. It is assimilated knowledge, which is more complicated. Because even the Lelièvres don't really have culture; they have areas of knowledge. Those areas that are necessary in order to hold their rank in society. But one suspects that they still need to go further in that direction. I have been struck by the number of people from the bourgeoisie who are ignorant about important, obvious things. You see them on game shows. Some of the answers by doctors and executives to fairly simple questions are hallucinatory.

YA: This film, more than many others, poses a moral problem. We wonder how much distance you take in looking at the world depicted in your films. What are the relative proportions of cruelty and caring?

CC: I think that in a certain way you can only get to caring through cruelty. I never try to excuse my characters, but I do try to understand them. And I shine the harshest light on them. From harshness to cruelty is a small step, even linguistically.[1] But nothing would be worse than wanting to hide things. Reality is always better than appearances. Always.

YA: The question of the distance the director takes in relation to his characters is of great importance in the cinema. *Short Cuts* is an admirable film, but it is difficult to believe in Robert Altman's empathy for his characters. Whereas the irony of a director like Dino Risi is only his disappointed realization about the state of the world.

CC: In general, we recognize mean people by what they say about others for no good reason. I don't believe that Altman is in that category. But I fundamentally agree with Risi, whose irony I hold in much higher regard than the tears of De Sica, for example. I don't ask the question about the distance of my perspective, because the spectator won't necessarily have the same perspective that I have. And it will be his problem, not mine. But I believe that accepting human nature is a sign of progress. That is no doubt one of the great advances of these past decades. I think I maintain a certain distance when I make a film. I am careful not to involve myself more than I have reason to do so.

YA: Does your involvement vary according to the person with whom you are writing? Caroline Eliacheff and Odile Barski don't have the same personality or the same life experience. And neither of them can be compared with Paul Gégauff.

CC: I don't know if it matters all that much. In reality, my screenwriters and I don't work together. The only time when we are working directly together is during the discussion we have at the beginning in which we establish the frame of the story. After that, the screenwriters go off and write. They write, and then I rework what they give me. Caroline and Odile don't work in the same way as each other. But in the end, there is, in spite of everything, the same work to be done. I have to bring the story they tell into my manner of seeing things. That is pretty much the same way I adapt a book.

YA: What about dialogue?

CC: There were really good things in Ruth Rendell's dialogue. In terms of my contribution, I would say off the top of my head that there is as much of it from my rereading the book as there was from Caroline's pen.

YA: Did you stay faithful to Ruth Rendell's novel?

CC: Oh no, we changed it enormously. The two protagonists in the book are two fat women. I didn't want the critical issue of the film to be a focus on their physical aspect. Ruth Rendell's book was written about forty years ago, and I told her that I had the feeling of adapting a book that she could have written twenty years later. She said she thought that might be true. And the fact that it was written that long ago doesn't take away from the fact that the book is great, and that it doesn't leave the reader unscathed.

YA: Another recent French film was adapted from Ruth Rendell, and it also deals with the divergent values of different social classes: *Alias Betty*, directed by Claude Miller. What do you think of it?

CC: It's a very good film. I am less taken with *Live Flesh*, which was adapted by Pedro Almodovar, a filmmaker I love. I like the way Ruth Rendell has of taking on the problem of social differences in a very direct manner. The fact that she is proworker plays an important role. What is funny is that I had thought *Alias Betty* was unadaptable when I read it. And I think that Claude Miller was able to avoid going in the direction of an exaggerated tenderness for the child, which would have turned into mawkishness; other directors would have gone much more in that direction.

YA: When *La Cérémonie* came out, you defined it as "the last Marxist film." Wasn't that really an advertising slogan?

CC: Probably. There was, in any case, a lot of provocation for it. It is true that the slogan was audacious and that I never considered the actions of the two young women to herald the coming of a new society. But I was annoyed, to say the least, when after the fall of the Berlin Wall people started talking about the end of class warfare, and even the end of history. What stupidity! I was even more outraged because I knew that this Pollyanna analysis of the forward march of the world was stuffed with ulterior motives.

Notes

1. In French, there is a phonic resemblance between the words *"cru"* (harsh) and *"cruauté"* (cruelty).

Selected Resources

Alexandre, Wilfred. *Claude Chabrol, la traversée des apparences*. Paris: Editions du félin, 2003.

Austin, Guy. *Claude Chabrol*. Manchester: Manchester University Press, 1999.

Bell, Dorian. "Cavemen Among Us": Genealogies of Atavism from Zola's *La Bête Humaine* to Chabrol's *Le Boucher*." *French Studies* 62.1 (2008).

Biette, Jean-Claude, Serge Daney, and Serge Toubiana. "Entretien avec Claude Chabrol." *Cahiers du cinéma* 339 (1982).

Blanchet, Christian. *Claude Chabrol*. Paris: Rivages, 1989.

Bonnet, Jean-Claude. "Entretien avec Claude Chabrol." *Cinématographe* 117 (1986).

Braucourt, Guy. *Claude Chabrol*. Paris: Seghers, 1971.

Braucourt, Guy. "Entretien avec Claude Chabrol." *Cinéma* 145 (1970).

Buss, Robin. *French Film Noir*. London: Marion Boyars, 2001.

Chabrol, Claude. *Et pourtant je tourne*. Paris: Robert Laffont, 1976.

Chabrol, Claude. *Par lui-meme et par les siens*. Paris: Stock, 2011.

Chabrol, Claude. *Pensées, répliques, et anecdotes*. Paris: Le Cherche Midi, 2016.

Chevrie, Marc, and Serge Toubiana. "Entretien avec Claude Chabrol." *Cahiers du cinéma* 381 (1986).

Collet, Jean, Michel Delahaye, Jean-André Fieschi, André S. Labarthe, and Bertrand Tavernier. "Entretien avec Claude Chabrol." *Cahiers du cinéma* 138 (1962). Reprinted in Antoine de Baecque and Charles Tesson, eds., *La Nouvelle Vague*. Paris: Cahiers du cinéma, 1999.

Dousteyssier-Khoze, Catherine. *Claude Chabrol's Aesthetics of Opacity*. Edinburgh: Edinburgh University Press, 2018.

Fassbinder, Rainer Werner. "Insects in a Glass Case: Random Thoughts on Claude Chabrol." *Sight and Sound* 45.4 (1976).

Gergely, Gabor. "Pruning Roses, Producing Space: Representing the Social Bond in the Melodramas of Claude Chabrol." *Studies in French Cinema* 12.1 (2012).

Graham, Peter, ed. *The French New Wave: Critical Landmarks*. New and expanded ed. London: British Film Institute/ Palgrave Macmillan, 2009.

Guérif, François. *Conversations avec Claude Chabrol: un jardin bien à moi*. Paris: Editions Denoël, 1999.

Guérin, Marie-Anne, and Thierry Jousse, "Entretien avec Claude Chabrol." *Cahiers du cinéma* 494 (1995).

Jacob, Gilles. "Entretien avec Claude Chabrol." *Cinéma* 109 (1966).

Jacobowitz, Florence. "*La Cérémonie*: 'The Last Marxist Film' by Claude Chabrol." *CinéAction* 39 (1995).

Jousse, Thierry, Nicholas Saada, and Serge Toubiana. "Entretien avec Claude Chabrol." *Cahiers du cinéma* 437 (1990).

Jousse, Thierry, and Serge Toubiana. "Entretien avec Claude Chabrol." *Cahiers du cinéma* 453 (1992).

Jousse, Thierry, and Serge Toubiana. "Claude Chabrol de A à Z." *Cahiers du cinéma*, special Claude Chabrol issue (1997).

Leigh, Jacob. *The Late Films of Claude Chabrol: Genre, Visual Expressionism, and Narrational Ambiguity.* London: Bloomsbury, 2017.

Magny, Joel. *Claude Chabrol.* Paris: Cahiers du Cinéma, 1987.

Magny, Joël, and Claude Chabrol. "Questions de Mise en Scène." *Cahiers du cinéma*, special Claude Chabrol issue (1997).

Monaco, James. *The New Wave: Truffaut, Godard, Chabrol, Rohmer, Rivette.* New York and Oxford: Oxford University Press, 1976.

Morrey, Douglas. "Le Creux de la Vague: Authorship, Adaptation, and Sexuality in *Les Godelureaux*." *Modern and Contemporary France* 21.4 (2013).

Neupert, Richard. "Red Blood on White Bread: Hitchcock, Chabrol, and French Cinema." In David Boyd and R. Barton Palmer, eds., *After Hitchcock: Influence.* Austin: University of Texas Press, 2006.

Pascal, Michel. *Claude Chabrol.* Paris: Editions de la Martinière, 2012.

Polack, Jean-Claude. "Chabrol and the Execution of the Deed." *October* 98 (2001).

Predal, Rene. *50 Ans de cinéma français.* Paris: Nathan, 1996.

Sellier, Geneviève. *Masculine Singular: French New Wave Cinema.* Trans. Kristin Ross. Durham: Duke University Press, 2008.

Simsolo, Noel. "Entretien avec Claude Chabrol." *La Revue du Cinéma—Image et son* 228 (1969).

Terrio, Susan J. "Food, Class, and Violence in Claude Chabrol's *La Cérémonie*." *Contemporary French Civilization* 27.1 (2003).

Thomas, Deborah. "'Knowing One's Place': Frame-Breaking, Embarrassment and Irony in *La Cérémonie*." In John Gibbs and Douglas Pye, eds., *Style and Meaning: Studies in the Detailed Analysis of Film.* Manchester: Manchester University Press, 2005.

Walker, Michael. "Claude Chabrol: Into the Seventies." *Movie* 20 (1975).

Williams, Alan. *Republic of Images: A History of French Filmmaking.* Cambridge: Harvard University Press, 1992.

Wood, Robin, and Michael Walker. *Claude Chabrol.* London: Studio Vista, 1970.

Index

About the Editor

Christopher Beach is a film scholar and author of several books on film and literature, including *Class, Language, and American Film Comedy* and *The Films of Hal Ashby*. He was named an Academy Film Scholar by the Academy of Motion Picture Arts and Sciences for *A Hidden History of Film Style: Cinematographers, Directors, and the Collaborative Process*.